THE LOST
BALI STORIES

VOLUME I

THE LOST BALI STORIES

VOLUME I

Created, Compiled and Edited by
Leslie Anne Franklin

Published by IngramSpark
Copyright © 2022 Leslie Anne Franklin

Editor contact: P.O. Box 1919, Big Bear City, CA 92314 USA.
lesliefranklinlcf@gmail.com
www.lostbalibook.com

Art direction by Natasha Berting
Cover design concept by Leslie Anne Franklin
Cover painting by Ketut Swardana

ISBN 978-0-578-35781-2

I dedicate this book to my children; Anouk, Yos, Katya, Morena, and to my grandchildren Sienna, Noah, Kesia, and Ethan.

ABOUT THE EDITOR

Leslie Anne Franklin was born in Newport Beach, California, USA. From the age of six, Leslie lived in Sydney, Australia. Leslie came to Bali for the first time in 1982.

During the thirty-three years she lived in Bali, she has witnessed social and environmental developments over time.

Leslie's love for Bali includes the fervent spirituality of the Balinese and their endearing hospitality, which has remained steadfast and unchanged.

Leslie founded the Lost Bali Facebook group, which at present has over twenty-eight thousand active members. The group shares memories and photographs that have captured a time before 1990 before mass tourism affected the island. The collective stories and images have served as inspiration for this book.

Leslie currently resides in her wood cabin in the mountain town of Big Bear, California.

She is the mother of four children and four grandchildren.

This is her first anthology.

I DEEPLY THANK the people of Bali, whom I offer my eternal and humble gratitude. The magic the Balinese bestow upon us by their loving acceptance, patience, grace, purity and smiles, will never be lost.

I thank the many authors of this book who took their time to return to Memory Lane and write about their experiences in Bali many decades ago.

Oṃ bhūr bhuvaḥ svaḥ
tat savitur vareṇyaṃ
bhargo devasya dhīmahi
dhiyo yo naḥ prachodayā

~

We meditate on the effulgent
glory of the divine Light; may he
inspire our understanding.

RIGVEDA 3.62.10

CONTENTS

Preface

The naming of the title of this book has its own unique story.

Sitting in a modern apartment in Umalas, Bali, in October 2011, I was scrolling through Facebook and came across a group called "Lost Sydney." The group's theme displayed old photos of Sydney, Australia, from the 1900s to the 1970s.

I liked the concept of this group and thought, *Why not form a group like this about Bali and call it "Lost Bali"?*

Five minutes later, I created the Lost Bali group.

My intent for the group was to honor Bali before mass tourism started in 1990. Hundreds of people immediately joined and posted photos and stories of the way Bali was before the massive changes. Many people reunited after decades.

All in all, the public response was overwhelming. Today we are twenty-eight thousand members and one enormous growing family.

At first, some members complained to me about the group name. Some wrote to me and said, "Bali is not lost!" and "Why are you so negative?" "Choose a more positive name for the group!"

Yet, I honestly never intended to give a negative connotation to my beloved Bali; I simply adapted the group's name from the Lost Sydney Facebook group.

To me, the word "lost" represented "something far away" such as *tempo dulu* (the before times). It had a nostalgic quality to it.

With the idea for this book in mind, I decided to write to my personal friends to see if they would be interested in sharing their experiences about their time in Bali. I also posted a blast to my Lost Bali Facebook group requesting story submissions.

The response was unbelievably enthusiastic. Eighty-five members sent their stories to me.

The tales in this book are love stories about Bali pre-1990.

Each story differs, as it is through the eye of the beholder.

Each author's relationship with Bali is unique.

I am grateful to those who have written so intimately and freely about their personal experiences in this book.

I asked each writer to add to the end of their story their own personal advice for the Bali visitor. One might find some pearls of wisdom or places to visit not found in any travel guide.

Bali is one of the most loved islands on Earth; then, now, and always.

It has been my greatest honor to create this book.

LESLIE ANNE FRANKLIN
— California, USA 2021

Foreword

After ten months of the COVID global travel freeze, Kuta and north-wards looks like a post-apocalyptic world of empty streets, encroaching vegetation, and shuttered shops. As if to rub it in, a peeling slogan on one of them reads:

DON'T LOOK BACK. YOU'RE NOT GOING THAT WAY.

Perhaps not, but as we don't know where we are and don't know where we're going, it seems appropriate to take an occasional look back-ward in case we forget what paradise on earth was like.

The mythology of "what Bali was like in the early days" has gathered its own momentum, like a meme, and is often as tenuously connected to the truth. It mesmerizes not only newcomers but also those of us who were actually here.

An old academic joke was that Bali was the world's worst place for an anthropologist to do his fieldwork. This was because so many of them spent years in their own corner of the island, meticulously cataloging the explanations the Balinese gave them for what things meant, only to find that their colleagues, in their different corners, had been given entirely different stories—thus rendering their cumulative years of effort completely useless.

This book doesn't have that problem. Yes, its viewpoints are as varied as the viewers, but it's more about the *feeling* of that narrow slice of time between a very ancient past—shared by us all in the Dreamtime—and the tech-connected globalism of today. It was when the island was still enveloped in thick vegetation and throbbed with ritualized animism and when constant offerings were made to an unseen world that seemed all too palpable. No wonder those of us who were already a bit fay when we arrived soon found ourselves experiencing "supernatural" events, like everyone else. This book reveals that Bali, for us foreigners, wasn't just a different planet but an altered state of mind.

Even reaching the island by plane was no easy task. If from Europe, you could fly Aeroflot with bodybuilding flight attendants, which advertised a stop in Moscow but might well skip that and bring you down in Tashkent or somewhere else you'd never heard of. Here you were deplaned, interrogated about whether you had any "documents" (film scripts, book drafts, etc.), and led to believe that if you did then your travels were over, forever.

Further east, you might land again in Kuala Lumpur, where you risked having your passport stamped with S.H.I.T., an acronym for Suspected Hippie In Transit. Or in Singapore, where if your hair—if you were a man—was longer than even a centimeter over the top of your ears, you could be denied the transit lounge and confined instead to a tiny holding tank until the departure of your connecting flight, which might be in another eight hours.

Ah, but the last hop down to Bali was bliss. The temperature was turned up to eighty degrees; there was no nonsense about having to fasten seat belts, even for takeoffs and landings; and the cabin filled with the thick smoke of *kretek* cigarettes. And as you crossed the equator into the southern hemisphere, below you on one side, you could see the sprawling jungles of Sumatra and, on the other, of Borneo and imagine them teaming with tigers and rhinos and never-contacted tribes, which to a degree they still were. Then, losing altitude over Java, you could make out not one but rows of smoking volcanoes before at last thumping down on Bali's rough tarmac. When the cabin doors opened, the blast of tropical aromas eclipsed even the miasma in the plane.

Outside the Customs and Immigration shed was a stand of frangipani trees. You could pick a flower to put behind your ear and chant a supplicatory mantra before navigating the final hurdle: the officialdom who could destroy in an instant the months of effort of a couple of penniless filmmakers, like us, who had imported all their equipment in disassembled pieces so as to attract minimum suspicion.

My dear, late brother Lorne and I had been filming adventure documentaries in the remoter islands of Indonesia for more than a year before finally making it to Bali in 1973. We liked to think of ourselves as explorers, so we tended to look down our noses at an island that already had an airport and international hotel. *Huge* mistake.

It was love at first sight, and we were immediately drawn into the embrace of the village community of Pengosekan, next to Ubud, where for about USD 500.00, they built us a two-story bamboo-and-thatch house in the rice paddies. In addition to being farmers and housebuilders, they were irrepressible sculptors, artists, and musicians. Their art of the time, created by such as Sena, Mokoh, and Batuan, are now in museums and private collections around the world. This was decades before Pengosekan, like so many other creative villages, was forced to abandon their art in favor of mass-producing more reliable tourist trade items such as carved wooden desk plaques reading "George [or Harry or Bob] is Gay" or the singularly successful flower-painted wooden penises, based on the black fertility carvings the Balinese had made for centuries to ritually to bury in the rice paddies.

Our village soothsayer was Ketut Liyer, who became globally famous as the wise man in Liz Gilbert's book (and the movie) *Eat, Pray, Love*. Wags on the island would sport bumper stickers saying "Eat, Pray, Leave." Sadly, Ketut only lived long enough for the first wave of fame and missed the second when busloads of international tourists began turning up in Pengosekan to ask for him. As about one in four Balinese males are named Ketut, the villagers of the right age did very well for a few years, providing a wide range of imaginative past-life readings.

Throughout the many years, Lorne and I were exploring the outer islands; our Pengosekan home was our decompression chamber between East and West, our spa of sensuous rejuvenation. We were nursed back to health by the village and enlightened and amused by Nyoman Batuan, our closest friend, who was also our key to understanding the island's complex practices and beliefs.

There was no electricity, and the only phone on the island was at the airport, ninety minutes away, and that closed at one a.m. So if you had to make a vital phone call to a producer or an agent in Los Angeles, you only had a one-hour window—between midnight, when the offices opened in LA, and one a.m. when the phone was locked in Bali. You might find the phone was already occupied, or out of order, or that your receiving party wasn't available yet, and you would have to drive home and try the following night again, and so on. Thus it was understandable, if unjust, that the outside world considered us Bali dwellers as somewhat flakey and unreliable.

Nature occupied our Pengosekan house as freely as it occupied the outdoors. The house had no walls or windows, and in the rainy season, we relied on retractable blinds to block the worst of the weather. Our mosquito nets, when furled up during the day, might trap fireflies or Atlas moths with ten-inch wingspans. So when they unfurled them over us at night, it was like being in a star-lit galaxy haunted by soft bats. Tokay geckos shouted, "Fuck you" from the ceiling. Yes, really. In different regions the tokays still have different accents. A few villages over, they shout, "Tickle me." I like the optimistic ones in Legian, who have lost their *t*'s and simply shriek, "OK!"

Snakes periodically curled up under the batiks on our sleeping mattresses, coyly waiting for us to come to bed with them. I had seen snakes on top of roofs, but once, while lying on the raised sleeping platform only an arm's length from the thatch above me, I watched a snake swim across the ceiling, from one end to the other—a technical improbability that still disturbs me.

There were days and nights when the house seethed with ants, and you could summon the Ant Shaman, who might announce that they were simply heralding the rainy season and would depart when it arrived. Or else, for a few dollars, he would conduct a complex ant-banishing rite, with bells and incense and ceremonial dress, which I remember as being astonishingly successful.

At first, we used paraffin lamps, like our village family, but they cast enough light barely to read by and caused us to nod off at the bedtime of a six-year-old. So we fired up the petrol-driven generator we carried through the field and ignited a couple of 100-watt bulbs—the first in the village. At one point, I was trolled for having the first electric typewriter too, powered by our generator, which was eighty yards away from the house. To keep the typewriter working evenly, I found I had to constantly run back and forth adjusting the speed of the generator, to the great amusement of the village, particularly of Batuan, who joked unkindly about it long after the typewriter had given up the ghost—which, admittedly, it did quite soon.

Lorne and I were rather smug about our two 100-watt bulbs, which were a quantum leap of radiance ahead of our neighbors, until our first Flying Termite experience. The termites still swarm here at the start of the rains but in nothing like the numbers of the early days. Even our real jungle adventures hadn't prepared us for the biblical massacre caused by our lights. Each termite, upon finding the light, abandons its wings and falls to the floor, where, as a crawling worm, it seeks to mate with another such fallen angel. This scene attracted armies of predatory lizards and rats and toads and frogs, which in turn attracted snakes and civet cats to eat *them*. An appalling murder-fest, among multiple species, in the heart of our home, film equipment, dinner, and mouths. But in barely an hour, it was all over. Not a beast to be seen, and the house was awash only with a rippling foam of iridescent wings.

The following day Batuan told us that nobody wanted to assist us, as the village had never had a better time of it: our light bulbs had attracted all the insects for miles around and left the village untouched. The correct procedure, he explained, is to sit in the dark, with just one low-level paraffin light placed in a tray of water. The water drowns most of the termites, and the rest are more tidily eaten by predators around the edge of the tray. Who knew!

Of the barely three or four dozen foreigners on the island in '73, just a small handful of us lived up in Ubud—mainly anthropologists, artists, and designers. The rest of the tribe—to use a zoographical term—"occurred" down in the beach area, and to visit them required moderately hazardous bike trips.

Our steeds were our motorbikes. They took us through torrential downpours and raging streams and midnight monkey forests back when the monkeys were better behaved. And, most memorably, in late sun-sinking afternoons, through golden rice paddies and intoxicating mists of rice husk burn-off mixed with temple incense. It was like riding a silver surfboard through a Walter Spies painting. At night, on the narrow asphalt roads, you could collide with "the black dog" or one of those gaping holes that announced itself with a warning sprig of greenery placed *in* them rather than *ahead* of them. And, in this era before insecticides, you might run into flack fields of flying insects, including beetles large enough to smack you in the face with the intensity of a tennis ball.

In addition to the one phone and no electricity, there were no road signs, street names, or navigational directions. This was when few Balinese ever traveled beyond their own villages, except for their annual pilgrimage to the Besakih "Mother Temple." So asking bystanders for directions initiated a promisingly eager response from an instant crowd but soon degenerated into everybody pointing in different directions. This was also when "north"—*utara* in Indonesian, *kaja* in Balinese—referred to the summit of the great volcano Gunung Agung. So if you were traveling around the base of the volcano, a circle of about fifty miles, and you asked directions to the north coast as you went along and got correct answers each time, you would end up exactly where you started.

On a bike trip, you were on your own. Particularly if the bike broke down and at night, when the island was asleep. In the daytime, at least you had the reassurance of a helpful crowd, but at night you needed a flashlight, a few tools, and an engineering degree.

The wild beach was a different planet again from Ubud. For a start, everyone in Ubud went to bed at about eight p.m., which was just about when the seaside tribe was rising and preparing for their exotic nights of dance and superb live music, mainly provided by escapees from various Indian ashrams. There was the sharing of tall but firsthand travel tales and essential alternative-medical advice. There was naked swimming in the bioluminescent surf and of course, love. Rather a lot of it. We were, after all, blessed by dancing in that narrow "Goldilocks" bandwidth between the invention of contraceptives and the advent of AIDS.

We were light of wallets, possessions, and clothing. You only needed a couple of sarongs and a toothbrush to see you through days away from home, plus of course, a bit of ethnic finery in the way of a Sumba scarf or a Dayak bead necklace. If the tribe couldn't put us up on the beach for fifty cents a night, you could always rent a *losmen*, a bamboo "gardening shed" with a very short bed, a dinky mosquito net, and a banana and cup of tea in the morning. For a bath, you sloshed yourself with cold water laced with mosquito larvae from a concrete tank and sometimes from a really old Chinese pottery urn.

When Lorne and I were heading back to Bali from our remote expeditions, which sometimes lasted six months at a time, we longed for three things: a decent hamburger, available at only one hotel on the island; our village community of Pengosekan, who would pamper and nurse us back to health; and our Bali tribe, who would connect us to the broader world and stretch our hearts again. They were a circus of self-sufficient individualists with great style, hailing from everywhere on the planet, including Indonesia. They were invariably beautiful, like plants in the right soil. I can attest to the fact that all the women who have contributed to this book were very beautiful and still are—but wiser. And the men—though I won't attest to this—were very stupid, and still are, but also wiser. And after all these years, I feel we still bring out the best in one another.

As I remember it, the tribe fell into broadly three categories:

1) The creative arty folk
2) The collectors of ethnographic treasures
3) The wild watermen

The first two groups would dress in exotic fabrics and jewelry either made by the first group or collected by the second. The second group were true adventurers, spending long months alone in remote islands gleaning tribal treasures and heirlooms to sell to foreign museums and private collectors.

The third group, mainly Ozzies and a few Americans, were the pioneering surfers and referred to the first two groups as the "scarfies." They dressed, day and night, almost exclusively in board shorts and had the bodies to get away with it. They hadn't traveled so far and were a bit more aloof but were physically the bravest of us all, by a long shot. Their passion was finding the most ferocious, never previously surfed wave breaks and flinging themselves into them. Their only lifeguards were each other. They were the first to broach the wicked sets of Ulu Watu and Padang Padang, which break over shallow coral, and the first to surf "G-land" in Java, when black panthers were still to be seen on the beach at night. They would gamely turn up at the parties wreathed in "reef pizzas" from coral wipeouts.

Decades later, it was the first group, the arty ones, that flowered the international stars of fashion, jewelry, textiles, and architecture, and hence who were responsible for putting Indonesia on the world map before the tourist tsunamis of the '80s and '90s.

And the second group—the pirate "scammers," as we affectionately referred to them—turned out to be less the grave robbers of the nation's treasury of ethnographic art as the key players in its preservation. For whereas in the early days such treasures rotted in, or were pilfered from, Indonesia's neglected museums, the best of them—thanks to the scammers—had been lovingly preserved abroad for half a century. And now that the nation is awakening to its cultural heritage, its gems are gradually being bought back again by Indonesian institutions and private collectors.

Tales of and by all three groups of the Bali Tribe are here revealed in the following pages. I only hope *Imigrasi* gets to take a look and sees what we little rascals were up to.

DR. LAWRENCE BLAIR
— Bali, Indonesia 2020

Introduction

Sitting alone inside my small wooden cabin set in the mountain town of Big Bear, California, during the COVID-19 quarantine of March 2020, my Bali memories became so vivid in my mind.

Life was so different now—not only for myself but also for the entire world.

I nostalgically reminisced about the thirty-three years I spent in Bali—of all the gifts I had received and the adventures I had experienced.

Having so much time on my hands and unable to travel, the idea sprang forth for this book. With the way the world was progressing, it seemed so important to preserve stories about Bali and the feeling of freedom it gifted to many. Hence, the book you are reading right now was born.

In my time in Bali, from 1982 to 2015, the island had changed dramatically—especially from 1990 onwards when mass tourism took hold. Of course, most societies grow and evolve with the times, yet to Bali, an ancient culture that had never been exposed to commercialism, the sudden change was shocking.

From 1990, the biggest real-estate developers in the world bought the island out from multitudes of Balinese in the blink of an eye. Also, Jakarta's money was flowing in giving birth to domestic tourism.

Over the time period of five years, the rice fields that I loved to bicycle through in the towns of Kuta and surrounding areas had slowly begun to diminish, replaced by modern buildings, and suddenly overnight, Bali had changed forever.

Tourists arrived on the island on cheap package deals that strictly escorted people from shop to shop. Large tour buses clogged Bali's heavily ingested roads.

Like Ibiza, Bali became renowned for its party scene, with more people frequently visiting to "see and be seen" at one of the world's most glamourous international hang-outs.

The lifestyle, that originally was casual and laid back had reshaped itself. A typical weekend consisted of a villa stay, a luxury spa visit, dinner at an exclusive restaurant followed by a high-priced night out on the town. A far cry from the parties held for free in private homes or on a beach under the moonlight.

More foreign investments meant the construction of stylish villas upon villas, each with its own swimming pool and neatly trimmed Japanese garden grass.

I admit—mass tourism had its perks. We could now buy cheese, wine, artisan bread, pastries, and milk, whereas back in the day, we would wait for one of our friends to bring goodies in from abroad in a suitcase. We would all be excited when a friend would arrive in Bali with some French cheese or a bottle of wine. We regaled in these simple pleasures. Today, in Bali, we can dine under the stars drinking exotic cocktails before being served four-course meals created by handpicked award-winning international chefs.

The island was now chasing the dollar. As mass tourism increased, everything in Bali suddenly had monetary value. Many innocent Balinese sold their family homes, including their family temples. Accepting the temptation of being offered more money than they could ever imagine gaining in three lifetimes; sadly now, years later could not afford to buy back their ancestral homes.

With the Bali boom, local expatriates started businesses—and lucrative ones at that. Many built homes (this time to rent out to tourists), some constructed hotels, others opened boutiques, and many started restaurants. Bali was running at a faster pace. It was rare to stay somewhere without hearing some kind of construction noise nearby (still today).

The evolution of such a beautiful island in this world was inevitable.

For the observer who witnessed Bali before and after the changes, he or she might think the purity of the island had been tampered with.

Bali had a way of teaching me a myriad of lessons—these being mainly freedom, joy, reverence, patience, and creativity. Having traveled across the globe and spending time in other parts of Asia, Australia Europe, and America, Bali had, and still has, a hold on my spirit and soul like no other place I have known. Bali nurtured me. Bali embraced me as though I was a long-lost child finally finding its mother. In Bali, I felt whole and loved. Returning at times to the West, I would suffer from culture shock, experiencing a world that seemed faster, dry in spirit and gentleness, and out of sync with nature's elements.

Bali drew us to her in various ways.

As for myself, I arrived in Bali for the first time in 1982. I was eighteen years old, wide-eyed and frivolous; I had no idea how much the mystical island would affect my life.

Only a few hundred expatriates were living in Bali at the time, compared to tens of thousands today. In the early days, those of us who were there were drawn to the island's freedom and beauty and became a close-knit family.

I left Kambala Church of England Girls' School in Sydney, Australia, when I was sixteen years old due to being heavily bullied by a group of four girls in my class. My parents had gone bankrupt with the Australian recession. My school was expensive, and I begged them to allow me to leave, and—with some level of relief to them and me—they did.

I joined Vivien's Model Agency in Sydney. I was successful modeling for magazines (including *Vogue*) and TV commercials, yet, through some connections; I was also offered a nighttime job as a (underage) cocktail waitress at The Cauldron, a famous nightclub back in the day.

One evening at work, a man walked into the club, took a shining eye to me, and invited me out to lunch. Gerald was a handsome, dark-haired Frenchman who wore a lapis lazuli and shark-tooth necklace, jeans with a silver belt, and a blue batik shirt. He seemed different from the other men in the nightclub who would usually ask me out for "dinner."

Lunch seemed harmless, so I accepted.

Gerald and I sat outside of the famous harborside restaurant Doyle's in Watson's Bay the following day. Gerald told me about many exotic places he lived: Goa in India, Ibiza in Spain, and Bali in Indonesia. "You would love all these places, Leslie. Let me show them to you. What are you going to do here in Sydney? Work at a nightclub for the rest of your life? Come with me. I will pay for your ticket. Let me show you a different life."

Being only seventeen at the time, I was unsuspecting and quite enchanted. I had a few friends who told me how much they loved Bali. One friend insisted I know this Balinese phrase if I ever go to Bali. "Leslie, repeat after me. *Sing ada apo 'de!*" I think she made me repeat it ten times. The slang phrase was to ward off haggling beach sellers to inform them I had no money. Gerald was very impressed with my knowledge of the Balinese language, just as much as I was impressed with his offer, even though initially I wasn't so attracted to him.

As naïve as I was, I believed his words about his profession as an international antique dealer (which later I found out to be "just words"). I introduced him to my parents, and they were charmed by his European ways. He sent me two dozen red roses every day (so his charm somehow was beginning to work with me too). He seemed educated, and we had mutual friends. The next thing I knew we were off to Goa, India, with my parent's permission.

So here I was, young, beautiful, and carefree, yet under the influence of a man I hardly knew, yet who would later become the father of my first child.

In India, my eyes were dilating to a new alternative way of living amongst Gerald's hippie and jet-setter friends. A few months later, Gerald took me on a flight to Bali.

Immediately as I got off the plane, I could smell the strong aroma of frangipani mixed with the smell of clove cigarettes. Driving through the back streets of Kuta in a rusty old taxi, I looked at all the little *warungs* (food stands) and a few *tokos* (shops) from the airport as we drove through Legian. Coconut and hibiscus trees abounded. The Balinese on their pushbikes wearing colorful sarongs mesmerized me. After about thirty minutes, we reached Golden Village in the town of Seminyak.

Golden Village was a group of about thirteen bungalows at the time, owned by Agung Boss. It was known to be where the "jet-set" stayed on the Goa/Ibiza trail. Agung Boss was "cool." Gerald told me Agung "tolerated" his guests hosting wild parties in their homes there. Agung's openness and patience with all the types of vagabonds who lived there created a sense of freedom for all. This type of freedom was worth gold to the jet-set tribe in the '80s.

Gerald opened the door to our two-story bungalow (which, strangely enough, ten years later became my family home for thirteen years and the place where I would give birth to my youngest daughter). I was enchanted to find an open, airy house with only a few *bedeg* bamboo mat walls. High coconut-wood columns supported the living room roof, and the home seemed to sprawl into the garden. The floors were terracotta tile. The vivid green of the plants, red hibiscus and frangipani flowers, and yellow bamboo walls harmonized together, dancing as one.

In our bedroom upstairs, I could see rice fields to the sea. I heard the clang of the *kul-kuls* (bamboo chimes) and a Balinese yelling in the fields at birds to stop eating his rice crop.

The air was humid and sensual. In Bali, I always felt the breeze caress me like a lover, brushing against my skin.

Gerald took me around Golden Village to meet his friends, who, like us, were going to spend many months in the homes they had rented. Everyone wore sarongs, and feet were almost always barefoot. There was Mariano the Argentinian, Adonis the Greek, Cushla the Australian, Patricia the Columbian, and Perry the New Yorker in the village. Everyone would visit one another's houses daily just for social visits. Someone might proudly show off something they designed, drink a Bintang beer, or enjoy a *kretek* (clove cigarette) or a *kopi susu* (coffee with milk) while sitting on our bamboo sofa, usually accompanied by a joint and talk about the plans for the evening that night. With the island's relaxed atmosphere, the humidity, the beach life, and the fresh fruits and seafood easily accessed, everyone looked beautiful, glowing, and healthy.

Everyone had positive energy. There was no complaining about life, taxes, the media, the government, or getting a job. Everyone seemed to either create jewelry, design clothes, organize parties, or plan road trips. Some were building their own houses on a piece of land they contracted for twenty years from a Balinese, not requiring building permits. One's imagination could go wild designing a home.

Being a young girl, I sometimes felt intimidated upon meeting all these creative world travelers, yet I also felt accepted immediately. Shy, I preferred not to say much and smile. In Bali, I was learning a new way of living and being. I would need some time to adjust.

That evening of my first arrival to Bali, Gerald took me to visit Milo. Milo had a beautiful home not far from Golden Village, closer to the beach. Milo owned a pet orangutan and was a stylish Italian designer. As I walked barefoot on the grass toward his home in the pitch black of the night, holding a flashlight, a green mamba snake slivered across my foot. I didn't realize it at the time, but the mamba is one of Bali's most poisonous snakes. I always felt in hindsight that the snake slithering over my foot was the sign of Bali initiating me; welcoming me to an island I would be connected to forever.

Gerald and I went on road trips around the island. I was blown away by this new world I was encountering. My love affair with Bali had begun. The smiles and waves from the Balinese opened my heart. The chanting I heard in the distance told me that spiritual life was vibrant on the island.

I remember one night I walked into Murni's restaurant in Ubud for the first time. The paraffin lamps on bamboo tables hypnotized me as I listened to fascinating tales from travelers' clad in heavy silver jewelry and ethnic clothing.

I met with Ian Van Wieringen and Shane Sweeney, eccentric and talented artists who lived on the Sayan ridge. I met Made Wijaya (Michael White), an Australian, prolific in Balinese culture, and so many other vivacious characters. These new acquaintances recounted tales about the richness of Bali and were living amongst nature and creativity, as the Balinese do.

The gentle morning light streaming through tall coconut trees and hibiscus flowers while I sipped my *kopi susu*, made each morning beautiful. In Bali, I felt beautiful, and the Balinese would always tell me I was. They saw my beauty and I saw theirs.

I fell in love with the misty mountains of Bedugul and Kintamani, and the changing landscapes of Karangasem. In many small villages, residents carved wood or made silver jewelry. I adored the white sand beaches of the south and black sand beaches of the north, the waterfalls, and the infinite variety of temples. I became interested in Indonesian natural medicines. *Jamu* is made from various concoctions of herbs, roots, and spices guaranteed to cure any illness.

I started to discover my creativity.

Bali was never boring—there was always too much to do and see.

In 1984 Gerald and I had our baby girl. Gerald was not the person I thought he was, and after some terrible times together, I ended our relationship; however, my relationship with Bali continued. Even though I returned to Australia for some months, I would visit Bali as often as I could. In 1987 I made Bali my permanent home.

The Balinese stay close to their religious culture. They are vigilant of the balance between black and white, good and evil, right and wrong. In finding balance, they abide by a correct way to live; in harmony with the world seen and unseen, the *Sekala* and *Niskala*; the before and afterlife; between humans and gods.

One of the most intrinsic values and lessons that one can learn from the Balinese is being calm inside and *sabar* (patient). I have seen the Balinese quietly walk away or look down in embarrassment at *bules* (foreigners) who get angry and shout—losing one's composure is considered undignified and rude in the Balinese culture.

The feeling the Balinese emit through their gentleness and kindness, love of children, and devotion to their culture and values can transform a person visiting Bali. They show us a softer and gentler way of living and being. Over the years, I have seen loud-mouthed, brash temperaments completely transform as individuals, becoming more peaceful and sensitive, simply by visiting Bali and staying there awhile.

I have seen countless people cry when leaving the island because Bali is not just an island; Bali is a teacher. Once it gets under your skin, you will be in love with Bali forever. Once you taste the true joy and freedom Bali offers, returning to old ways is difficult. Yet, too, I have seen visitors wanting to leave Bali as soon as they arrive, not coping with the island's intensity.

Bali will be your best friend and grow with you if you are kind to Bali, showing you the lessons you need to learn. On the flip side, Bali's teachings can be severe. If you disrespect the island and its culture, somehow Bali has a way of showing you your mistake, and you risk getting whooped by the island. I have seen visitors suffer strange sicknesses; experience bad luck, or have accidents. Some go amok there (amok is an Indonesian word). The energy of the island is intense. One must be humble in its presence.

~

My wish is that by reading the stories in this book, the reader will get a sense of the freedom we experienced. In this challenging era with the current lack of liberties due to COVID-19, the control by government over our lives, and for many, the inability to connect with loved ones, hopefully, the stories in this book will inspire those that read it while keeping Bali's magical spirit alive.

Just as for those of us who chose to be in Bali in that innocent time to live entirely against the norm in the tropics, may this book inspire you to discover your freedom wherever you may be.

We came to Bali. We loved Bali. We returned again and again.

Bali forever beckons to those who love her.

Bali will never be "lost" in our hearts.

Matur Suksma! ("Thank you" in Balinese.)

LESLIE ANNE FRANKLIN
— California, USA 2020

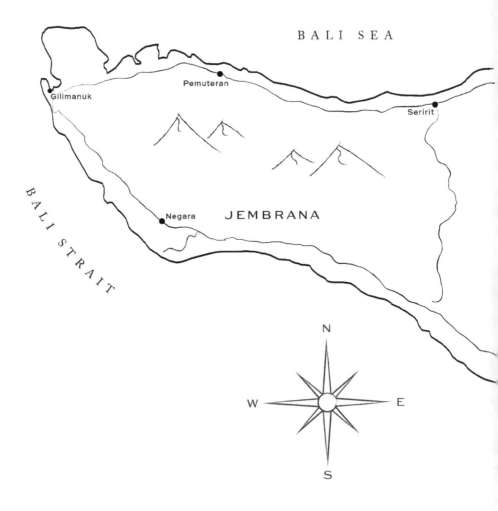

BALI SEA

Pemuteran

Gilimanuk

Seririt

BALI STRAIT

Negara

JEMBRANA

N

W   E

S

MAP OF
BALI

PART I

BALI
PRE–1970

Air filled with cloves
Frangipanis abound
Bells clang on golden cows
Island blessed, its people proud
Kecak dance extremely loud
Black rice pudding feeds the day
Adorning altars bend and pray
Daily tasks of sweeping, raking
Calendar festivals in the waiting
My first impressions of Bali pure
But for how long, days are fewer
Island paradise but at a cost
Before a way of life … a Bali lost

KEN JOHNSON
AUSTRALIAN ARTIST

Legong
Time Ago

RHETT HUTCHENCE

Rhett Hutchence is a Bali-based artist who has lived more than half his life outside Australia. Best-selling author and ex-naughty boy, his current business, Skull Bali, produces unique chic skull art and contemporary fashion.

After the war, in 1948, my dad, Kelland Hutchence, had secured a job with Qantas in Surabaya. In March, having two weeks' vacation, he decided to go to Bali. Bag packed and armed with a letter of introduction, he flew on a DC3 into Denpasar and was met by a local driver. Dad knew a little Malay, similar to Indonesian, but the driver, not understanding, thought it best that he drive him to the only other people he knew of who spoke English. A little while later, my dad was on the beach in Sanur at the house of Adrian-Jean Le Mayeur. Adrian was a Belgian-born impressionist artist who painted Bali culture and his muse and wife, Ni Pollok. Ni Pollok was a famous *Legong* dancer who had met Adrian at age fifteen and married him three years later. Considered royal entertainers, these girls usually married into noble families, so it was a shock to her family when she announced that she and Adrian had decided to marry—Adrian being nearly forty years her senior.

Traditionally, Legong dancers were girls who had not yet reached puberty, and after marriage, they would stop dancing. Dad had been asking Ni Pollok to do a dance one night for his dinner party guests, and she declined, stating that her *gamelan* orchestra was back in her hometown of Kelan. You can imagine the roads, or lack of, in 1948. However, one day Dad rented a truck, a driver, and an interpreter, and drove the track to Kelan, found her orchestra, explained the reasoning, loaded them up, then drove them back to Sanur. That evening, unable to decline, Ni Pollok danced the Legong with a sunset background on Sanur Beach. My dad told me it was incredibly mesmerizing and worth all the trouble. He also said there was an American there who hadn't stopped talking the whole time, telling this and that. When Ni Pollok started dancing, for the first time in a week, this New Yorker dropped his jaw and shut up, adding to the island's beauty.

In 1997, my father grieving from the loss of a son and me a brother, we both decided to return to Bali and its healing qualities. I went with my dad to the house, which is now the Le Mayeur Museum. It was fun to hear him reminiscing: "Oh, that's the room I stayed in, we ate there and had sunsets here …"

I presented some photos Dad had taken of Adrian painting back in '48 to the museum, where they currently hang.

Dad described his 1948 trip as the most beautiful two weeks of his life—life-changing.

I always wished my father had stayed in Bali and bought land or something. It was not until years later I realized that I would not be here to enjoy my life in Bali if he had, as he would never have met my mother.

That said, these stories and the photos my father took helped instill my love of Bali, which he had firmly cemented by taking our family there in 1972.

I kinda wish he had bought a painting too.

MY ADVICE FOR THE BALI VISITOR ———————————————

Visit Museum Le Mayeur, located on Sanur Beach at Jl. Hang Tuah, Sanur Kaja, Kec. Denpasar Sel., Kota Denpasar, Bali.

Five Decades Later: Looking Back at Bali

RIO HELMI

Rio Helmi was born in 1954 to an Indonesian diplomat father and a Turkish mother. A photographer and writer, Rio has been capturing images of Asia and writing since 1978. His work can be seen in magazines, documentaries, and more than twenty large-format photographic books.

Once upon a time, Ubud really was a village. During an early child-hood trip here with my family in 1963, my older sister left behind a bag with all our tickets and belongings that my father put her in charge of in the *wantilan* (town pavilion) by the side of the main road in Ubud, where we had stopped. Discovering this hours later in Besakih, she went into a teenage panic attack, but my father was completely assured and said, "We'll get it back", which we did with no fuss at all. It was still there, exactly where she'd left it several hours before, untouched. The main street of Ubud was a much more leisurely place in those days. This is not something I would like to test now.

Eight or so years later, when I came back to Ubud as a teenager, some things hadn't really changed. There was one public bus a day to Ubud from Denpasar. An old Ford with a wooden body "made in Bali" atop its chassis, it carried high priests, merchants, commoners, goats, chickens, and the odd stranger like myself at a stately pace. As the Balinese were much more attentive to the spirits back then, it was necessary to make offerings at certain corners or "dangerous spots." The conductor would hop off and trot alongside the groaning bus and put the offerings down, mutter a prayer while waving the essence off to the spirit, trot back alongside the bus, and hop on. The driver never took his foot off the accelerator.

A sixteen-year-old with almost waist-long hair, loose pajama pants, a shoulder bag, and sandals, I stepped off that bus from Denpasar late one afternoon in 1971 in Ubud. Broke but optimistic, I wandered south through the market, which in those days spilled out onto the monkey forest road. It had already shut down for the day, the stalls with their flat woven bamboo shades empty. Rice fields began right where the football field is now—nothing downhill from there but rice fields and the narrow dirt track that led to the Padang Tegal cemetery in the forest, which is now known by its English name: Monkey Forest.

Across the potholed main road, Ubud's *wantilan*—the closest thing to a town hall—had a big banyan tree towering over it to the north. It was under this tree that two of Ubud's most iconic warung food stalls of the time were to be found. Ibu Rai's *nasi campur* (mixed rice plate) on the eastern corner, and just next to it, separated by a woven bamboo *bedeg* "wall" to the west of it was Okawati's, who had already began to cater bit by bit to Western tastes. At Okawati's you could have "proot salad" (fruit salad)—fresh fruit, condensed milk, and fried peanuts—even if she only she was catering to the three or four non-Balinese living in what was still the village of Ubud at the time. If fruit salad wasn't your thing, you could also order instant oatmeal!

But most importantly that morning was the presence of a big, burly young Balinese man with a large head and a big beaming smile. I would add that he wore a Balinese sarong, but in those days everyone did. "*Selamat pagi*," ("Good morning") he said in a deep, booming voice. Nyoman Suradnya, aka Badung, was the first person in Ubud who befriended me. I think he found me an interesting oddity, and he was always curious about the world around him. Young and somewhat innocent (not that many thought that of him), that morning we chatted like old mates. He had a spontaneous openness and a seemingly endless sense of humor.

Often we sat there eating Ibu Rai's nasi campur, washing it down with a glass of steaming black coffee, and finishing it up with a clove cigarette (you could buy just one cigarette out of the packet in those days). It all added up to the grand total of twelve and a half rupiahs, or what we would call five *ringgits*. A ringgit was a two-and-a-half Rupiah unit that has long gone out of print and style. Nyoman always had jokes to tell and puns to deliver. He also knew everyone in town. He would fill me in with short, pithy descriptions of who they were. And everyone in town knew and liked him. Already then, he was a bit of an icon.

One by one, I got to know many of the people who would walk up from the main road to the dirt track that was to become Jalan Suweta. There were no road names, no house numbers, no electricity, no asphalt beyond the main road, and no phones. Addresses were by *banjars* (village council center), *subaks* (irrigation systems), temples, or in the vicinity of large trees. But it really didn't matter because it was a community. Everyone knew one another and where they were at any given time of day. It was an endless web of interrelationships sealed by marriages and loyalties. Outsiders like myself were a tiny minority. An outsider could be forgiven for not registering that this community had experienced the horror of dreadful bloodletting only six years before during the 1965 massacres.

I drank it all in with the thick, gritty *kopi Bali* and the long laughter-filled chats with Nyoman. When a rather distinguished man appeared across the road from an imposing brick gateway, I learned from Nyoman—both by his change in demeanor and his words—that this was the Tjokorda, the king of Ubud. I also got to know many of Ubud's movers and shakers while sitting there. This was Badung's world. Badung, too, was to become a mover and shaker in Ubud.

It seemed as if the entire population of Ubud was remarkable. On good days the late Tjokorda would make an appearance outside the palace and give you a hearty hello. He was one of the very few who had a car. Pak Roda—in real life a bit of an artist and quite the Balinese flute player—was the startlingly naïve and rather comic local "constable." Pak Klepin, in real life an unrepentant prankster, was the local tailor who somehow never could make five meters stretch into a pair of trousers (though later you would see his grandson wearing a cute little pair of pants and shirt with what seemed exactly the same fabric, while you walked around in trousers that were a couple of inches shorter than ordered). Pak Getén, the temperamental and coarse market sweeper cum *wayang* (shadow play) agent, would wobble his pushbike all the way down to Sukawati and back to arrange for Dalang puppeteers to perform in Ubud.

By nature gullible, Getén was once conned by the tailor into rolling a used forty-eight-gallon drum all the way up to Tegallalang in the hopes of recouping good money from a supposed buyer there. The road was mainly cobblestones, and there were no pickup trucks for hire then. No one in Tegallalang had heard of said buyer, nor did they have any use for what was by then a badly battered oil drum. Needless to say, Pak Klepin avoided him for many months after that.

Slowly, as electricity, asphalt, and TV made their way into all the corners of Ubud, and the local population multiplied, things changed. The tourist boom also arrived, and Ubud isn't such a simple village anymore. In the aisles of the local supermarkets (heavens, *now there's* a telling sign of change), once you have run the gauntlet of Ubud's traffic, you might run into young Russians and other Westerners in leathers and feathers, or a Japanese female saxophone player, or an Australian lady who has rented a villa to look after stray cats. Activities are not restricted to cooking classes or batik painting, but on the bulletin board outside Bali Buddha you can find notices for Cherokee Medicine Woman healing sessions or "Discover Your Inner Child"—or, if it's your lucky day, you can get a combination retreat of both for the price of one!

Ubud might not be quite so quaint anymore, but it's still a pretty colorful place.

MY ADVICE FOR THE BALI VISITOR ──────────────────

Tread lightly; you are a guest in someone else's house. Be respectful of the Balinese culture—whatever your opinions are of their traditions; they are just your opinions. (For example, beachwear is for the beach: please ladies, don't go exploring the island in your thongs and a short, flimsy, extremely see-through top—you would be amazed how many women do this.) The Balinese are very appreciative when you are respectful, and when you are not, they judge you harshly whether they show it or not.

I Have Arrived, I Am Home

ARTHUR KARVAN

Arthur Karvan was born in April 1943 in Australia to Greek parents. He married Gabrielle Godard in 1972 and had three children: Rupert, Claudia, and Paris. Arthur was involved in building restoration and construction in the inner suburbs of Sydney. He created the infamous Arthur's nightclub in Darlinghurst, Sydney, in 1976. In Bali, Arthur designed fabrics and produced traditional method batik fabrics. He also designed numerous restaurant venues specializing in Trompe-l'œil and painted finishes. He presently resides in Bali.

It was 1968. I wanted to run away from a broken heart. "I'm sick of love, and I'm in the thick of it," sung Bob Dylan.

I chanced on something, which was to be a solution to this love-sickness. At a cocktail party, I told my strife of a life to Lesley Walford, a renowned Sydney interior designer, and he suggested I speak to his boyfriend, Dicky Keep, who ran a travel agency. They had just come back from a place called Indonesia and stayed in one of its islands called Bali.

It didn't sound like much of a solution to me. I'd sort of heard of Indonesia. Bali I thought was somewhere near Tahiti or Hawaii. I associated it with Rodgers and Hammerstein's film *South Pacific*, with some island paradise called *Bali Hai*, all grass skirts, and leis. Not coming from the surfing world, which at the time was discovering

Bali as a surfer's paradise, I resonated a lot more with what was happening in our new youth-centric world, which had finally arrived in Australia thanks to the influence of the Beatles, the Stones, Carnaby Street, and the whole California scene, along with Flower Power and the protest movement against the war in Vietnam. I had already been to San Francisco and New York and seen what was going on with the students and young people generally. I had actually joined the March in Washington to protest the Vietnam War.

In Australia, there was an underground youth-oriented movement, but so many of our most creative and best minds had gone to London and made waves there. Martin Sharp (who designed the psychedelic album cover for Cream's *Disraeli Gears*), Germaine Greer, and Richard Neville, who shared the Pheasantry on the King's Road with the likes of Eric Clapton and others. And Neville's *Oz* magazine, which made history with Neville and his crew being jailed and charged with obscenity for a special edition for school kids. They won their case largely due to the inspired pleading of Geoffrey Robertson, who'd made his name as the go-to lawyer of the day when it came to human rights. It changed the censorship laws in Britain in the process.

A few years later, I too fell foul of the law and got locked up for making a film with my lifelong mentor Albie Thoms. *Vision For A New World*, a well-produced and creative short movie, included an abortion scene with an actress lying on a table with her legs open. The vice squad took a serious view of it because abortion was illegal. So the premiere itself was aborted, and we were dragged off to the lockup for questioning (held but not charged and later released).

My middle name is Urban, but you will always find me somewhere associated with nature!

I grew up in a New South Wales country town called Cowra, with a basic education and parents from an impoverished Greek background. My parents tried to Australianize us fast and hid our Greek culture to the extent of locking away the olive oil if visitors came to call (visitors hated the smell of olive oil, as they only used lard when they cooked). Speaking Greek at home wasn't allowed, in case we spoke with an Aussie accent. I became quite conflicted about my place in the world. So, by the age of twenty-four, I was gravitating toward a more free and progressive approach to the world. Without help, I was more than a little confused, and Australia was not doing it for me—back then, it just didn't seem to be the place to find the meaning of life, which is why so many of us at the time felt the need to leave and seek answers in other cultures.

I bought my ticket and was Bali bound.

From its rocky start as the Republic of Indonesia, Indonesia has presented a prickly pear face toward foreigners. Due to various foreign interventions in the run-up to and following its successful establishment in 1948 as a nation, Indonesia had a very xenophobic foreign policy and tried to keep foreigners and their influence at a distance. A few years before my arrival (1965–1966), the country had been engulfed in a traumatic reaction to a perceived Communist takeover, during which half to one million Indonesians—so-called Communists and their sympathizers—were slaughtered. As the killings spread throughout the country, local feuds and past grievances added fuel to the massacre. When peace returned, the army had taken full control of the country and decreed a new order. This was to involve an opening to foreign investment and development. A key component in this plan was the development of tourism, and Bali was to be the jewel in the crown. The program was kicked off by building a hideous government-owned eight-story hotel on the beach at Sanur and a new international airport a few miles down the beach, near the island's capital, Denpasar.

The Boeing jet with just a dozen or so people landed, and the doors opened. Stepping out onto the tarmac, I was hit with the intoxicating smells and the tropical heat, all enticingly new to me. It was a mix of frangipani, satay, *kretek* (clove) cigarettes, coconut oil, and the aroma of burning of rice stalks, all of which permeated the air. I loved it immediately, and within the hour I felt light and carefree. The immigration and customs agents were amiable. People were helping and carrying things for me, and the service was so polite and kind—it was heaven!

True, the airport was very basic, but then so was the one I'd just left in Sydney; the age of mass travel was in its infancy. This was even before the writer Diana Darling, who summed it up so well in her wonderful essay "You Missed the Best of It": "If you came to Bali as a young thing in, say 1976 [or 1980 as I did], you would have seen things that you can't capture in a selfie. You would have seen the movement of the invisible. But these days the old holy has become shy."

I had nowhere in mind to go, no map, no phone numbers—though, there weren't any phones in Sanur, which is where I decided I was going. My only contact was Donald Friend, an Australian artist, writer, and diarist, who had come here in 1967. I knew him slightly. He was very much a big name on the Australian art scene at the time, which by world standards back then wasn't very well known. Donald had established a name for his work in Europe and was also well known in the London art world. He was well-traveled and well connected. He had lived for a time in Sri Lanka, encouraged by his friend Bevis Bawa, who (pre-independence) had been aide-de-camp to the British governor.

It was through him he met his architect brother, Geoffrey, which then led Donald and his Indonesian friend and collaborator, Wija Waworuntu, to invite Geoffrey Bawa to Bali. That led to the creation of the Batujimbar Estate, which gave birth to what is now known worldwide as Tropical Asian architecture. The rest is history, particularly when it comes to tropical resort architectural design and development.

Donald was someone I knew through listening to his marvelous stories while sitting in the front bar. Actually, it was the bottle shop, which became the cozy bar of the Windsor Castle Hotel in Paddington, Sydney, for a select few who enjoyed the intellectual stimulus. His cleverness made him a bit scary, and I was shy about arriving out of the blue at his Bali villa, so I checked into the cheap government hotel near his house on Sanur Beach. It was basically just bamboo huts with a shower—which meant a bucket of water you poured over you, that was refilled twice a day.

The Indonesian rupiah then was 100 to the US dollar, so everything seemed cheap. I paid what was asked and had no concept of bargaining. Food was hard to work out. Nothing was familiar, and there were no restaurants. Supermarkets were still unknown in Australia. At home, there were cake shops, butchers, or corner grocery stores; there were greasy spoons where you got fish-and-chips, chiko rolls, and milk-shakes when out and about. Fruit from *warungs* (food stalls) was all I could find. The Balinese didn't eat bread, so that was off the menu. I hoped Donald would enlighten me.

I hit the beach. As now, Sanur Beach is a breathtaking part of nature. Its shallow waters behind a coral reef is seven kilometers long. Depending on tides, it is a plentiful fishing place, with the fish trapped behind the coral wall at low tide. The colorful *jukung* single-sail fishing boats lay on the sand or were being trawled off the beach for fishing. The place was hypnotically exotic.

This beach was part of a number of small villages that relied on it for their existence. From it they used the dead limestone coral to build their houses, temples, and walls and the bounty from the sea to eat. The catch is enormously varied—turtles, octopus, and squid forming some of it. Large grassy meadows common to the villages are grazed by the deer-like Bali cow amid the coconut trees. Very few structures were built from the main road down to the beach. It was all a nature wonderland with no fences and shared by the many villagers.

Because of the coral reef, the beach encompassed beautiful white sand. A little further north and extending along a long coastline, the sand changed to black due to the currents bringing in volcanic sand. Here on the beach, I found part of the solution of what to eat: seafood grilled over coconut-shell charcoal and sometimes whole small rock lobster from a little further along the beach, probably brought in by the fishermen from the large island sitting a mile or two off Sanur called Nusa Lembongan. Rice was almost another first for me! This was a fishing village, and I found out later that Sanur is a very spiritual area, home of the Brahman caste and also known for its sorcery that is sometimes called black magic.

Here I received my initiation into the things that welded me to Bali and why it became my home. I was drawn to the simple life, modest and contented, whose beacon is beauty. Bali engages with such amiability and kindness and is ever so sweetly polite. There is no describing it and the spell it casts. I gulped it up and could never get enough of it. And, at this point, I hadn't even seen the drive to the city of old Denpasar—its smelly market, its history, and a visit to the old Dutch colonial-built Hotel Bali.

The initial reaction to the question "How am I going to get through ten days here?" shifted to "Do I have enough time to see more?" On my first trip to Asia and I was bitten and smitten but didn't know what part of me and how. Slowly I started to see more closely the faces of the men and women I encountered. It was all so subtle because here, everything proceeds at the pace of nature; nothing goes any faster than the environment surrounding us. There are no machinery and manufactured noises, just the wind, and the ocean waves. As I realized the Balinese are always smiling, are so genuine and soft as they are, I started acting and feeling the same. No longer was I protecting myself and staring suspiciously out of a dark corner. Bali eased me into being myself. After the first few days, I slept like a baby.

When the time came to see Donald, I couldn't announce my arrival, so I just arrived cold around what I thought was a good time—the cocktail hour. It was good timing. There were some other guests, and I was again just an audience listening to Donald, the master raconteur. It was the environment he lived in that held my interest the most—a house with largely no walls that met the edges of the garden surrounded by beautiful walled courtyards. Young men with only sarongs and sashes were gliding around the place, helping with the drinks and snacks, and two lone musicians created the soothing music on instruments I'd never seen before.

At some point, I strolled outside and saw the house was almost on the beach, sheltered by large tropical trees. The site had been hand-picked for its unique vantage point over the ocean, slightly protected from the elements by the adjacent cape, which was the site of the nascent Tandjung Sari Hotel owned by Wija Waworuntu, a collection of bungalows catering to tourists, the only other one on Sanur Beach. It was all magnificent and seemed out of a fairy tale. Donald dropped in bits of information between his stories about what I could see and how.

It seemed transportation was limited to a couple of old American cars—a Chevy and a Plymouth from Mah Patimah's taxi service.

Now I was starting to realize that Bali had more of a Western presence than first appeared, given 350 years of Dutch colonization of Indonesia (only 100 years in Bali). It was enmeshed in the woodwork. Quite a few Europeans had resided in Bali. Austrians, Belgians, and Germans had settled here since the 1930s. The aristocrat-artist Adrien Le Mayeur lived at the other end of the beach from the 1930s until the mid-1950s, when his house became a museum. Predominately those who came here, like the artists' Spies and Bonnet, chose the mountain areas as the place to live, as did the American anthropologist Margaret Mead and British musicologist Colin McPhee, the latter two in Sayan, next door to where I would eventually live intermittently over a period of forty years. In the 1930s, Charlie Chaplin and Miguel Covarrubias came to the mountains too and fell in love with the culture.

So there I was, feeling a little less the pioneer and a good deal more confident as I headed off to the Bali Hotel in Denpasar in the big Chevy. Denpasar is not that much of a capital—it was a bit too small for that, but I was fascinated. Goods were pushed on makeshift carts, the beautiful *Dokar Hias* (horse-drawn passenger taxis) decorated in their finest. Gajah Mada, the main street, sold food, from vegetables to poultry, meat, fish, and spices that you could smell over the entire area. The market was a central distribution point selling to smaller traders in their villages, and so it was very busy.

There was a large Chinese presence with traders selling hand tools, ice-shaving machines, and scales with their beautiful bronze weights, and Bineke, the first coffee roasters, still there to this day. The Chinese store selling traditional medicines from local sources and the Chinese mainland, smelling strange and unfamiliar, drew me in for a closer look. Here in the adjacent market, there were stallholders selling cooked food, and I was introduced to my very first satay; then *Panggang* Chicken, *Betutu* Chicken, Chicken *Goreng*, endless chicken dishes, curries, and fish. More choices than I'd ever seen in Australia, which at that time had practically no cuisine at all, except "one meat and three veg." I went for something that sort of looked a bit like a batter thing from home—it turned out to be frogs' legs floured and deep-fried in coconut oil. An excellent choice, and by then, I wanted to try everything else. I'd truly hit upon Asia. The major element that drew me here was food—food so delicious, cooked home-style by people who had done it for centuries and served it road-side while sitting on plastic chairs, sucking in the charcoal fire fumes, the noise, and smell of a busy marketplace, which, after all, is all about food. It's so casual and natural; it still gets me.

I met a German girl on the beach with whom I spent a little time, but time was short, and I still wanted to visit the other recommended place before I left—Ubud, the genteel center for tourism. There was nothing there then that resembled a tourist location. You needed a lot more time than I had to get into the swing of it.

Donald said to go to the Royal Palace, Puri Kaleran Mandala in Peliatan, a village on the outskirts of central Ubud. The palace was familiar with foreigners, and some English was spoken. Here I heard the haunting music you hear all over the island and found out it was called *gamelan*. I was starting to understand how ignorant I was about the island. Its history was overwhelmingly rich, and its presence in the world was quite well known in some quarters (but not in the uncultured Australia I knew). The palace I stayed at was the backdrop to the dancers and musicians led by A. A. Agung Mandera, the Peliatan gamelan group and its young dancers, among them Ni Gusti Raka, who had become stars overnight in 1952–1953, delighting audiences around the world during the troupe's triumphant world tour.

I was invited to stay, as the palace was set up for paying guests. Breakfast was served the next day in the garden, consisting of fresh fruits, rice cakes, and *kopi Bali* served by the most beautiful smiling hand-clasped bowing staff—a pleasurable memory I've never forgotten. I kept thinking about how could I come back here again.

Naively, I thought in due course, everything about Bali would be-come widely known, but it never did. Modern Bali has gotten in the way of our finding out more of Bali's culture, and I have to reread the excellent books by Adrian Vickers, Colin McPhee, John Coast, Vicki

Baum, Bruce Carpenter, Made Wijaya, and Diana Darling to immerse myself again to know again how it was.

A few knowledgeable expats in the region and a handful of Australians already had—and many more would subsequently—beat a path to Sanur. Wija Waworuntu was instrumental in influencing the World Bank's plans for tourism development in Bali sufficiently to ensure that no buildings ever got built in Bali taller than a coconut tree. This cultured sense of ease and style led to a golden period before it was lost to a wave of mass tourism. A time when monarchs, aristocrats, old money, media barons, prime ministers, Elizabeth Taylor, John Wayne, Henri Cartier Bresson, Salvador Dali, Gore Vidal, and Buckminster Fuller all came to Sanur. The younger set—Jagger, Yoko Ono, Bowie, Barry Humphries, David Frost, David Byrne, Grace Jones, and bringing up the rear, Princess Di—are those who saw it before it was lost forever to overdevelopment. It continues remorselessly today—greedy operators build permanent structures on the sand of Sanur's beach so that they can cram a few more tables into their seaside restaurants.

"How and why did Bali become the world's most gorgeous culture?" demanded the late, great Made Wijaya. It had a violent and warlike past, some of that from internal conflicts and slave trading, some from European interlopers and Dutch colonists. It had had to stand up and defend itself many times, as in 1906 and 1908, when its chances of defeat and humiliation were so great that the Balinese preferred to undergo the mass ritual suicide called Puputan to mark their defiance and protest the inevitable.

I don't know the full answer to Made's question. What I do see is how Bali's culture and people are so loved for their politeness and good manners and how their culture so greatly affects nearly everyone who comes in contact with it.

What does occur to me, despite my limited knowledge of such matters, is that it must have something to do with the Balinese connection to nature. I once had an extremely talented woodworker with whom, as so often happens in Bali, I became good friends, and we would visit each other in our homes, and that is where I met his family.

His two daughters were angels, and I said so to him. He said, "Yes, it was planned like that," and he went on to explain that they were conceived on the exact right date according to the Bali calendar. With a full moon and before intercourse, they prayed in the forest to the gods, making offerings and supplications for a divine birth to follow.

My first impressions of seeing the harmonious life in the villages, on Sanur Beach, or the workers in the rice fields, all toiling in collective harmony in non-competitive activities to support their livelihoods and in sync with nature, has had a lasting impression on me. The underpinning spirituality of it was something I was to yet discover. Some years later, I became an early practitioner of biodynamic farming, from which the modern concept of permaculture grew. My sons went to Rudolf Steiner schools, and whenever I wasn't consumed by my urban existence, I tried to get back to something connected with the environment. After my kids grew up I came back to Bali, and it has been my home for twenty-five years.

Am I ready to return to my old life in Australia after all these years under Bali's spell? It's hard to say.

"I have grown to appreciate the refinements of the Orient, which is such a relief after the determination determinism of the Occident," observes the artist John Olsen.

Me? I'm just thinking—I wish my parents hadn't hidden the olive oil.

MY ADVICE FOR THE BALI VISITOR ───────────────

A trip to the old city of Denpasar. Start at the Museum Bali, then move on to Jl. Gajah Mada with its shopkeepers selling basics. A crossroad street is Jl. Sulawesi, also known as Arab Street, where you can find fabric galore including traditional batik. End up in the Pasar Bandung/Kumbasari Markets—this is the central distribution point for Denpasar for fruit, vegetables, fish, poultry and spice sellers. This gets going at 11 p.m. and trades all night until dawn when it turns to a chaotic scene of pickup trucks loading up, women to and fro with great loads on their heads and local breakfast and coffee smells wafting amidst the hustle and bustle. This is Asia. Sit on a plastic chair and suck up the atmosphere.

PART II

BALI
1970–1975

What you have taken has been from here
What you gave has been from here
What belongs to you today
belonged to someone yesterday
and will be someone else's tomorrow.
Change is the Law of The Universe.

BHAGAVAD GITA

The Old
Road to Bali

Janet DeNeefe

Melbourne-born Janet DeNeefe is the founder and director of the Ubud Food Festival, established in 2015, and the Ubud Writers and Readers Festival, established in 2004, one of the region's most successful and important literary events. It has recently been named as among the world's top six by the UK Telegraph. *She is the proprietor of Indus and Casa Luna restaurants, as well as Honeymoon Guesthouse. DeNeefe also runs Casa Luna Cooking School. Her books* Fragrant Rice *and* The Food of My Island Home *chart her on-going love affair with Balinese food, culture, and traditions.*

We would never have come to Bali but for my father. It was his idea, a quick decision, to take us on a family holiday after Christmas. He loathed the fuss and bother of time-consuming organizing and preferred the thrill of intrepid travel—spontaneous adventures to lesser-known places. My sister and I had heard about Bali from the *Morning of the Earth* surf film that heralded a new awakening for Australia's neighboring island. My mum thought it must surely be a destination full of swanky, glam hotels like Hawaii. My dad knew it as an artists' refuge from the tales of a painter friend who took art groups to Ubud. And so, out of the sky, within the crammed confines of a Garuda airplane, we swooped, swayed, and descended into Denpasar Airport on a single landing strip framed by lapping waves and palm trees.

January 1975. It is here my story begins.

The memories of our arrival are still very clear. The plane doors were flung open, and a gust of hot air loaded with the sticky scent of a verdant landscape caught me by surprise. My dad took photos; we were all in various stages of excitement and bewilderment, standing on the burning black tarmac. The thick, intense humidity was overwhelming. Rivers of sweat trickled through my hair, down my arms and legs, and collected at the back of my knees. My cotton kaftan clung to my body in folds around my thighs. Even the tangle of palm trees in the distance seemed to be melting with heat fatigue and dissolving like a mirage. The blistering hot midday sun beat on our backs as we made our way to the airport terminal, which looked more like a country schoolhouse, with tin roof and patchy white walls. Arched frangipani trees, with tufts of delicate leaves and a thousand small buds, framed the entrance, their shade offering both welcome relief and an alluring, delicious scent.

Queuing for Customs seemed to take an eternity. Small, carefully groomed men, skin the color of milk coffee and dressed in tight navy-blue uniforms, slowly examined our passports with definitely more intrigue than was warranted. Large stamps almost the size of their hands slammed the page. We eyed each other with curiosity. The sound of a different language, a puzzle of words, voices of a different pitch, rhythm, and passion rang in my ears. We were in unknown territory in a chaotic ocean of people—or, rather, men. And they were everywhere—sleeping flat on their backs on the floor, lazing on bench seats, waiting for guests with painted signs, hawking drinks and peanuts, or just passing time to see the tourists, some with shirts lifted to cool their bellies, and all were smoking. Our bags were grabbed enthusiastically, and we pushed our way outside into the open air.

Our young driver was waiting for us; our names scrawled on a large board. He was dressed in navy polyester flairs that swam around his skinny legs and a body-hugging pale-blue batik shirt. A layer of coconut oil kept his thick black hair slicked into place and framed his smooth, round caramel-colored face. A single frangipani blossom was tucked behind his ear. He was ready and dressed for tourist action.

With a huge radiating smile revealing large pearly-white gapped teeth, he politely introduced himself as Wayan. "Nice to meet you, Wayne," replied my father, towering over him and shaking his hand briskly. We piled into his sparkling-clean white Holden car, our bodies moist with sweat, and reclined against the hot vinyl seats.

The drive to Ubud took us along an endless narrow road lined with the tallest trees I'd ever seen that cast patterned shadows across the street. You had to strain your neck out the open window to see a patch of sky. Balinese dressed in faded sarongs—some topless—sauntered slowly alongside, at arm's length from the car window. I was tempted to hold out my hand and touch them as we drove by. We passed mud-brick, grass-roofed cottages half-hidden behind ancient-looking crumbled stone gates, rows of frangipani trees covered with yellow-white blossoms, papaya trees with huge cut-out leaves, red hibiscus hedges, roosters, pigs, barking dogs, cyclists on old Dutch-style bikes, and the occasional car. Giant shocking-pink bougainvillea's draped over leafy mango trees laden with dusty-green fruit, enormous ferns bathed in sunlight bursting forth under fringed palm trees, and small roadside food stalls drifted past in a vivid blur. The tiny patch of distant sky was framed by a riot of pink, red, and green. And between the lush growth were stretches of rice fields, massive banyan trees, moss-covered shrines, faded black-and-white-checked umbrellas, and piles of small sun-dried offerings. People washed in the shaded streams that lined the streets. It was a slow-motion movie of life and color. I could instantly feel myself retreating into my own world, getting lost in this oversized film set that was Bali back then.

Our holiday began when we arrived at the Hotel Tjampuhan in Ubud. Set on the slopes of the Tjampuhan River, this cluster of grass-roofed bungalows was our first experience of a tropical paradise. Tjampuhan refers to the meeting point of the two sacred rivers that converge here and become one. Our room was the lofty two-story Walter Spies bungalow that held enough beds for the whole family. The large terrace overlooked a picture-perfect lily pond where peacocks roamed. Beds for the children were on the timber mezzanine floor upstairs under sheer mosquito nets and a hand-stitched grass roof. Every morning the water carrier, with an enormous smile, brought two buckets of water, strapped in tandem across his shoulders, to fill our *bat mandi* with fresh spring water. The bat mandi was a square cement tub, like a large, deep sink, where you stored water for the morning and evening wash. With a small hand-held bucket, you drenched yourself until thoroughly clean and cool. There were no showers or bathtubs.

Each night, summoned by the call of a wooden gong, we gathered in the open restaurant pavilion that overlooked the sprawling garden. The scent of coconut candles floated through the air and provided a romantic light as we mingled with the guests, listening to their life stories. There was no electricity yet or what they called "electric city." Balinese bamboo music was played during dinner and tinkled down to the river. Mealtimes were *Rijstaffel-style* (Dutch Indonesian meal), with a procession of beautiful smiling young Balinese men and women wearing traditional shirts and patterned tea-colored sarongs, each adorned with a red hibiscus flower and bearing platters of Indonesian food to a seated audience. Frogs' legs, red fried rice, green leaves tossed in peanut sauce, a variety of satay, fruits poached in palm sugar, and other unknown dishes were part of the ongoing feast. It was the most intriguing food I had ever tasted.

Days were for exploring. Together with my family, we walked west of the hotel to Sanggingan, the next village. This small road now zooms with traffic and runs past our restaurant, Indus. We passed hundreds of ducks quacking in the rice fields that were tended by sturdy bare-chested farmers who were dressed in cotton sarongs tied between their legs like a nappy. They waved and smiled as we passed. Children greeted us with "Hello, hello" and gathered around us as we wandered up the hill. They laughed, sang, and chatted as we made our way to the next village. Years later, I was to learn that "Hello" is the name children call tourists.

Sometimes we took the other direction into town by walking down the hill and over the small bridge across the Tjampuhan River. Back then, the river was the communal bathing ground in the mornings and afternoons where young men and women flirted from their designated swimming areas (women upstream, men downstream), and Tarzan-like vines suspended over the cool water provided outdoor gymnastics for swinging into the river. The sound of splashing and laughter could be heard from the road, and later in the day, the voices became those of older women washing the family clothes, scrubbing them on the flat grey rocks that lined the water's edge.

The Tjampuhan River was also a hive of building activity with the construction of a new bridge beside the existing one. A daily procession of women carrying enormous rocks on their heads would appear from the steep riverbed, dropping their burden beside a pile of stones and cement, where Bridges Restaurant now sits. The pace was slow; there was no urgency. The bridge would be ready in the fullness of time.

The main street was lined with simple mud-brick compounds, some that rose above the road, tucked into the hillside. Everybody and everything was on the street—people, dogs, roosters, and black-bellied pigs, their tails swinging frantically to keep flies at bay. The market was much smaller back then and set in the same corner of Jalan Raya and Monkey Forest Road. No parking space needed, for humans were the only vehicles. The palace was more modest too. Swanky white geese—spiritual security guards—wandered freely and noisily around the crossroads: feathered traffic cops with no sense of humor!

The third day was market day. By sunrise, in the golden morning light, throngs of locals descended on this makeshift "shopping mall," buying before the heat of the day, a buzzing vortex of Balinese from different villages, a busy hum of haggling for chilies, ginger, dried fish, meat, coffee, and everything else they needed. It was a simple open-air setup with folks laying their provisions on mats on the ground, their wares shaded by flat woven bamboo "umbrellas." In the middle of the wet season it was a muddy, gruesome affair.

I was mesmerized by the women who heaved their baskets full of the morning's purchases on top of coiled towels on their heads and sauntered home with side-to-side precision, backs as straight as marching soldiers. And then there were the betel-chewing grandmas with red-stained lips and earlobes with drooping holes from wearing traditional earrings that became makeshift purses for rolled-up rupiah. Monkey Forest Road was a dirt track that eventually petered into rice fields. Canderi's, just a few meters down the road, was already up and running in 1975 and was the proverbial "home away from home" for many off-the-beaten-track tourists.

Across from the market, the grounds of the village pavilion became a betting ring for cockfighting after midday—a different sort of marketplace that focused on gambling rather than bargaining. We watched out of curiosity, crowded by thick rows of men and the scent of clove cigarettes, coconut oil, and body odor, to a chorus of mad chants with each new game played. I've never understood throwing money away on the sport of two fighting roosters. The government eventually banned cockfighting, and it is now limited to ceremonies and wherever else they can play in secrecy!

Afternoons brought rain falling in sheets and as regular as clockwork, a shimmering water show of delicious coolness that sent filtered shades of silver light across the terrain. Sometimes I would float in the Tjampuhan Hotel's spring-water pool carved into the hillside, gazing up at a sky framed by coconut palms, relishing the glorious downpour. I was wrapped in a silken web of wonderment, a spinning, gossamer dreamworld I never wanted to end.

At night, we watched spellbinding performances by slender young girls who wore brilliant pink, green, purple, and gold-patterned costumes and crowns of fragrant white frangipani flowers. To the vibrant sound of the *gamelan* music, they danced with curved fingers, flashing eyes, and movements like swaying palm trees. Every day I'd practice the sliding eye movements, secretly wishing I could be a Balinese dancer. After dinner, when conversations with staff and guests had dissipated, we watched a ballet of fireflies from our terrace, enjoying the balmy indigo-black evening while sipping rice wine to the sounds of a wild orchestra of frogs, owls, dogs, crickets, and peacocks performing on a shadowy forest stage, moon suspended overhead with nature as our theatre.

Our driver, Wayan, took us to Kintamani and proudly showed us the dramatic vista of Mt. Batur, Lake Batur, and the distant, lofty Mt. Agung—active volcanoes in a gentle landscape. Our viewing area was a simple dirt overlook, unlike the paved decks of nowadays. There were no other buildings in sight, just a panorama of nature's magnificence. We visited Besakih too, which was a collection of simple shrines with matted black coconut-fiber roofs. The journey took us past rice fields, mud-brick cottages, and fields of tangerines, corn, and sugarcane. Clove, coffee, banana, and cocoa trees grew wild along the road's edge.

I especially loved the sparkling sun-drenched mornings and waking up to an alarm clock jungle of birds, from cooing pigeons to the *cheep, cheep* of sparrows, the soprano shriek of peacocks, and the *swish, swish* of bamboo brooms sweeping the grounds of the family compound. If it were early enough, a silky mist would hover above the river, as if suspended in thought, before dissolving into the day. I was told it was the smoke of angels cooking. Hibiscus in Gauguin reds and pinks were placed daily in a small bowl on our table. Breakfast was papaya and banana with a slice of lime, white bread toast that was a tad too soft, served with waxy weird Blue Band margarine and sweet pineapple jam.

I was immediately enchanted by this ornate culture where the intense colors of the tropics were matched only by the graciousness of the Balinese. I thought they were the most beautiful people I had ever seen with their smooth, polished skin, elegance, and warmth. This fragrant paradise was seething with sensuality and beauty, and I will never forget the impact of this first visit.

My second visit, in 1984, nine years later, was the turning point of my life. On the second day of my holiday, I met my future husband, Ketut, and the rest, as they say, is history. Six months later, in 1985, I was back with a mission to write a Balinese cookbook and introduce the world to the food I had grown to love.

It felt as if nothing had changed. I moved into Nani House, a small guesthouse owned by my future sister-in-law, Kasi, on Monkey Forest Road, south of the soccer field. I spent my mornings in her kitchen jotting down recipes and drawing mysterious ingredients while she created a breakfast of exotica: small fish with chilies, blanched greens with coconut, tofu with tomato *sambal*, braised pork, slow-cooked jackfruit, eggs, sambal, and rice. My Balinese culinary studies had officially commenced. My day started at six a.m. with a cup of hot Balinese coffee—*kopi tubruk*. More than thirty years later, I still start my day the same way.

After breakfast, I would walk up Monkey Forest Road to the crossroads to catch a public *bemo* (minivan bus) to the Pantheon, Ketut's wood carving gallery, in Mas village. Monkey Forest Road was mainly rice fields back then, with a few small homes here and there. I'd pass the primary school and soccer field, watching the students line up for speeches or simple exercise routines before the heat of the day, marvelling at their iridescent white shirts and immaculate uniforms. At the market, I'd squeeze into the back of a bemo, pressed between as many humans as possible, as well as chickens, sacks of rice, and vegetables. I loved catching these beat-up open-back trucks and enjoying the camaraderie of so many passengers in ridiculously close confines, an egalitarian people-journey. Invariably a *kebaya*-wearing grandma would sit next to me and press her hand firmly on my knee for stability while the bemo swayed and jolted to a halt when anyone flagged the driver down. There were always kids, too, who would either stare at me nonstop or cry. Some people talked to me, mainly men, practicing their English. "Wherrre you prom, miss?"

I spent my mornings at the gallery, sitting in the simple kitchen, watching the girls cook the staff meals, notebook and camera in hand. After lunch, I would return to Ubud and wander through the Ubud market, which now had a covered section. I'd meander through the network of crammed stalls and pungent smells, practicing my makeshift Indonesian with often embarrassing results. Ketut had advised me about the correct clothing to wear, which included no hems above the knee, shoulders covered—preferably arms too—and definitely no armpits showing. A friend told me later how her thighs were pinched by Balinese grandmas when she wore short shorts in the market.

Afternoons were spent in local restaurants lazing on bamboo chairs around small bamboo tables. We'd sip freshly squeezed lime juice with loads of crushed ice while Ketut would tell us tales of Indonesian myths and legends. "If you want to understand the Balinese character, you should read the *Mahabharata and Ramayana*," Ketut told me. At night, we'd visit Canderi's restaurant and spend hours among assorted eccentric Balinese and others, the likes of which Ubud will never see again. They played guitar and chess and told stories of crazy mishaps, black magic, and the terror of 1965. The tragedy of that time is still buried deeply within the hearts of many.

Ubud was a quiet, sleepy town in 1985—Bali, "the morning of the world," as Nehru had called it. Traffic comprised of Vespas, Holden cars, pickup trucks, bemos, cyclists on old Dutch bicycles, and pedestrians. Late in the day, farmers would walk along the main road with their cows in tow or a flock of ducks that obediently followed the farmer's white flag. On the tiered steps of Toko Tino's, next to Casa Luna, we would sit and watch processions of animals in the fading light. (There was a lot more sitting around back then!)

Oka Wati's, tucked in the rice fields behind Monkey Forest Road near the primary school, was another favorite eatery. It was run by the enigmatic Oka Wati, who was known for her *nasi goreng* and other more adventurous specials, such as mixed salad and toasted cheese sandwiches. Another regular haunt that overlooked the rice fields was Ubud Restaurant, run by Ketut's brother. He served the finest Balinese food in town, all made to order (meaning it took ages!), and his dishes were the inspiration for our first restaurant, Lilies. Monkey Forest Road was now a narrow paved thoroughfare lined with flowering purple orchid trees. It ran all the way to the tangled jungle of monkeys, continued past the Padang Tegal cemetery, and then curved a path through to Pengosekan.

The rivers were still a hive of washing activity, providing additional time to socialize with friends before nightfall. Kasi's young daughter, Nani, and her schoolmates would wash in the cool rock pool in the Monkey Forest, carrying buckets filled with towels and clean clothes on their heads. They would return, refreshed and laughing, with their buckets brimming with spring water for the next day's cooking. In time, everyone had running water and built bathrooms.

What is it that draws us to another country and to create a home there? John Le Carré said, "To have another language is to have another soul." I think about my life between cultures and can't imagine it any other way. I still live happily in Ubud, and my life continues to flow in many directions. I thank Bali for allowing me to make my dreams a reality.

MY ADVICE FOR THE BALI VISITOR

Dine at Casa Luna! Established in 1992 and set in the main road of Ubud, Casa Luna is an iconic, multi-leveled eatery that dishes up a mix of Balinese and Mediterranean fare, as well as, artisan breads and baked goods from the Honeymoon Bakery. It is also the home of the international Ubud Writers and Readers Festival and the Ubud Food Festival.

Letter
to Bob

PETER REX THOMAS

Peter Rex Thomas is an Australian who traveled overland from Timor through Asia to London in 1971. He wrote this letter to friend who was en route to Bali. Peter worked in London and New York before returning to Bali in 1975, where his son Putu Jai was born. He worked in Bali for both the Florida Folk Art Museum and the huge Ron Jon Surf Shop USA chain. Peter is a published poet and the owner of Shelf Respect Booksellers in Australia and is married to Marie. They have a dog named Saffron.

Bangkok, June 1971

Dear Bob,

Bali, needless to say, is paradise.

Arriving by plane, you'll land at Denpasar Airport—that's about ten kilometers from the city, and the only road runs almost parallel to the beach. I think the beach is the best place to stay. The motorized trishaws are so cheap that you can go into the city every day if you want. Don't take one of the big taxis from the airport; take a *bemo*. It is about two km along the road. Just as you turn a corner, turn left down a dirt road for about three hundred yards, and straight in front, you'll find a nonstop six-foot-high perfect wave about a mile long. On both sides of the road are small hotels and stalls, all the way down to the beach. They are quite cheap, as low as you will find in the town.

There are about 375 rupiah to the US dollar and no black market. At any of the *losmens* (homestays), you can expect to pay about Rp 150 a night, although we once got it down to Rp 50. They are quite clean and will get you anything. A bemo to the "city" shouldn't cost you more than Rp 25. Not bad for quite a long trip of eight kilometers. While you are on the beach, say hi to Jenny, an exquisite woman who runs the local salad stand. I'd love to know if she remembers me (her real name is Jenik, now the owner of the Poppies group). Denpasar is the capital; the only other large towns we found were Singaraja in the north and Kintamani at the crater of the volcano. Both are worth the trip. But Denpasar is where everything is based. This is where you can cash traveler's cheques and buy *Newsweek*, although you won't be as starved for news as we were (Australian Prime Minister Gorton had just been sacked!).

Go to the Three Sisters, a cafe about four cross streets from the Hotel Bali and the main street. Just ask any other traveler—they all know it. It is run by three girls, and they are bloody good cooks. There is a chance that my (passport) photo will be on the wall somewhere, and the middle sister may still have my old army hat. It would be great if so!

It is much better if you speak some Malay. It's simple and quite logical. *Nasi goreng*: fried rice; *es jeruk*: ice lemon or lime; *mie goreng*: fried noodles; *babi guling*: roast pig. *Minum* means drink, so *minum air* is boiled drinking water (they get sick too). *Berapa?* How much? *Dimana?* Where (is something?)

Where to stay? In Denpasar: Arjuna 39, Adi Yasa, or Two Brothers. The first two are near the Three Sisters cafe. You can rent a small 90 Honda for about two dollars a day. That is usually for twenty-four hours, if more than one day at a time. With two on the bike it is very cheap—all you need is your international license, and a day's riding will take you anywhere on the island, although it can be a long way back. Make sure you get one in good condition.

I think the bike is essential for you to get around. There is the volcano (still active), the Elephant Cave Temple, and the Grand Temple at the top of the mountains (along with about 9,998 others). The wood-carving center, the painting centers, the evening bath ritual... and the morning one too! The music and the dances—there is just so much to see and discover.

If you have a few spare bob, the Balinese are the best woodcarvers in Asia, and their paintings are very distinctive (and curiously Cubist in influence). The Ramayana wooden books are unique, and the ceremonial swords (*kris*) are beautiful. However, the batik is just as cheap in Jogjakarta—they make most of them there and have a much larger range to choose from.

The thing about the Balinese is that you are treated as a friend, not a mark. They'll try to sell you something, sure, but I think they often enjoy the bargaining more than the sale. I am sure one fellow I met made a loss on a painting he sold me. I know his wife was furious, but after spending nearly three days solidly with me, and coming down to about 7% of his original price, he was so delighted that I finally bought it, and had so enjoyed the battle, that he took me to his home for dinner!

Don't forget the sunsets on Kuta Beach. With the "right utensils," they are even better (if possible), and try the coconut wine! To Surabaya, take an "Eletha" bus from the booking office near the Bali Hotel. It is a good trip for Rp 850, and the ferry trip is a pass-way into another world.

Safe travels,
Peter

MY ADVICE FOR THE BALI VISITOR ——————————

Visit Tirta Empul Temple. Tirta Empul Temple is a Hindu Balinese water temple located near the town of Tampaksiring. The temple compound consists of a Petirtaan or bathing pool, famous for its holy spring water, where the Balinese go to for ritual purification. This place is ancient and awe-inspiring. You will need to wear a sarong and a sash.

Magical
Mystery Tour

SIMON DAVIS

Simon Davis first arrived in Bali in 1972 from Australia on the yacht Kimbala. *He has been trading and traveling throughout Southeast Asia ever since his retirement in 2000. He is married to Teresa, whom he met in Bali, and they have worked and traveled the world together for some forty years. They now live in the Northern Rivers region of New South Wales in Australia and still travel the world.*

I first arrived in Bali in 1972 onboard the yacht *Kimbala*. I had a quarter share in her, which I and George (another co-owner) sailed from New Zealand to Sydney via Lord Howe Island and then on to Bali via Thursday Island and Dili Timor.

We finally made it to Bali and sailed through the outer reef into the comfort of Benoa Harbor. In those days, there was not much in Benoa: a fishing village to one side and a couple of warungs on the side we anchored.

It was a beautiful spot surrounded by coconut trees, mangroves, and a myriad of small fishing boats whose owners would paddle over to our yacht and offer us untold amounts of seafood for a small sum. The Balinese were beautiful people—all smiles and laughter—and made us feel welcome.

After a few days, and having located the harbormaster, we decided to leave the boat and go over to Kuta, which in those days was also just a fishing village and a few shops with a dirt road running down to the beach.

We found a place to stay—the *losmen* Radiasa—with super friendly owners and their children. Our days were spent walking down to the beach, lazing in the sun, and surfing in front of Kuta. Every day we would do this, and we became friendly with three young Balinese girls—Wayan, Made, and Nyoman—who would sell us pineapples, papaya, bananas, and other fruit. I remember these girls because I'm still friends with one Made Jadi, who now travels around the world representing her clothing company.

Kuta was great—friendly faces, big smiles, and a few good rustic warungs to eat at.

The sound of the *gamelan* was ever-present, as well as friendly cock-fights in the streets. At night there were puppet shows called *wayang kulit* in the coconut groves, where a sheet would be strung up between coconut trees and lanterns held behind the sheets to illuminate the puppets for an adoring audience of Balinese children. On other nights the word would go out about a trance dance to be held in a cemetery behind the beach dunes down toward the airport. We walked over there at midnight with the Balinese and saw lanterns and fire lights everywhere, gamelan musicians, and colorfully dressed Balinese in their sarongs and *kebayas* (women's traditional lace tops). The trance dance was otherworldly.

After a week of this, I thought I had to see more of the island, so one day, after I had taken some magic mushrooms, which were for sale in a small restaurant, I decided to go exploring.

I hopped on my motorbike and headed out into the country. Wow, was I blown away—golden rice fields as far as the eye could see undulating in the breeze, like waves on an ocean. I felt like jumping into them and immersing myself. I didn't though and continued on, and at some point, I realized I was going toward the mountain and decided that this should be my destination.

As I approached what I thought was the top, my bike ran out of gas.

I started to push, and a young Balinese boy came out of the jungle and offered to help me push to a gas seller. The boy and I became friendly, and he asked me if I would like to go to a festival his village was having. Of course, I jumped at the chance.

Well, the festival was on the other side of the volcano lake at the base of the volcano. The view of the volcano was magnificent from where we started. We wove our way down toward the lake via a small path, and there were small horses carrying the frailer, older villagers, and goods. At the bottom, I was ushered into a small canoe and paddled over to the other side to what was the base of the volcano and the festival site. It was truly magnificent and colorful, with food stalls, gambling mats, Balinese dancing, ceremonial rites, and plenty more.

Night came, and I was ushered into an eight-man canvas tent— bloody cold too, but with Balinese bodies and a dog sleeping at the top of my head, I survived. In the morning, we climbed the volcano.

This was my introduction to Bali in 1972, and I returned there to work for many years after that.

MY ADVICE FOR THE BALI VISITOR ————————————

Go to Amed!

Our First
Bali Family

CHRISTOPHER HAZZARD

Christopher Hazzard is a Trinidadian-born Australian-trained doctor who grew up all over the world. He and his wife, Veronica, discovered that Bali was their spiritual home in 1972 and have spent time there every year since. Refusing to be just one thing, he is an artist, surfer, ex-beachcombing grandfather, enjoying being alive.

We arrived in Bali with our heads filled with stories of how inexpensive it was to live. "Just get off the plane, catch a *bemo* (small bus) to Kuta, and find a place..." was the advice we'd been given. When the plane stopped, gangways were brought alongside and we walked across the tarmac to the airport building, which was a simple building with a tin roof and open like a classical Javanese *joglo* (traditional home).

We had the name of the *losmen* (homestay)—Mandara on Kuta Beach Road—and that is where we went. The only room they had available was terrible—a bunk in a *lumbung* (rice barn) accessed by a ladder, through a small rice barn door and with no windows and a dirty toilet. We could not stay.

On the flight, we had befriended a New Zealand girl called Emily, who was even less ready for Bali than we were. We walked together down to the beach and along toward Kartika Plaza. On the walk, a Spaniard joined us. He was already at home with a deep tan and wearing a sarong. He recommended the Garden Restaurant, and so we walked up Jl. Pantai Kuta with him to Buni Sari where the restaurant was. We asked for a room, and they told us that they would have one the next day.

The night was falling as we walked out onto Jl. Pantai Kuta. A *Barong* dance was being performed. The barong, I think, from Bajar Tegal. "Oh, another amateur barong," our friend said dismissively, and he left, but we stayed. It was just in the street between Bemo Corner and Airport Road. The dance progressed to the stage of the *keris* (sometimes spelled *kris*, these are Balinese and Javanese swords that are said to have magical power) dance, in which the warriors start going into a trance, rushing at *Rangda*, and then when repulsed, stabbing themselves and falling to the ground. The crowd pressed forward, and as we were in the front, I was pushed so close to the dancers and their flailing keris. The emotion generated was so strong it engulfed me, and I felt that any minute I was going to vomit.

Our Bali adventure had begun. Only in retrospect, I realized that the events of that evening were sort of magic. For instance, our Spanish guide disappeared; we never saw him again. To see a real barong—not a tourist performance—in which there is a magical battle between good and evil sealed our fate. Bali had captured us.

The next day we moved into the Garden Restaurant. On the eastern side they had built a losmen with six rooms, each with a bed and a dressing table, and in the back, the *kamar mandi* (bathroom). The kamar mandi consisted of a squat toilet and the cement *mandi* (tub), which was filled each day from the back of the building with water pumped from the well by hand. There was no electricity. Each room opened onto a communal verandah with a small table and two chairs in front.

Over the next few weeks, we became members of the family. Ibu Made was the female head of the household, married to Pak Pugug. Pak and Ibu were not able to have children, and so Ibu adopted a boy and a girl from another part of her family. Ketut Wenten was a strong, bright boy in his teens. He was very keen to learn and a good worker. He helped in the losmen pumping water and cleaning. The girl we called

Little Wayan. Her task was to help Ibu in the kitchen. Little Wayan was pregnant, but there was no father. When asked about the father and his whereabouts, she said that she did not know.

Because she was not able to conceive, Ibu had chosen a second wife for Pak. Wayan wife number two was a good woman, very helpful with temple offerings and other responsibilities. More importantly, they were able to have children. The infertility in the marriage was due to Ibu Made as time was to tell. Wayan wife number two was less beautiful than Ibu, and I think that this was why she was chosen. On the surface of things, everything was fine, but we sensed some tensions in the family, which sometimes erupted into noisy arguments (in Balinese, so we had no idea what was the cause).

The following year we came again and discovered the cause of those angry words.

We had intended to stay at the Garden again, but Ibu said that we should stay in Pusuh Sari, the cottages that Pak had built on his land in Tuban (or it may have been Kuta Kelod—I am not sure) just south of Kartika Plaza Hotel. Pak and his family had owned all of the beachfront land, which is now Kartika Plaza, but the government commandeered it, paying him a small compensation and leaving the small parcel of land on which he had built Pusuh Sari.

Pak lived there with little Wayan. He was the father of her first child, and she was pregnant with the second. Wayan told us that at the time of the birth, she had gone crazy and run away. She gave birth alone in a rice field. The baby was born with cerebral palsy and mild retardation, possibly a result of birth trauma. Almost every year, we would arrive, and Wayan would have had another child, eventually totaling six sons.

Our life in Pusuh Sari was blissful, but it could not last. Tourism was developing at a great pace, and some of the changes due to this development made staying in this part of Bali intolerable.

The end of our staying at Pusuh Sari became inevitable when Pak had built some losmen-style rooms at Pusuh Sari, which he rented out to parties of Japanese businessmen, who, after concluding their business, would acquire the services of some local *kupu kupu malam* (which translates as "butterflies of the night"—working girls). They first would eat and drink in some establishment, and around about eleven p.m. they would arrive at our place, drunk and noisy. There were cars arriving and leaving with lots of slaps and tickles.

We needed to find a new place, and so the next time we arrived in Bali, we did.

For many years we have had no contact with the family, and we have never revisited Pusuh Sari. I believe that Little Wayan is still alive, and the baby Pak had with Wayan wife number two now has a restaurant in Jimbaran, and we are now Facebook friends.

MY ADVICE FOR THE BALI VISITOR ───────────────

Walk to Kuta market at daybreak. Buy some fresh fruit and have a coffee. It has hardly changed since the 1970s. Actually, you can go to any village market in Bali and have a similar experience.

The Keepers of the Light

BRUCE W. CARPENTER

Anglo-American Bruce W. Carpenter is a respected art historian and Bali resident who has authored and coauthored more than twenty books on the art, history, and culture of Indonesia and Bali, including the newly released Heroes, Gods and Guardians *(2021). He currently resides on Sanur Beach and is actively involved in numerous cultural projects.*

Om Mahajwalay Vidmahe Agni
Madhyay Dhimai Tanno Agnih Prachodayat.
"Meditate on the great flame, grant me with higher intellect,
let the radiant God of Fire illuminate my mind."
— AGNI GAYANI MANTRA

Since the dawn of history, the keepers of fire and light have always held an esteemed place of honor in mankind's collective myths and legends. According to Hindu belief, the universe was a black void until Agni, the god of fire, brought light, thus creating day and night (Mairtrayani Samhitastate). Worshipped until this day, along with the sun god Bhatara Surya, Bhatara Agni's name is the root of the Balinese and Indonesian words for fire—respectively gani *and* api. *This is the story of my own magical encounter with these mythological beings on the island of Bali in 1976.*

Like most young travelers bound for Bali in the 1970s, the last stop before embarking on the final leg of our journey to the fabled island was Yogyakarta, a royal Javanese city that served as a restorative oasis and acclimation zone after the shock of being suddenly confronted by the confusing urban chaos of Jakarta, the usual port of entry. In contrast, Yogya with its charming palaces, ruins, and bustling native market was a laid-back re-creation of *tempo dulu* (time before), the romantic vision of Indonesia that prevailed in nineteenth-century travelogues like Eliza Scidmore's Java: *The Garden of the East* (1897).

Here we were in the realm of Nyai Roro Kidul, the jealous goddess of the South Seas, immersed in the aroma of clove cigarettes, sweet jasmine tea, and coconut oil at a time that the batik sarong and *kebaya* ruled supreme. Our interlude included full-moon bicycle rides down to the churning waters and cliffs of Parentretes Beach and the solemnity of the Kraton palace with the slow intonations of large gongs and endless ancient Hindu-Buddhist temples, including Borobudur, which lay in the shadow of Gunung Api, a still-smoking volcano.

Yogyakarta was also the place that my traveling companion, Charles Junod, alias Chan, and I would start meeting the colorful band of gypsies who were on the road. Adventurous nomads all, we were fleeing the madness and contradictions of the West with naïve expectations of achieving enlightenment, fame, or fortune. At the time Chan and I were theater vagabonds who had performed with the Friends Road Show, a raucous troupe of anarchistic clowns headed by Jango Edwards. The people we met in Yogya included Alfie, a comical Italian fruitarian from Sicily sampling local varieties and collecting seeds to plant in his homeland; his tall, long-legged German girlfriend, who deservedly called herself the goddess; and Robert, a burly and charismatic American from the Midwest who had discovered that the local pharmacies were happy to sell him all types of prescription drugs after he told them he was a doctor. Together they shared a house with John Barker, a studious, mousy outsider who was constantly bickering with Robert's nonstop gatherings. He later went on to author a thin book on how to learn Indonesian that was kept in print by Periplus Editions long after many of us realized that it was in many ways rather useless. It was during this period that I met Michel Picard, a budding French scholar, who later became an acclaimed Balinese expert. He remains one of my closest friends to this day.

After two weeks had flown by, Chan and I decided it was time to make the final move onward. So we left the Asia-Afrika Hotel next to the train station to buy tickets on a *Bis Kilat* or Lightning Bus from a dingy *biro jasa* (agent) found on the rabbit warren of streets behind us. That night I replayed the events that had brought me to the brink. My first taste of Bali occurred as a young lad. Playing hooky, I would ride the Long Island Railroad to the 1964 New York World's Fair. While I was much amazed by Futurama, the vision of the future—which featured phones with TV screens, the first presentation of the Ford Mustang, and other such sights—the pavilion that truly gripped me belonged to Indonesia. As I entered in through its doors, I was overwhelmed by an exhilarating exotic feeling. I remembered an amazing image of a *Kecak* dance in a 1966 edition of *Life* magazine. Taken with the newly invented fisheye lens, the circle of distorted dancers with bare tops and checkered over-sarongs had triggered an epiphany of sorts, the first in a series of "signs" that led me to believe my destiny was inextricably linked with a South Sea island imbued with the cosmic mystery of Shangri-La, about which I knew little if anything. This was the place I needed to go.

Our trip to Bali proved as terrifying and exhausting as it was thrilling. Climbing into a brightly colored iron box on wheels, a primitive local precursor of bullet trains, I found myself cramped in a middle seat barreling down the narrow potholed northern postal road at speeds that rattled the body and mind. Our short muscle-bound driver, with no neck and bloodshot eyes, took few breaks, leading to the suspicion that the little red pills he gobbled down with sweet black coffee were bennies. Swerving violently as he changed lanes to avoid oncoming traffic and the giant rain trees lining the roads, which had been planted to give shadow in the age of horse and buggy, there were moments I thought that my end was nigh.

Every two hours or so, between warp-speed jumps, the bus would suddenly screech to a halt in a series of terminals, such as Surabaya's notorious Joyoboyo, where it would be boarded by a bustling chaos of vendors, pickpockets, street musicians, and beggars wandering the aisles colliding with disembarking and newly boarding passengers. Too exhausted to join the melee. Instead, we sweltered in the heat in an age before air conditioning and took care that our baggage wasn't washed away with the tide of humanity. The bus would also stop at remote ramshackle bamboo restaurants for fifteen-minute toilet and feeding frenzies.

At a certain point, the lack of sleep, constant inhalation of the smoke of thick pungent clove cigarettes—not the tame filtered ones sold nowadays—and general sensory overload caused me to feel I was in a confusing alternate universe. All this changed as I peered out my window at the break of dawn to see golden rays embrace a surrealist chain of undulating mountains from a fairy tale. Shortly later, we stopped to eat breakfast at Pasir Putih, a beautiful stretch of white sand with crystalline turquoise waters, multihued outriggers, and even a pelican that had somehow been blown off course. As we inhaled, we sensed we had reached the borderlands of paradise.

After crossing the Bali straits in a wooden boat—a windy trip along the south coast—our bus abruptly dropped us off on the streets of Denpasar. Our journey to Kuta proved to be the final gauntlet as we boarded a series of *bemos*—miniature Mitsubishi pickup trucks equipped with parallel wooden planks as seats. They were our first intimate experience with the Balinese. Jostling with old ladies with rolled-up towels on their heads and large baskets, we were overwhelmed by the smell of fresh coconut oil, with which the women copiously anointed their hair, mixed with the honest sweat of hardworking people. The chewing of betel nut, now a past memory, was ubiquitous.

Faces changed as riders chewed carefully prepared quids wrapped in pepper leaves to a mash. Cheeks bulged and teeth and lips were stained red as the teeth constantly grinded. At last we reached Kuta's nearly abandoned Bemo Corner, the last trip of the day. Our greeting party was a gaggle of young boys in sarongs and shirts who smiled and invited us to come and stay at their family *losmen*, the Indonesian pronunciation of the original French word *logement* or pension house. Chan and I followed along narrow sandy paths through a endless plantation of swaying coconut palms. The only other beings around were deer-like Balinese cows with white rumps that ran from us in terror as the wooden bells around their necks clanged. In the distance, we could hear the exhilarating roar of surf and smell a still-invisible sea.

At last, we arrived at Losmen Satria, our new home, a Balinese compound surrounded by a thick bamboo fence interwoven with thorned plants. Within its perimeters sat a newly constructed lodging house hastily built to accommodate the growing stream of young travelers. It consisted of a row of six rooms, each with a verandah and small bathrooms with a squat toilet and mandi basin for washing, equipped with bamboo chairs, a table, and two single beds. We were delighted, and our hosts could not have been more hospitable, as tea and bananas suddenly arrived.

After putting on our bathing suits, we walked the sandy path past dry seagrass to the beach, a magnificent curve that stretched as far as the eye could see. The crashing waves were like champagne. Musing at the strange spiral patterns created by crabs digging in wet sand, we watched the sunset, a fiery globe descending into a shimmering sea. I knew that I was home.

In the next weeks, my time was spent between the beach and fascination with the Balinese. I quickly came to admire the beauty and miracle of their ancient rhythm of life. Although the men seemed dominant, it was the women who stood as the foundation and shouldered the greatest responsibilities. I did not understand Balinese, but I understood that the power behind the throne was a magnificent matriarch, the *dadong* (grandmother). Like all women, with the exception of those who went to school, this proud woman wore no top unless she left home. Rising early in the morning, she would oversee the trip to the market, the restoking of the fire in the kitchen, the drawing and boiling of water, and the preparation of food for the entire day. I was surprised to learn that the Balinese rarely ate together. Rather, if you were hungry, you ventured to the kitchen, make a plate of whatever was available, and fed yourself.

The women also swept the compound with their left hand behind their back. It was the men who tended to the cows and the coconut plantations; however, for the most part, they seemed more preoccupied with sitting around smoking hand-rolled cigarettes and drinking gritty black coffee as they preened their fighting cocks. I was also incredibly impressed by the attention paid by both sexes to personal hygiene. Their routines demanded at least two baths a day and always a change of clothes, perhaps simple and even threadbare but always clean.

Having come in search of spiritual wisdom, Bali defied what I had learned about classical Hinduism but mesmerized me through its visceral elegance and beauty. One of the chief tasks of women was to make and distribute offerings, multihued wonders constructed of woven unopened coconut leaves, blossoms, old coins, and dabs of magical substances destined for the ancestors and high spirits that visited the family temple. There were also cruder hastily made offerings unceremoniously upon the ground to propitiate the less discriminating *poltergeisten* (bhuta kala). Naïve fool that I was, I tried to follow the prayers and rituals, much to the amusement of the family who apparently thought I was hilarious.

My meeting with the Keepers of the Light was delayed by a lack of attention. At least the cobbler in the Grimm Brothers' fairy tale *The Elves and the Shoemaker* was immediately aware of the miracle and cognizant of the existence of secret helpers even if he did not know who they were. Each day I would leave the compound in the afternoon to explore and visit with a growing circle of friends. When I returned later, I never asked why or who had placed the glass lamps on the balcony table or why they disappeared without a trace the next morning. My ignorance was pierced after a powerful dream caused me to awaken before dawn. Sitting on the porch, I sat and contemplated as the sky turned from black to dark blue and the compound came to life. To my amazement, a team of boys and girls, some barely six and often carrying babies, suddenly arrived with trays to extinguish the flames and ferry away the now soot-covered lamps. I followed them to the back and watched as they carefully dismantled and cleaned them, then stored them carefully. The same night I would see the other side of the dance: the silent delivery of the lamps to each room, the lighting of flames, then the trimming and adjusting of wicks to perfection before the children slipped off to study for school and sleep.

My discovery caused a minor epiphany. Taken one by one, the oversight of the lamps was a minor task; however, in the thousands of villages throughout Bali where electricity had never been known, it was a major industry that had once encompassed most of our entire globe. The idea that the guardians of this ancient cycle of illuminating the night, which had existed for over one thousand years, were mere children was mind-boggling—all the more so because of the grace by which they fulfilled their duty. In my mind, it was nothing short of divine.

Of the many great wonders I experienced in Indonesia, I did not realize at the time that I was witnessing a final brilliant efflorescence of an ancient rite or tradition that would soon be extinguished. The death knell, as with so many things at the time, was delivered by modernity and progress—in this case, the introduction of electricity as the New Order government implemented an ambitious program to run the grid to every Balinese village in the 1980s. Within a few years virtually all hotels, restaurants, and homes were equipped with low-watt tube-shaped fluorescent bulbs that gave off an eerie and depressing blue-green light that oscillated at a high frequency accompanied by the annoying buzz of transformers.

Another disturbing development that came on the heels of electricity was the sudden appearance of VCRs and Betamax machines playing inane American sitcoms like *Starsky and Hutch* in all the hostels, hotels, and restaurants serving young travelers along what was later dubbed the Hippie Trail by the BBC. From my perspective, electricity turned most people into zombies and thus assassinated the age of magic and poetry that had preceded. Whereas we were once bathed in a golden light that made us all look like gods, bards, and heroes, exchanging tales of adventure, dancing, and singing, the ugly side of the West that we had fled was howling at our heels and forcing those of us who wanted no part of the new landscape to find new escapes.

We were not the only ones confronted. After electricity, the Indonesian government ordered televisions be installed in every village. In Bali, these were the *Bale Banjar*, or open public pavilions. Being expensive prestige items, every boob tube was locked inside an iron cage to prevent theft. Broadcasts begin at six p.m. sharp with the national anthem, followed by the one-hour propagandistic news broadcasts with endless boring speeches by government officials. As soon as the novelty wore off, the Bale Banjar emptied out. That would change at eight p.m. when the programming switched to American sitcoms. One of the most popular was *Lancelot Link*, a comedy that featured talking chimpanzees. Attracted by bellows of laughter, I joined a full house of squatting viewers in Ubud one evening. At the end of the show, three members of the audience struck up a conversation.

"Are you from America?" I was asked. I nodded, and my interrogator digressed into a monologue. "We Balinese were surprised to see that monkeys still talk in the West. Long ago, they spoke here on Bali, but since the days of Hanoman and the Ramayana they have lost their knowledge of speech. Do you think we can bring some of your monkeys here to teach ours?" This triggered in me deep thoughts about the mystery of culture and myth. Who was I to gainsay this hopeful proposal? Had I not come to Bali myself on a quest to find a magical world?

I muttered something to the effect that I would look into it and wandered back to my room at Munut's Cottage in Penestanan, long before it became a yogi-healer–new-shaman ghetto. In those days, there were only rice fields full of frogs croaking deafening love songs. These were the days before the coming of the green rice revolution when myriad fireflies hovered over the placid waters, their soft green tails blinking. Catching some, I held them carefully in my cupped hands before releasing them, not realizing that they too, like the Keepers of the Light, would soon be sacrificed in the name of progress. For although green rice multiplied the harvest, the obligatory pesticides needed for this bounty killed the fireflies and countless songbirds.

Despite what has been lost, there are also countless stories of miracles and wonder that live on. I cherish these memories—not as dried specimens but living things. They are akin to carefully wrapped embers carried by nomadic tribes on the journey to their next destination, where they will light bonfires to illuminate their new home. There is continuity from the past to the heat of today and hope for tomorrow.

MY ADVICE FOR THE BALI VISITOR ──────────────────────

Like all things, culture is in constant flux. Bali is a world in which the wonders of the past live side by side with cappuccinos and Instagrammers. Cherish your experiences in Bali, but do not deceive yourself into believing the fixed image you record in your memory is forever. Remember, too, that we are all guests and that the destiny of the Balinese belongs to the Balinese.

The Migration of Goa to Bali

GILBERT GARCIA

Gilbert Garcia is a multi-talented musician, gathering his musical flavors from exotic destinations and incorporating performances into his journeys to every corner of the globe. As an inveterate world traveler, a few of his favorite locations—which include Goa, India; Bali and Ibiza, Spain—have now become home to his schools of music, where he performs and instructs students from all over the world. Gilbert continues to perform on a worldwide basis in prominent clubs, concert venues, retreats, and resorts while actively seeking new musical influences.

Although it may seem too unusual to start a Bali story with some Goa history, it is my belief that they are absolutely intertwined.

In the 1970s, the overland global trek toward Goa and the rest of India had indeed commenced in earnest. Most of us came overland from Europe by every imaginable means of transportation available. There are millions of stories out there, and all are unique and genuinely interesting, especially when one arrived in the Afghan region. But, after all is said and done, Goa was one of the main focus points and where most of us ended up eventually, me included.

As the years passed, many of us stayed on permanently in Goa, India, and Nepal, spending our monsoons in the Himalayan mountains trekking and the dry seasons in Goa partying. Because Goa had a weekly market, people started doing business and making a life of it. Over time, the boundaries started to expand. First slowly into Thailand and then, obviously, down south through Southeast Asia, eventually ending in Bali.

The difference between the Goan Freak lifestyle and Bali has been discussed to death. We won't go there, but, as we all know, Bali was a paradise for creative artisans. Hey, get serious—who didn't fall in love with Bali in the early to middle '70s? No further discussion is necessary. The quality of life, the Balinese people, the beautiful temples, the lifestyle, the food, the *losmens* (homestays), the parties, the Bali family together for the sheer fun of it all was intoxicating! So, lots of "Goa Freaks" immediately settled in Bali and started to create a life for themselves.

Friends such as Jean-François, Richard, Jorge, and many others were all Goa neighbors of mine who, once bitten by the Bali lifestyle, seldom returned to Goa. They all went on to achieve their own successes and never looked back. These are but a few examples (apologies to the many others who are not mentioned) of the Goa family that went on to build their empires (so to speak) in Bali. And, who could blame them?

A little-known fact is that after the Goa season, I, together with Jean-François, met in Kathmandu in the '70s and set off through Burma, Thailand, and eventually down to Bali. At this point, J. F. had never been outside of India or Nepal, and the idea was for me to introduce him to Southeast Asia. We never completed the entire journey, as he was, shall we say, an unusual traveler! He traveled with huge Indian metal trunks filled with shells, feathers, trinkets, and assorted other unimaginable weird items, which caused complete chaos at every border we ever crossed! Hours and hours were spent in Customs examining his "treasures." Finally, around Koh Samui, Thailand, I threw in the towel and went on alone via Sumatra and Java. Jean-François didn't wish to join in on my adventure.

In my opinion, Goa and Bali are intertwined with a shared history represented in the people who came, stayed, created, and profited from the rich Balinese culture. Bali certainly enhanced my life—and I'm certain everyone else's too.

Although I'm not a permanent Bali resident, I continue to come, "stay long time," enjoy, and am always enriched by our Bali family and our million different stories, which I could never even begin to include in this brief recounting.

May we all enjoy, be healthy, and prosper...

MY ADVICE FOR THE BALI VISITOR ───────────────

I recommend total surrender. Surrender yourself to the loving Balinese total experience! Bali's culture, temples, charm, food, dance, artisans, smiles, and people will become the best part of your total surrender. Sit back, open your heart, and absorb the experience, which will remain unforgettable and an integral part of your life... Spread the word... Om Swastyastu.

Made's Warung

PETER STEENBERGEN

Peter Steenbergen was born in Amsterdam in 1948 and lived there until he found Bali in 1973. After marrying Made Masih in 1974, they both developed the concept of turning a warung into a more mainstream food destination. In 2019 they celebrated Made's Warung fiftieth year of existence and are still going strong with outlets in Bali, Jakarta, Amsterdam, and at the airport in Bali.

The reason I went to Indonesia was that I had a friend who was born in Sumatra and wanted to revisit the country of his parents and his birthplace. We decided to prepare a minibus and drive from Amsterdam to Sumatra through Europe, into Turkey, and then through Iran, Afghanistan, Pakistan, and India. We had to take a boat from Madras, now named Chennai, in south India to the island of Penang in Malaysia, as Bangladesh and Myanmar didn't allow foreigners to drive through their country. From Penang we had to take a ferry to Medan in the north of Sumatra, where we arrived in Indonesia sometime in May 1973.

My friend visited his place of birth in Sumatra and then decided to go back to the Netherlands. I had come halfway around the world and wanted to visit Java and Bali as well. We shipped the car back to Holland from Medan, as we had to put up a bond—*a carnet de passage*—which was a sort of a passport for a car, assessed at 200% of the value of the car in Holland, and didn't want to lose this.

I continued by bus and train to Java and finally arrived in Bali in June 1973.

The only place to go in Bali at the time for young people like us was Kuta. By "people like us," I mean the travelers, or, as we were called, hippies.

From Denpasar bus station, you took a *bemo* (public transportation minivan) to Kuta and got out at Bemo Corner, where Kuta started in those days. Kuta was a small, sleepy fishing village with a dirt road leading to the beach called Jalan Pantai. Accommodation was very basic: bamboo huts between coconut fields alongside sandy paths and small roads. I checked into a *losmen* (homestay) on Jalan Pantai, not far from the beach but, more importantly for me, close to a roadside stall called Made's Warung. This tiny little warung would change my life forever.

From day one, I felt at home in these tropical surroundings, a feeling I didn't have in any other place I had visited previously. After two weeks, I moved to a family compound on Jalan Legian about fifty meters from Bemo Corner. A few months later, I made an arrangement with the family that allowed me to build a small house in their compound, much more comfortable than the little rooms in the losmen, which were the typical accommodations of the early '70s. A row of rooms next to each other, each of them with a small bathroom attached, a concrete floor, a squatting toilet, and a *bak mandi*, which is a tiled water reservoir next to the squatting toilet with a little plastic scoop to throw cold water over your body as a form of a shower and to clean yourself after using the toilet. Since then, I cannot use toilet paper anymore and looked on, stunned, at the toilet paper runs in Europe and the US during the beginning of the COVID-19 pandemic in 2020. Tip of the day: just buy a bottle of water, put it next to your toilet, and clean yourself and refill—it saves a lot of paper (trees) worldwide. And is a lot cleaner than using toilet paper.

Changing the losmen-type accommodation into a more luxurious living space with a shower and a Western-style small kitchen is

probably the first step toward changing the basic living ways for foreigners in Bali and of the Balinese people. There was no electricity yet in
Kuta, so air conditioners and fridges could not be used unless one had
a power generator, which was the next step. However, the romantic and
basic way of living with StormKing lamps (pump lamps) and concrete
cool boxes with ice blocks as fridges is what we are now looking back
at with nostalgia.

Going to restaurants for food was very basic. In Kuta there was
Made's Warung and Poppies, which started as a warung near the beach
and later moved to Gang Poppies, where it still is today.

The only places to buy food supplies were the market in Denpasar
and a few shops in Jalan Gajah Mada.

My favorite hangout was Made's Warung on Jalan Pantai in Kuta.
Not only for me but also for most semi-foreign residents there.

A warung is an Indonesian-style food stall, usually on the side of the
road, where the local people drink their coffee; have a little sweet snack;
gossip about the day-to-day life in the village; and buy little hanging
sachets filled with *sabun rinso* (soap to wash your clothing), mosquito
coils, and other basic essentials for living.

Made's Warung was a little roadside stall like that in the sixties.
Run by Made's grandma and her mother and assisted by the daughters,
they catered to the villagers in Kuta, which was still a sleepy fishing and
goldsmith's village.

In the late sixties and early seventies, the first tourists, hippies, surfers, and holiday travelers came to Bali and stayed in rustic Kuta Beach,
which slowly started to change. People wanted a little more than unfil-
tered coffee, rice cakes, fried rice, and rice desserts such as the delicious
black rice pudding.

Made, the oldest daughter in the family, started to help out after
schoolwork was done and slowly changed the Balinese warung into a
more suitable eating place for foreigners, without changing the concept
and the structure of a warung.

The environment of the warung was fine, and foreign guests from
abroad as well as from other Indonesian islands were very happy chatting

and hanging out at the warung. The only change needed was a bit more variety in the menu. Surfers introduced jaffles, an Australian type of grilled sandwich. Other people asked for fruit salads, then came pancakes (still a best seller), and Western-style breakfasts. Japanese showed Made how to make sushi and sashimi. Made adapted quickly, and so the menu grew and became truly international, from *gado gado* (vegetables with peanut sauce) to sushi, pasta, and Pad Thai dishes.

Made's Warung became a must in Bali for the local Jakarta crowd and the foreign guests, a hangout where people wanted to see and be seen. After I got married to Made (more about that later), I got involved in renovating the old warung in Kuta about six times but didn't change the atmosphere.

I preserved the concept of people eating together in an environment that was informal, friendly, and in line with the Indonesian warung philosophy. In a warung, complete strangers sit together at a table and eat, drink, and talk together. A table for one or two does not exist. New contacts are made. We decided to stick to the warung concept, which by now is widely accepted in Indonesia. In the '70s, when people asked what business you were into and you told them that you had a warung, people would look at you and say, "You mean a restaurant, right?" Now even multinationals such as Telkom use the word *warung*, such as Wartel (Warung Telecommunication) and others.

For me the food and the ambiance of the warung were not the only reason I frequently visited the warung. Behind the counter stood this beautiful girl helping her mum with the business. She would ground peanuts all day on a earthenware flat plate. With a mortar she would grind and make the most beautiful and delicious sauce for the gado gado. She had long hair all the way to her knees. Standing there in a tight sarong wrapped around her waist, in a *kebaya*, which is a traditional top, part of her stomach would not be covered, revealing her navel. A very sexy look.

Her face was round, like a full moon. Her smile would mesmerize not only me but also a lot of other people. I visited the warung more and more, just to sit there and look at Made. I didn't speak Bahasa very much, and she didn't speak much English. Communication was done only through looking at her eyes and smiling. The peanut language came soon after. I would buy a plate of peanuts, sit on a bench, and throw a peanut at her from behind. Quickly pretending I was in conversation with one of the other guests, she would look around and not know what hit her and where it came from. When she turned away and made another plate of gado gado for somebody, I would throw another peanut. It took her a little while to find out where it came from, but after a few plates, she knew it was from me. This was the beginning of our communication. After getting hit, she would turn around and give me the most beautiful smile every time.

It was not common for a tourist—or, as the Balinese would call us, *tamu*, which means guest—to date a foreigner. They were very much into their own culture, and mixed couples were very few. And in Kuta there had never as yet been an instance of a foreign man marrying a Balinese woman (as far as I know). A Balinese man marrying a foreign woman was more common, and I knew a few guys that had married a Western woman.

One couple who became our very good friends were Ketut from Denpasar and Jean from the US. Besides being our neighbors, they also advised me on how to pursue the quest of getting more involved with Made. It would take a lot of patience and perseverance. Not only did I have to win the heart of Made, I also had to make sure her parents and brothers, and sisters would like me. The politician and diplomat in me were born.

I needed a motorbike to get around, and renting one all the time was a bit of a waste, as I was planning to stay for long periods of time. I bought a Honda CB 125, a top-notch bike in those days, and put it in her brother's name. I could use it when I was in Bali, and he could use it when I was away. Everybody was happy.

For me to get to know Made required me to learn the language quickly. Learning Bahasa Indonesia was not too difficult for me and was also handy in Java for my business. Reading and writing the Indonesian language properly is a whole different story. People who say that the Indonesian language is easy to learn don't know what they are talking about. To be able to get around and speak Bahasa Pasar or market language is indeed not too complicated, but if someone told me that Bahasa Indonesia is an easy language because they could speak some, I would give them an Indonesian newspaper, and they would not be able to read any of it.

Made, her sister, and her mother were always in the warung. The men worked elsewhere. Her father took care of the rice field, and her brothers were both goldsmiths and silversmiths. It was because of them I got into the jewelry trade in the early days, having classic Balinese rings made in gold with stones I bought in Thailand to be sold in Europe. More and more, I felt at home in Bali. After a few months I was able to talk a little bit with Made, her mother and her sister. In the beginning, they were only the women that I had contact with, which suited me fine anyway.

I started helping out in the warung, giving some advice on equipment, suppliers, and other technical information. I had fallen head over heels in love with Made and was several times a day in the little roadside stall, drinking more coffee than was good for me, just to be in her presence. Going out together was out of the question. If I wanted to see a movie in Denpasar with Made, I had to take half her family with us. If I wanted to take her out for a day trip to Kintamani or Bedugul, I had to rent a minibus so part of her family could join us. The two of us were never alone, which made it more exciting than I ever thought was possible. I grew up in the sixties in Amsterdam, where dating with a chaperone was unheard of. Here I was. I had fallen deeply in love with a beautiful young Balinese, who was protected by her family, like the most precious thing ever, which she was and still is.

After dating like that for about eighteen months, I decided to ask her to marry me.

Asking for her hand was like asking her to give up her life, as neither she nor her family knew who this foreigner was and didn't know his family or background. She didn't give me an answer, instead told me not to tell her father or brothers about my proposal. She needed some time to think it over, but for me it was time to make a decision, and after a few days I asked her again. Again, she gave me no straight answer, and I could see in her eyes that she had doubts, and I didn't want to push the issue. We were both in love, but she was afraid she had to move to Europe and give up her Balinese culture and religious activities. We talked about it in secret in the back of the warung after it was closed. Her mother, who slept in the warung on a bench, pretended to be asleep. I told her that I wanted to live in Bali and would never keep her from her daily religious and *adat* (customary or traditional law) routines, which are very important to the Balinese people. I also told her that for me, eighteen months of courting was very long. Finally, she agreed.

If two lovers in Bali want to get married, but one of the partners is afraid of being rejected by the other's family for whatever reason, there is another way to get married, namely *Ngeroro*—which in Balinese means "kidnapping" with consent of both partners. We both decided not to ask her parents and instead run for it. If her parents and brothers would not agree to the marriage, we wouldn't be able to see each other again. Therefore we decided to do it that way and not take the risk of rejection by her family.

I realized that this was an enormously brave move on Made's part, as her life would have been completely different had I not taken this proposal and marriage very seriously. My cousin, who was in Bali at the time, helped me with the logistics of the kidnapping by consent. We acquired a big Chevy Impala, and my cousin pretended to take Made out to Denpasar. Her parents didn't suspect anything suspicious, as it was daytime, and two women together couldn't possibly be doing something inappropriate. The car was parked around the corner, and Made got in and joined me. We drove off into an unknown future. I had left a letter with my Balinese friends Ketut and Jane to give to Made's parents, which explained that their daughter had decided to marry me and that we were "disappearing" for a while. We kept our hiding location to ourselves.

The Hyatt in Sanur had recently opened, so I decided to go there, as I figured nobody would look for us at this hotel, and there was good security there. The *adat* or custom law in Bali is such that when you have slept together, usually the marriage is accepted by the family without any repercussions, and so it was. We returned to Kuta, the family arranged a ceremony to legalize the wedding, and we have lived happily ever after, married now almost fifty years.

Our life together has been a blessing; we have two sons and four grandchildren.

For Made and I, Bali continues to be a blessing. Has it changed since the early seventies? Yes. Has it been lost since the seventies? No.

Every generation looks back at the past and thinks it was better, but this opinion would not be fair for the next generation.

MY ADVICE FOR THE BALI VISITOR

In Bali, you are not considered to be a tourist but a tamu, *which means guest, which to me is an honor. Please respect that. Bali is not just a party place. Find some time for the mountains, ceremonies, culture, and wonderful people. Don't just eat pasta and sandwiches. Try the local cuisine—nasi campur (mixed rice), for instance. To me, Indonesian cuisine is one of the best in the world.*

My Cherished
Bali Nostalgia

MAS NGURAH WAGENDAWATI

Mas Ngurah Wagendawati is Balinese, born in Bali and lived in Seminyak while growing up. Mas's father is Pak Agung Ngurah, mostly known as 'Agung Boss' by many in Bali. Agung founded and owned Golden Village, which was the first bungalow-style accommodation in Seminyak in the 1980s. Agung also owned the infamous Chez Gado Gado disco on Seminyak Beach. Mas now lives in the Netherlands with her husband Eddy, and their two sons, Jerry and Dez.

When Leslie sent me an email to write about Bali before mass tourism arrived, I got such a feeling of longing for those days.

I was introduced at age nine to the expat crew around 1974. My friend Michael Palmieri described that time as "The Bule Age" (the Balinese use *bule* to represent anyone not from Bali), when many visitors started to descend on Bali.

Papa started to build Golden Village Inn (GVI) then on his land in Seminyak. I loved to help him, along with my cousin (known as Agung Boy by the crew) and some locals from the village, who are also seen to me today as members of my Seminyak family.

I loved cutting the high grass used for the roofs and carrying stones for the foundations and walls.

At first, there were four rooms built. Tourists started to come.

Bit by bit Papa continued to build *rumah-rumah lumbung*. In Bali, *lumbungs* were normally traditional-style bamboo huts with straw roofs used to store rice. Papa used this model and scaled them much larger to create live-in homes. A very simple design, and the tourists loved them.

Sometimes guests couldn't pay their rent so Papa would accept their cassette recorders, books, or cameras in lieu of payments. I loved the books because I could continue to learn English.

Then, at one point, Golden Village Inn became a popular meeting and party place. Through the guests, I learned many things, and one of them was to eat a delicious raw spinach salad. In Bali, eating raw salads was not part of our cuisine.

The parties were fabulous. I became used to recognizing the smell of marijuana.

One day something funny happened. Wayan Dana, the *silat* (martial arts) master from Karangasem, was there. There were some other guests. They all started to smoke, sitting in a circle, and I had joined the circle with them, including Wayan. The stuff went around (I then understood why it's called a joint). Wayan Dana wanted to pass it to me. One of the circle members, Milo, said, "No, skip her." Ha-ha-ha. I was sixteen years old then, I remember. I suppose I had been passively smoking a long time.

Papa was not always happy about his guests smoking, or with me sometimes joining the gatherings in GVI, but he didn't mind taking me along to the many places he went. We would visit Made's Warung in Kuta, the Goa bar, and Poppies restaurant.

Papa would say, "Mas, you know what you may and may not do."

I recall that once, someone asked me whether Papa was a widower with one daughter because he was often seen alone or with me. My mum and my other siblings were not really into the Kuta, Legian, or Seminyak scene.

Once I attended a party at Perry Kesner's house in GVI, with Papa. I saw a man sitting alone in the corner, with dark-brown curly hair playing his harmonica. I wondered whether he was Bob Dylan. I guess he was, because there were a lot of celebrities in Bali in those times, enjoying the anonymity and the hippie way of life.

Another of our guests in GVI, Uncle Michael, was friends with Richard Gere and chaperoned him on his visit to Bali. That guy in the corner just as well may have been Bob Dylan.

Then, the "Chez Gado Gado" era came. Party on, guys! Chez Gado Gado was opened by my father and was the first disco in Seminyak. It was a large open-air pavilion located on the beachfront.

Papa would do his rounds, praying with us every night before opening. I remember in the early days of Chez Gado Gado, Papa would instruct me: "If there is no one on the dance floor, go and start dancing!" in hopes of motivating others to come join me and dance. I loved doing that and hated it when he came to stop me—which he did because, when the dance floor started to fill, we needed to work in other areas. My next job after dancing was to put bowls filled with roasted salty peanuts on bar tops and tables. The philosophy was, if our guests ate peanuts, they would grow thirsty and buy drinks. We needed to sell booze.

It was a lovely time in Bali then. It was hard work for me but full of memories, pure and without a "show-off" mentality, now apparent in the Bali social scene today.

I'm happy I experienced all that.

Now living in the Netherlands, I think often about those days, missing the hippie time.

I'm glad I still have the current residents—Michael Palmieri, Tamara, Thomas, and Christopher—in GVI to talk with about those days.

Also, it gives me a nice feeling knowing that many beautiful memories were made in Bali for many.

Against all odds, I do hope that Bali will soon have tourism back, like in the '70s and '80s. I wish for friendly tourism, of which the human connection is more important than money and based on universal love.

MY ADVICE FOR THE BALI VISITOR ————————————

I'd like to thank all the people who love Bali. When you guys are there, take a nice long walk on the beach from Kuta to Petitenget Beach, and watch the sunset there. Explore the beauty of central Bali and its rice fields, but please keep the nature pure.

The Dance of
Good and Evil

TERRY TARNOFF

Terry Tarnoff is the author of four novels, one play, and ten screenplays. He spent eight years traveling throughout Europe, Africa, and Asia in the 1970s, where he helped run the Spirit Catcher Bookstore in Kathmandu and co-founded the Anjuna Jam Band in Goa. He currently lives in San Francisco and has frequently given readings at City Lights Bookstore, the Beat Museum, and bookstores throughout the Bay Area.

The ocean roared against the beach in Legian. Rising over vast coral reefs, the tides swelled, swirled, surged, and crested, then dropped like a ledge against the jagged rocks. The amplitude built with each series of waves, but it was in every ninth wave that the full fury of the ocean was unleashed. Every ninth wave is the biggest. Every ninth wave comes crashing over the sea.

As the sun set over an endless horizon, I watched hundreds of tiny sand crabs fighting against the incoming tide. They burrowed into the sand and held on valiantly for a second or two, then lost their grip and were funneled a little further out. As the water passed over them, they dusted themselves off and, quite comically, made a mad dash on their minuscule legs for dry land. Again and again, they repeated this sidelong dance of survival—until the ninth wave. For if they weren't on high ground when the ninth wave hit, they would be dragged out and disappear forever into the sea.

I felt a shadow and looked up to see a strange-looking man standing a few feet away. One of his eyes was glassy and rolled back in its socket, while the other had too much white around the cornea. He stared at me for a moment, then began cackling and walking backward toward the trees. It was creepy, him edging away like that, laughing and leering, and I wondered if this was the man I'd heard the Balinese talk about—the man from the Black Magic Forest.

A *Barong* dance was planned for that night. Wayan told me it was a special ceremony, not one of those tourist performances, and that he himself would be dancing. There wasn't much of anything around when I arrived, just a dusty open space inside a grove of trees and a few dozen villagers listening to a *gamelan* orchestra. The group consisted of drums, gongs, flutes, and a vibraphone-like instrument that was struck with steel mallets. The music built and released like waves in the sea, and I felt myself floating off to the hypnotic beat.

A short while later, four *Legong* dancers appeared in shimmering sequined sarongs and performed the traditional opening for the ceremony. Then the Barong, a great leonine figure, danced into the clearing. His head was a large wooden mask and his body a mass of cloth and hair that was slung over two men wearing striped leggings. They danced in perfect conjunction, their legs moving not precisely together but slightly apart—like a real lion—as the head and mane dipped and swayed to the music.

After the Barong carved out his territory, *Rangda* the witch appeared, and everyone instinctively moved back. Rangda wasn't much more than a giant mask, but she was so horrific, it was hard not to be frightened. Her orange eyes bugged out in a malevolent glare, her mouth opened to reveal enormous fangs, and her tongue hung all the way to the ground, bright red, as if she'd just tasted the blood of her latest victim.

Rangda did her dance and challenged the Barong, and then the two of them were in the center of the clearing, the feet of the Barong and the hooves of Rangda kicking up great clouds of dust as they faced each other down, good and evil going at it, while children hid behind their mothers' skirts and men watched with nervous smiles.

I smelled a wave of heavy incense and glanced over to see a priest blowing clouds of sandalwood into the faces of a half-dozen men as he intoned a prayer. I noticed how their faces were totally blank. One of them was Wayan. The men were led into the dance area, each of them carrying a long *kris* knife. The kris, a wavy beveled blade, was sharp and jagged and annealed for maximum strength. After dancing as a group in front of Rangda and the Barong, each of the men did an individual dance to the Barong. They held the tips of the kris knives against their hearts in a personification of the fight of good against evil. Their hands were wrapped around the pommels as the spirit of Rangda tried to force the blade into their hearts and the Barong fought back, pulling the blade away. Back and forth the battle went—played out in the biceps of the dancers' arms—while two husky men stood a few feet away, watching the eyes of the dancers and the muscles in their arms. Every once in a while, when things looked like they might spin out of control, they stepped in to grab the knife.

Last to dance was Wayan, and he entered the ring with an energetic leap. As he swung the kris in a circle and placed it over his heart, I noticed the two burly men watching him closely. The point of the blade pushed against his skin, then released, then pushed again. Back and forth it went, Wayan's blank expression never altering. Then—maybe it was the raising of an eyebrow or the twinge of a muscle—the two men leapt upon him and struggled to pull the knife away. Still, Wayan's expression didn't change—he was in a deep trance—and even the strength of two men wasn't enough to stop him. The gamelan abruptly stopped, more men rushed over to grab Wayan's arms, and finally they pulled the kris away before he managed to kill himself.

The priest doused the dancers with holy water from Mount Agung, and one by one, as the droplets touched their faces, they came out of their trances. All but Wayan. He was still struggling on the ground, kicking and screaming, when the priest pulled a live chicken from his satchel. He held the frantic bird in front of Wayan's face, and then, in one quick motion, snapped its neck with his bare hands and shoved it into Wayan's mouth. Wayan sucked the warm blood, his body shaking uncontrollably, until he finally collapsed onto the ground. The priest disappeared, the two burly men picked up Wayan, and the crowd quickly dispersed. As I headed out of the clearing, I noticed Madé, Wayan's wife, standing by herself against a tree. She watched Wayan from a distance, then turned and walked home alone.

~

"What's good today?" I asked the young woman behind the counter of a tiny *warung*.

Kortis looked up, and a smile played upon her round brown face. "F*rrrr*uit salad good today," she responded, the rs rolling off her tongue like a gymnast coming out of a somersault.

"What fruits are in season?" I asked, just as I had every day for the past two weeks.

"Eve*rrrrr*ything in season," said Kortis, continuing our routine. We went through this at least once each afternoon. Always the same question; always the same answer.

"Well, then, I'd better have a fruit salad."

"*Bagus*," she said, indicating I'd made a good choice as she cut up a banana, then added mangosteen, jackfruit, and papaya. She poured a few drops of sweet condensed milk over the top, and then dusted the whole thing with grated coconut and peanuts. "When you take me America?" Kortis asked, batting her eyelashes like a hummingbird.

"As soon as Papa gives me four goats and two cows."

"Papa no *have* cows!" she moaned, still following the script, feigning disappointment.

"Well, you know the deal, Kortis—no goats, no marriage; no cows—"

"No New York!" She looked at me with terribly sad eyes, and then burst out laughing. "How is f*rrrr*uit salad?"

"Fruit salad *bagus*."

She waved to me as I left the warung and walked along the dirt road of Legian toward the ocean. Legian was a new village, a few miles past the more established Kuta Beach, and the road was lined with palm trees, a few acacias, and sweet-smelling jasmine. Several pathways led off the road to *losmens*—guesthouses that had manicured stone gardens and tiny ponds filled with water lilies. The walls were covered in hibiscus and the archways in bougainvillea, and at the sides of the entrances were shrines to the gods.

"*Selamat jalan*," called out Wayan, wishing me a good journey as I passed the Pala Ayu. He was preparing the evening offering, a few morsels of cooked rice that he placed upon a bed of flowers. He slid a banana leaf on top of the shrine, to honor the gods who lived in the mountains and in the sky, and put another down below to appease the demons of the ground and ocean. Almost immediately, birds flew down and nibbled at the rice—a sign that the gods were pleased. Then a dog came by, sniffed around, and slobbered up the food down below, confirming that evil—easily identifiable by its sharp fangs—would be put off for at least another day.

"*Selamat sore*," I called to Wayan, wishing him a good evening as I headed for the beach to watch the sunset. The Balinese weren't all that comfortable living near the beaches. They preferred it up in the mountains, closer to the gods. The ocean, with its strong undercurrents and sharp-toothed fish, was a good place to avoid. The Balinese were lousy swimmers and reluctant fishermen, and they looked at the sea not for sustenance but as a place of great danger. It didn't really take long to figure out the ABCs of Bali: up, good; down, bad. Smile, good; fangs, bad.

MY ADVICE FOR THE BALI VISITOR ———————————

Find a good time machine and dial it back to 1974. If that doesn't work, avoid the yoga classes and head for the hills, the more remote the better. There are cultural treasures still to be found in those mountains.

Lekas-Lekas

RUCINA BALLINGER

Rucina Ballinger is a writer who co-authored the book Balinese Dance, Drama and Music: An Introduction to Balinese Performing Arts *with Wayan Dibia. She has been a dancer, a comedienne who founded Grup Gedebong Goyang, a director of nonprofits such as YKIP and Desa Les Community Center, a tour guide that worked with the Obamas in 2017 when they came to Bali, and a teacher/lecturer on Balinese culture. She has lived in the same house in Peliatan since 1988 and is currently there with her two sons, their wives, and their children. She originally came to Bali in 1974 to study dance and theater.*

I originally was going go to India to study South Indian dance (Bharata Natym), but due to new visa regulations in the early 1970s, I had to turn my sights elsewhere. As an undergraduate at an American university, I wanted to go somewhere where dance was still a viable part of the culture and performed on a regular basis. Well, Bali was one of the few places on the planet that fit all those descriptions.

With a major in dance, religion, and folklore, I felt I was ready to take on this strange, new culture. I read as much as I could, but, unfortunately, where I lived did not offer any language courses that would be useful in this venture.

So in 1973, I set off to study Balinese dance at the American Society for Eastern Arts in Seattle, Washington, with Nyoman and Nanik Wenten. My two-year LIPI (Indonesian Research Institute) visa was granted within a few months (unheard of at that time), so I jumped on a plane for the grueling thirty-plus-hour flight. In those days, we used Cathay Pacific, stopping in the tiny airport in Biak for a quick layover complete with a dance performance by very bored-looking dancers. This was January 1974.

Arriving in Denpasar near midnight, I touched the tarmac, and the smell of *kretek*, the ubiquitous clove cigarette (which I adored then), hit my nostrils. I breathed in deeply and felt, in true Ubudian fashion, that I was home.

I knew very little Indonesian, and Wenten had taught me the word *lekas-lekas* (which I pronounced le-kas-slaw-kas). It means to go quickly, and in my more than forty years in Indonesia, I have never heard anyone use it. Go figure. But it sounded funny, so I guess that's why he taught it to me. He also taught me how to say "I love you" in Balinese, which I have never used either.

I overnighted at a small Denpasar hotel and the next day meandered over to KOKAR, the High School of Performing Arts, where I was to begin my study of dance. I was dressed in a *kamen* (sarong) and very carefully stepped around the small *canang* offerings in front of every shop. I was twenty-one at the time and much older and bigger than the students at KOKAR. In my discomfort, I quickly asked permission to go study in the village privately with the renowned I Nyoman Kakul, who was one of Wenten's teachers.

One day I went to visit Wenten's family in Sading. I rode in an open-backed *bemo* (public transport minivan) filled with chickens, eggs, fruit baskets, and cigarette smoke—as well as people spitting and snoring—from Batuan to Kereneng in Denpasar and then hopping on another one to Tabanan. I was dropped off by the side of a tiny road and began walking in the heat of the day. I had no idea where I was going really, nor how to get there. But I had a small Indonesian-English dictionary in one hand and walked through the dusty streets looking for Meme Kursi's house. Her name means "second-born chair," and I never got the skivvy on why she was called that.

When I finally arrived there, she hugged me like a long-lost daughter and immediately made me a meal of rice, tempeh, and veggies. It was to become one of several meals I ate there, as she became my surrogate mother. She spoke no English, and my vocabulary had expanded a bit from lekas-lekas, but I was still more nonverbal in nature.

Wenten comes from a family of artists. His grandfather was a famous *dalang* or puppeteer, his uncle and several cousins well versed in *gamelan* music. There were a few xylophone instruments called *gangsa* at the house, and the men—as only men at that time were playing music—would gather in the evenings and drink their glasses of *kopi Bali* or Balinese coffee. They made it in a small tempered glass by putting in a small spoonful of coffee and three heaping spoons of sugar, giving it a stir after adding water, and waiting for the grounds to settle and the heat to fall away. The glass was never filled more than halfway. And all the men smoked kreteks, as did I in those days, and I never saw another Balinese woman smoke in public. As kretek are made of cloves and tobacco, the pungent aroma was intoxicating and addictive.

They would begin playing simple melodies on the instruments, and then one of them—usually the oldest man—would show a more complicated riff, and they would all fill in their parts until a thick tapestry of sound had been created. Once in a while, one or more of the young girls would get up, put on a kamen and begin to dance. Sading was quite well known for its dance and music, so this was a delight for me. I watched as their small bodies would move from side to side on the balls of their feet, eyes darting left and right, elbows carving out shapes to the sides of their body, and I luxuriated in their elegant yet sharp movements.

Whenever I spent the night there, Meme Kursi would make me a meal but put out two place settings. She never ate with me, which was a typical Balinese thing in those days. I asked her, in my broken Indonesian, whom the place setting was for, and she replied, "Your future husband." Little did I know that my future husband would in fact come from a nearby village and that her family and his already knew each other!

Wenten had given me gifts to bring to his family, and I remember distinctly the one for Grandpa, as it was cologne. When I gave it to him, he opened the bottle and started to put it to his lips, thinking it was a form of whiskey. I had to mime rubbing it on my arms and sniffing it. I think he would have preferred the booze.

I had moved to the village of Batuan, where Kakul lived in a typical dusty compound. Several pavilions surrounded a central courtyard, each with its own porch area. The kitchen was a dark and grimy place in the southern part of the compound, where his wife and daughter-in-law would spend many hours of the day preparing the meals. Next to the kitchen was the bathroom, where there was a long cement trough (but high up) that was filled with water from a bucket from the nearby well. The pigsty was close to the kitchen so the critters could lap up the slop more easily. In the northeast corner was their family temple with several shrines. We often would rehearse here, as there were also a number of shade-giving trees.

Coming into the compound, I saw a slender man in his seventies, with a shock of black-grey wavy hair, caressing a fighting cock. It turned out Kakul loved to go to cockfights and had a number of his own birds. I let him know I was a student of Wenten's, gave him his gift, and asked if I could study with him. He looked me over and asked me to show him what Wenten had taught me, which was *Pendet*, a dance of welcome done by females. After a chat and some kopi Bali, he said he'd teach me, but he wanted to teach me *Baris*, which is a strong male warrior dance. He thought that suited my energy better.

Good judge of character, I thought. "When can we start?" I asked, eager to begin learning with this renowned master as soon as possible. "Let me check the calendar," he said, and I thought he had to see when he was free. But, no, he had to check to find an auspicious day for beginning a dance class. So, a few days later, we started. For three months, all I studied was *malpal*, a type of walk where you put your feet under you, splay your legs out in a very deep plié, then alternate kicking your foot up to your opposite knee. This all while walking in a figure eight, with one's shoulders hunched up to one's ears, stomach sucked in, and eyes wide. In the beginning, I probably lasted five minutes and was drenched in sweat.

What is interesting about having a traditional teacher in Bali is that if you are having trouble with a particular section of the dance, they just begin all over again. Breaking it down into segments is not within the spectrum of teaching (though this has changed drastically since the '70s). With my long-term memory needing to be seriously rebooted, I ended up starting from the beginning several times.

The lessons progressed, and after several months, when I had my "foundation," he began teaching me the rest of the choreography. In the evenings, we would sit on the *bale* (pavilion), next to the Strongking lamp (pressure lamp that we would have to pump up) while he would cut the shells for the Baris headdress and play with his grandsons. I never performed Baris, in the end, as I felt I wasn't ready.

There was another woman studying with him—Ana Daniel, who wrote a book about Kakul's life called *Behind the Mask*—and she performed the Baris at a temple festival the first month I was there. I had never gone to an *odalan* or temple ceremony with the dancers before and remember Kakul cackling and telling people we were his girlfriends. Nothing was further from the truth. I felt like I was invading someone's private space at first, as I didn't know all the norms and niceties—not to mention being stared at quite blatantly. I remember we were fed before Ana and Kakul and his troupe were to perform and how embarrassing it was for our hosts. You see, I was a vegan at the time, so all I could eat was rice and *sambal* (salsa *à la* Indonesia). I still sometimes get that feeling of being a total outsider if I am invited to someone's home that I don't really know for a ceremony. It comes completely from me, as the Balinese are nothing but gracious and hospitable (but at the same time don't pay you much attention). But after nearly thirty years of marriage and going to countless ceremonies in people's homes and temples, I have gotten used to being the "odd white girl."

But I digress.

After about six months, Kakul felt I was ready to perform *Topeng Keras*—a masked dance of a prime minister. We had progressed from Baris to Topeng, which is how one is supposed to learn Topeng: get the footwork down first. In rehearsal, we didn't use a mask, as Kakul's masks had been consecrated and could only be worn in context. So I hopped on my bicycle and went to the Sukawati Art Market and bought a "tourist" mask and used that in rehearsal so I could properly understand the feel of the wood against my face.

If you have ever done mask work, you know it is hot, sticky, and hard to breathe when wearing one. Much less if you have only been rehearsing with one drummer and one xylophone player and then... *bam*! There's a twenty-five-piece orchestra that you can't really see because the slits for eyes are miniscule. And if you look down to see where to put your feet, it changes the visage of the mask. But I got through it, and it felt good. Then, a few hours later, Kakul came up to me and said, "You are now going to be a *bondres* clown. Tell the others that you are looking for souvenirs from the sunken ship."

For context, when one is going to do a Topeng show, the story is secondary. In fact, one doesn't know what story one will do until after arriving at the host's home or temple. When we first arrived for a local wedding, we sat around chatting with the host and then Kakul decided which story we should do and assigned roles accordingly. The entire thing is improvised, although some of the clowns will have "bits" that they have rehearsed, and the musicians follow the dancers. This was problematic for me as I was doing transitions at the "six" count instead of the "eight" and totally confusing the players. So the clown mask was put on me—I didn't even see the mask before putting it on—and I was shoved onto the stage. In deference to my not yet speaking decent Balinese, the other actors used Indonesian so I could understand. It was only a few minutes long, mercifully, and afterward the play was soon over. We walked home, and I went to bed.

As the show had been in Batuan, when I walked around the village the next day, people came up to me and said, "Your Topeng Keras was good, but you sucked as a clown." And they were right. But, ironically, I now am one member of a very well-known comedy troupe in Bali called Grup Gedebong Goyang. We are all Western women who are married to Indonesians, and we do skits and songs in Balinese.

I've come a long way, baby.

MY ADVICE FOR THE BALI VISITOR ———————————————

Try not to just go from one destination to another, but stop at a local warung, have a drink, talk to the Balinese there. The best part of Bali is its people.

A Bali
Love Affair

MIRA STANNARD

Mira Stannard was born in New Zealand in 1937 and moved to Australia in 1968. She is a psychic, healer, midwife, and filmmaker. She lived permanently in Bali from 1997 but returned to Australia in 2014 when her beloved husband, Tansen, became ill; however, she still has a home in Bali. She is a mother, grandmother, and great-grandmother.

In May 1974, as we descended from the airplane to the very basic airport at Denpasar, I was hit by the heat and the smell of coconut oil, incense, and cloves. It was overwhelming, and for me it will always be the fragrance of Bali. I felt I was on another planet.

My partner, Tansen, had fallen in love with Bali on his first visit in 1969. This was his third trip. We were students at an acupuncture college in Sydney, and I was enthralled by his tales of the magic and mystery of Bali. At that time, we were known as Carole and Norman. After attending the famed Aquarius Festival in Nimbin, Australia, we had hitchhiked to Darwin, where we boarded a Merpati Airlines flight to Bali. My left thigh was frozen by air escaping from a small hole in the side of the aircraft, but that didn't distract me from the spectacle of fellow hippies and surfers hanging out in the back of the plane with the fun-loving hostesses and rummaging through their medical kits for uppers and downers.

We had a brief stop in Kupang on a small dusty airstrip, with pigs, chickens, and dogs on the runway. Finally, we arrived in Bali, slowly approaching the island over a brilliant blue sea dotted with little fishing boats and a palm-fringed green coastline. We made our way down a narrow lane—it may have been Poppies Lane—to a *losmen* (homestay) near the beach in Kuta. The losmen was a concrete building of four rooms, each having a door and a small window. Inside was a cupboard, two basic wooden single beds with hard mattresses, pillows, and a striped cotton sheet that barely covered the mattress. The Balinese owner welcomed us warmly with coffee made with condensed milk. What a sugar hit! We drank it sitting on the two simple bamboo chairs at the table outside our room.

"Hey, let's see the sunset. You won't believe it!" said Tansen, hauling me to my feet. He was right. The sunset was stupendous—a huge red globe slowly sinking below the horizon, with striations of vibrant red, orange, and gold, gradually changing to subtle greens, blues, and violets. Suddenly the show was over, and we were surrounded by the dark velvety fragrant tropical night. Upon returning to the losmen, we showered in the communal bathroom. Another new experience. Next to a squat toilet, there was a large square-tiled container—a *mandi*—built out from the wall and filled with cold water, plus a plastic scoop to throw water over oneself. Later, we lay in bed listening to the sound of the wooden bells hanging around the necks of the graceful deer-like cows, the sighing of the fronds of the coconut palms, a distant *gamelan*. I was in an altered state. Was this heaven?

I awoke the next morning, to find a thermos of fragrant black tea, fried bananas, and sticky black rice pudding on the outside table. Delicious. We met our neighbors and much appreciated the pile of Thai Buddha marijuana heads laid out on a table for all to share. Unbelievable to think of that now! We spent the day on the beach, swimming, sunbathing and buying snacks from the friendly Balinese women parading the beach in sarongs and *kebayas*, with baskets of fruit, many I had never tried before—rambutan, mangosteen, salak, nangka—and coconuts on their heads. At that time, there was no plastic. Everything was wrapped in banana or teak leaves. So refreshing. Amazing to me were the number of Balinese who remembered Tansen from his first visit. The Balinese memory is prodigious, remembering us in years to come.

The next memorable experience occurred that evening when we attended a Balinese dance called the *Legong*. The grace and beauty of the dancers, the gorgeous costumes, the vibrant exciting energy of the gamelan with its unfamiliar rhythms transfixed me. An out-of-body experience that drew me into another dimension. My mind was blown by this exotic, mysterious culture.

On an earlier trip, Tansen had become friends with a local Balinese woman called Kompiang. She had several small businesses, including a tour guide agency. She invited us to accompany her on a tour around Bali. The island was stunning: volcanoes, lakes, waterfalls, hot springs, deep ravines, forests, huge banyan trees with their vast aerial roots and shrines, the spectacular paddy fields laid out according to ancient knowledge, the beautiful people bathing un-self-consciously in rivers. I was entranced by the culture—the architecture, the temples, the religion, and the lifestyle reflecting the natural rhythms of nature.

Not all experiences were so benign, however. Packs of barking dogs and screeching monkeys could be intimidating. One time, after ordering chicken in a restaurant in Singaraja, we didn't much like the taste, and Tansen held up a piece of meat with a long back hair. It was dog! We also became very wary walking along pavements because if there was a missing paver, one could fall into the malodorous sewage mix below—a terrible fate.

Above all, I was overwhelmed by the Balinese themselves. Both men and women in sarongs wore flowers behind their ears. "*Selamat Datang*" was a greeting so welcoming, warm, and friendly. When we asked for brown bread, they obliged by giving us bread containing chocolate, probably a holdover from the Dutch colonization. They were so willing to please! Life seemed so unhurried. There was a complete lack of urgency.

Ceremonies honoring their gods seemed all-important to them and informed their everyday lives, in harmony with natural cycles. I had never encountered people so good-natured, always laughing and smiling. We met priests, *dukuns* (healers), painters, dancers, musicians, woodcarvers, stone carvers, and jewelers. We watched *wayang kulit* shadow plays, trance dances, dramas, and *Barong* dances. An abundance of experiences uniting mind, body, and soul. Ceremonies were everywhere. Long processions of Balinese in their temple clothes. The women were graceful and erect, tall pyramids of offerings on tables, and baskets balanced on their heads, while the men beat cymbals and drums.

One time we were held up to make way for a funeral procession. A huge tower in the shape of a bull was being carried by many men seesawing this way and that to distract evil spirits. A sense of joy and celebration was evident as they made their way to the cremation ground, and later with flowers, offerings, and the ashes to the ocean—so different from the mournful funerals to which I was accustomed.

The offerings to the gods, which so intrigued me, were everywhere in Bali, exquisitely made from intricately cut palm leaves, containing flowers, fruits, incense, rice, cakes, and sometimes money and cigarettes. These were made mainly by women who could be seen at crossroads, compound entrances, inner courtyard shrines, outside and inside public buildings, as well as temple compounds. These rituals and ceremonies inform the way of life of the Balinese and come before all else. This deeply spiritual society, so unfamiliar to me—having been brought up on the Western work ethic—was very attractive. I was amazed by the concept of *jam karet,* "elastic time": no rush, no hurry, spending time just hanging out.

When we returned from our first marvelous exploration of the island, we moved from Kuta to a homestay in Legian owned by Lodji, another friend of Tansen's from a previous trip. Legian was quite isolated at that time, so we'd walk on the beach to Kuta and often travel by *bemo* (public transportation minivan) to the market in Denpasar, a sprawling, colorful affair where we'd buy fruit and eat at the night market. At that time, there were very few cars and not many motorbikes. People mostly walked, rode bicycles, or took a bemo to get around.

The bemo experience was unforgettable. Two benches opposite each other in the back of a small van, crammed with men, women still wearing the coiled towels on their heads that would support their baskets, pigs, chickens, and children who regarded us seriously as strange, possibly devilish, animals. Everyone laughed and talked loudly, and just when we thought nothing else could possibly fit in, the bemo would stop, and the bemo boy would cram someone else in with their belongings.

The street life seen from the bemo was a kaleidoscope of images, colors, and smells. A woman riding a bicycle with a huge basket of eggs on her head. Men selling brooms, feather dusters, and other household items. A constant movement of people and things. Babies were adored. They had special ceremonies at three months, then six months of age, and were never put on the ground until they were six months old. They were always being held by loving relatives.

There were no bemos from Kuta to Legian in the evenings, so we walked along the road bordered by fields of coconut and other trees, passing cows and the occasional small toko or shop. There was little electricity, and light was mostly provided by kerosene lamps. Sometimes just a small wall lamp with a blurry mirror behind it.

In the following years, we lived in Europe and India but always returned each year to Bali on our way to visit family in Australia. We usually spent extended periods in Bali at these times. We delivered many babies at home there (including the first water birth in Indonesia) and continued our healing work and psychic seminars. In 1997 we moved permanently to Bali, fulfilling our dream to build a house there. Many of my children, grandchildren, and great-grandchildren visited us and fell in love with Bali too—some even staying, to my delight.

A traumatic experience was surviving the Balinese bombing in 2002. With our grandson Sai, we were attending the opening of a new store almost diagonally opposite the Sari Club, the center of the blast. I was thrown on top of a friend, and we were covered in rubble. I'll never forget that night. Driving away from the terrible scene, we found Phil Britten, who had been in the Sari Club with his football club from Perth. Phil was very badly burned, covered in blood, and in a terrible state, wandering the street looking for his mates. He nearly died. We took care of him until he got to the hospital and informed his mother.

In the following days, we interviewed victims and the amazing helpers, primarily expats, who performed miracles of organization and help of all kinds at the hospitals, which were completely unprepared for a catastrophe of this magnitude. But that is another story. *Through the Ashes* was a film we made documenting the disaster. We followed our personal story and the stories of Phil, other friends who died or were badly injured, survivors, and helpers, but focused particularly on the Balinese and their extraordinary response to the tragedy with an enormous powerful cleansing ceremony. Their deeply spiritual response was the essence of their culture of harmony with nature, each other, and their gods. This film was shown on Bali TV.

We forged many deep, lasting friendships in Bali. We experienced many momentous occasions, fabulous parties, and inspiring ceremonies, but I will never forget my first meeting with Bali and its people, still indelibly imprinted on my mind and heart. It has been hard not being able to return, due to the pandemic—particularly not to be able to attend the funeral of my beloved friend Milo, but Bali is more than a place; it is a state of being. So very beautiful! I feel such gratitude to the Universe for guiding me there.

Om Shanti. Shanti Shanti.

MY ADVICE FOR THE BALI VISITOR ————————————

If you have the great good fortune to visit Bali, the Island of the Gods, do leave the tourist spots and explore the beauty and wondrous experiences that Bali offers. Go to Kunung Kawi, Batu Karu, Lem Puyang and the waterfall at Bedugul—Sekumpul. The Balinese are welcoming and happy to share their ceremonies and ways of life, but please respect their customs and wear appropriate dress at temples and ceremonies.

Coming to Bali –
The Last Destination

ANITA LOCOCO

Anita Lococo, originally from California, has been a world traveler her entire adult life. She graduated from the University of San Francisco with a degree in anthropology, while also learning traditional dances from around the world. She first traveled to Bali in 1975. Later, she became a fashion designer under her own brand and then an art dealer in the US. Having lived for five years in Japan and a year in Brazil, she then decided to permanently move to Bali in 1991, starting the first real estate company on the island, called Bali Tropical Villas, which operated for twenty-four years. Anita is now a painter and has written books such as Living in Bali *and* Women in Bali. *She has been living in Bali for the past thirty years with her husband, Alec.*

My first trip to Bali was on April 30, 1975. It was the day the Vietnam War was officially proclaimed to be over. During my university days, my antiwar protest marches in Golden Gate Park, San Francisco were history now.

It had been an auspicious date foretold by a back-street fortune-teller in Kathmandu a year before, who noted that it would be an important date in my life, at twenty-five years old. And it was—it was indeed.

I disembarked from the Thai Airlines flight with about twelve other tourists at a tiny airport with a soft tropical wind blowing my hair and ruffling the hem of my pink dress as I walked across the runway. I was excited with wonder to have finally arrived at a place I had heard about on my journey overland for the past eighteen months on the hippie trail from Europe. Australian backpackers traveling in the opposite direction had told me about a tropical island of beauty called Bali. My boyfriend, with whom I had been on this journey, opted to return to our homeland in California, but I had to make Bali my final destination, so I went alone.

As the taxi left the airport and drove along Legian Road, I wondered if I had come to the right place, with coconut fields lining the road and no one around. Its beauty instantly grabbed me, but there were no people or buildings—nothing but endless coconut groves and a few shacks on the roadside. My first night was in a little losmen, like a pension or small hotel, with an earthen floor covered with a woven mat. I had just come from Bangkok, where I'd been hanging out with a group of international drug smugglers driving around in a fleet of dark-tinted-windowed Mercedes and partying in Pattaya. There was no electricity here either. Even India had electricity!

However, the next morning, on a rented bicycle at dawn, I rode down Legian Road and people—even bare-breasted women—were bathing in the clear rushing water of the gutter-like ditch along the road and waving to me, asking me, "Where are you going?" Further down the road were verdant green rice fields, and people waved to me from the fields, asking, "Where are you going?" As the sun rose with a golden hue, casting shooting rays over the fields, I knew then that this was not just another country I had come to explore as a tourist. I even asked myself, "Where are you going?"

That first day, I also ventured to the beach and looked in awe down an long empty stretch of a U-shaped shoreline with no people—just huge ocean waves, reminding me of California. I stayed there for a while, and before long, a young Balinese came over to sell a cold drink. Then another came to sell a coconut. I felt alone, missing my boyfriend, yet oddly enchanted. I had dreamt of a tropical island and seen a thatched-roofed bungalow in my escape place, in my imagination. The second day, I found the thatched-roof bungalow while wandering around and moved into it immediately, since it faced directly to the ocean and sunset.

It had a large room with a huge verandah overlooking the ocean (costing USD 10.00 per month) and happened to be next door to the hangout of young travelers called Legian Sunset Beach Cottages with rooms and a restaurant. On my third day in Bali, while I was on my way, venturing to the seaside, an old woman emerged from behind a coconut tree and gave me a folded leaf with a few mushrooms inside. I put them in my bag and continued walking further down the shoreline. I saw a small group of Balinese children sitting on the sand with an old man, and they waved for me to join them.

As I approached them, the old man looked at me with a grin and asked, "Are you a fairy?" in perfect English. I did a double-take, and he repeated, "Are you a fairy?" I was stunned by such a question and could only feel as though I had really gone down a rabbit hole. This was my first encounter with Papa Wayan, which turned into a long story of opening doors to a new world—the world of Bali and its unseen side, steeped in tradition and mystery.

I had never stayed for more than three months in a country during my past travels, but here I decided to stay for as long as I could, Bali being my last destination of my round-the-world sojourn. Knowing I would have some time, I felt it best to pursue my desire to learn Balinese dance. I already had a background in classical ballet, modern dance, African Haitian dance, and flamenco.

Within the first month, I contacted the professional dance school in Denpasar called Kokar. There I received private dance lessons from a lovely lady, Miss Susilwati, who later I discovered was one of the best dancers in Bali. It was such a delight to learn the *Legong* dance, the most elegant and classic of Balinese dances, so quickly with the patience of my teacher holding my arms in the correct position from behind and pushing my derriere into a protruding squat position. It was the op-posite of ballet with hips outward, feet outward, and moving to the strange sounds of *gamelan* music with lots of chang-chang xylophonic infections. It certainly was not Debussy, and it featured a rhythm that was a mystery and required understanding the gong sound at intervals. Each private class cost USD 1.00.

My days were becoming quite busy. I was writing in my diary, painting, and making collages with a new energy. I engaged in creative activities like designing a carved wooden writing table, designing my low bed near the window for sea viewing, decorating my room, designing some jewelry and clothes, and buying paintings from a cute young guy on the beach. The seller's name was Agung Rai, who now owns the well-known Agung Rai Museum of Art (ARMA) in Ubud. Bali had so many creative avenues for discovery and exploration.

I started to make friends—Balinese, Javanese, and Westerners alike. The Balinese were so friendly and curious about my ways. I remember performing to a few of them from my verandah, a ballet dance wearing my satin toe shoes that I picked up from a store in Thailand. They loved it. We would indulge in the favorite Balinese dish of *Babi Guling* (roasted baby pig) together. Although I never fancied the local food, the gathering of the feast together was never without laughing and lots of smiles.

Westerners from all over the world usually gathered on the beach. The beach became the ultimate goal in my daily schedule. There, one would meet friends; exchange Bali experiences; inform each other of gatherings, local traditional dances, ceremonies, immigration rules, and gossip; and become part of a community of world-travelers—young people open to a new way of life. There were no bars or discos. Everyone seemed interested in discovering the rich culture around them, and nobody was judged by how much money they had or how famous they were. We all just knew that we had found a special place.

I remember a group of us traveling by *bemo* (the only local transport, in an open-backed truck with benches) in the middle of the night to the special ceremony to be held at the mother temple, Besakih. We all piled together, traveling on winding full moonlit roads to the temple, which was shrouded by a wispy fog. It was a magical night, and the locals performed in front of the temple a new dance called the "Frog Dance," with the young boys comically impersonating dancing frogs with very realistic masks and movements. It stunned us all. Afterward, we went to a ceremony in the area of Klungkung, down about two thousand steps into a valley, where I could hear four different gamelan orchestras throughout other villages of that valley playing music in unison and creating reverberating echoes into the distant hills. I returned to my room at about four a.m., and the moonlight by then was shining directly onto my bed, embracing me and making flittering, simmering diamond patterns on the ocean waves outside as the moon set into the sea. I felt something that night, a magic that intrigued me and took me to the next level of my Bali experience—the invisible.

I had already been in Bali for six months and had a better understanding of its people and the lifestyle. Before I arrived, no one had told me how primitive this place would be, like in another century, or like traveling back in time. I eventually had to pump my own water from the well, and kerosene lamps became my night-time companions, so to speak, with hours of watching the dancing flame behind the glass coverings and lots of candles all around too. The intense daytime humidity without fans was a constant adjustment. One needed a plethora of mosquito coils at night after a shower, which was always cold since there was no hot water either.

I actually did not mind these aspects, as I was growing to love this time-travel episode. My previous adventures on the trail had been tough at times, like exploring remote Northern Pakistan to Gilgit and the Everest Trek, but those were just passing-through travels. This new experience was more; it was becoming a way of life.

I had a degree in anthropology, and this cultural adventure became even more intriguing as a study experience. None of my friends and family back home had ever heard of this place. At that time there was very little literature about Bali, although some publications written in the thirties by foreign visitors, like Margaret Meade, were available in the West. The APA publication *Insight Guides—Explore Bali* and Miguel Covarrubias's book *The Island of Bali* written in 1937 (still a classic) were the only sources of written information available in Bali. They both described the communal social/village structure, the *subak* (community rice association), family structure, ceremonial rituals, and local religious beliefs. It was evident that this culture and its people believed in the unseen forces of life and death, good and evil, and spirits. It was a collective belief exhibited in sacred yet sometimes fanciful ways with humor.

The main entertainment activity for all, including Westerners, was going to the village dance in the local *banjar* or community center, shaded by an enormous banyan tree. Three times each week, there would be a rotation of the *Legong* Dance, *Ramayana* Dance, and *Barong* Dance. I am sure that I saw all of these at least a hundred times. A tiny stall in front of the dance area would sell a shot of *arak*, the local alcohol of very strong rice wine, for two cents. I would join the men at this stall for a cocktail prior to the dance starting.

The Barong dance was the most dramatic, with a selected group of village men, in trance, pushing sacred *kris* knives into their chests with all of their might and incurring not even a scratch. Sometimes they would become so entranced they would push the kris into their ear, eye, or nose, very tenaciously too, with no penetration. The collective good vibrations of the trance were protecting them as gallons of holy water were being showered upon them by the village priests.

The Balinese call the seen world *Sekala* and the unseen world *Niskala*. I came to realize that since I was physically present in this community, the forces of these two worlds coexisted in the community's reality and could be experienced on levels of aware observation, even as an outsider. The influences of the scientific, technological, and fact-based modern world were nonexistent among the one million inhabitants of Bali at that time. Their beliefs were a reality of balancing the good and evil forces of the gods, man, and nature. On rare occasions, sometimes the unseen world would reveal itself, falling through the cracks of reality, even to the neutral observer like me. Still to this day, I wonder about some of the phenomenal sights I encountered. For instance, I remember sitting on the stairs of my verandah and looking into the dark night, and darkness was so dark then, with a million stars drawing their constellations across the night sky. Oddly, I observed flashing small lights, like fireflies, but moving in directions toward one another in a crisscross fashion.

The next day, I mentioned this occurrence to my Balinese friend, and he told me they were fighting *magic lights*. Visions, too, could happen in Bali. I was with Papa Wayan, my little old Balinese rice field worker friend I had met on my third day in Bali, with whom I experienced these extraordinary, inexplicable moments. One day, we walked through a nearby forest together, and he would show me some magical apparitions, like people from my past walking behind me, who were actually not there. I came to know that he could even foretell the future and read my thoughts. One time he told me I had had a bad thought. He came to my house every day with a coconut, and one time he slept on my verandah at night. That night I had dreams of whirling mandalas in the most vivid forms. I usually kept these stories to myself; I did not want to appear weird. Telepathic connection was more intensified out of need since there were no telephones or communication devices. Friends seemed to show up at the right time, in the right place. Parties and events spontaneously came together. There were no coincidences; it was all a coincidence of living in Bali at this time, before mass tourism tipped the balance toward hiding the unseen world.

All my expat friends were deeply interested in the culture of Bali and its people. The goal was to find a way to live in Bali and be able to stay comfortably. No one was aspiring to be a "big shot." As a result, several expats became, over the decades, experts in their chosen field, be that tribal art, textile weaving, garment manufacturing, jewelry design, or whatever. Bali afforded an abundance of opportunities, an open frontier for entrepreneurial ideas, and pursuits for exporting or producing products. Many succeeded, too, as it later turned out.

My best friend, Milo Migliavacca, an Italian fashion designer, pioneered the ready-to-wear garment industry, receiving an award from the Indonesian Ministry of Trade. I remember him experimenting with different types of fabric dyes in his losmen bathroom using old coffee tins. And then he became an international fashion exporter. Some notables from this era were Linda Garland, international interior designer and founder of the Environmental Bamboo Foundation; John Hardy, international jewelry designer; Michael Palmieri, tribal art dealer; Kent Waters and Perry Kesner, textile connoisseurs; Lawrence and Lorne Blair, who explored the archipelago and produced their classic film *Ring of Fire*—and the list becomes quite long from those early expats of the '70s who expanded their interests in Bali and Indonesia on a larger scale, internationally.

There were many extraordinary times together among the expat community during the 1970s. The parties were not as elaborate as during the '90s and onward, but there was a deep comradery in experiencing Bali, a place that was still quite unknown to the world, where life was like a fairy tale. I remember, in particular, a great party in the lobby of what is now the five-star Oberoi Hotel, then called Kayu Aya. I danced all night and even pole danced around one of the pole beams in the lobby, swinging around and then jumping into the lobby pond with friends. It was, however, not always easy, this fairy tale. There were tough times too.

I always considered Bali to be like a human entity, a relationship. For any foreigner who wished to stay and make a deeper connection to Bali; there always seemed to be a rite of passage. Usually, this rite tested you, and it was not easy. It was as though if you passed this test, you were permitted by this entity of Bali to stay and be embraced by its gentle arms. Sometimes though, this entity would slap you in the face for wrong, careless, or thoughtless actions. These moments would be wake-up calls of instant karma bringing you to a better understanding of yourself and others, if you learned the lesson of your actions.

I've been lucky to have lived in Bali for the past thirty years with my husband, Alec. I was fortunate to have had a successful villa rental business for twenty-four years with notable guests ready to explore the wonders of the island, which I hope I contributed to their experience. Now a painter, I am recording the moments visually of mostly the Bali magic and its timelessness.

The decade of the 1970s in Bali seemed to have had a theme of being an exceptional period of another era, with the last glimpse of traditional Balinese living without the interference of excessive tourism. We were lucky to have experienced it with youth and timing on our side and to be able to savor and share the story of a vanishing moment in time. As author Diana Darling so aptly put in an article entitled "You Missed the Best of It": we were blessed to have known this time on the Island of the Gods.

MY ADVICE FOR THE BALI VISITOR ─────────────────────────

Take a great scenic bicycle ride through rice fields, local villages and gorgeous tropical settings outside of Ubud.

I Found Exciting Men in Bali

NOELLE SIMPSON

Noelle Simpson was born a rebel on a horseracing stud farm in New Zealand. She was sent off to boarding school in Switzerland and the United Kingdom. She is a lifelong artist in fashion, design, painting, and jewelry design. Since 1969 she has been living between Australia, New Zealand, the US, London, and Bali. Noelle fell in love with Bali in 1975 and has never missed a year as a part-time resident since 1984.

Many people have asked me, "What made you choose to live in Bali?"

Usually, I respond with a laugh and with something like "Only someone who hasn't been there would ask that!"

Being asked again, one day I replied, "Well, it may have had something to do with all the wonderful men I met there!"

Of course, I fell in love with Bali for its culture and beauty, the vista of the rice fields, the people, the temples and ceremonies beyond imagination, the balmy air, the sacred mountains, and the exquisite arts everywhere.

To me Bali represents the cornucopia of beauty, delight, and abundance of all the good things we imagine.

But I also fell in love there more than once with fascinating, vivacious, fun, creative, artistic, intelligent souls who took me on adventures and showed me parts of Bali and myself that revealed mysterious aspects of life.

My first two trips in 1975 were magical, and I knew I would come back. It took me until 1984 to return after being seriously sidetracked to Hanalei Bay in Kauai, following my heart.

Arriving from Sydney, the first day I stayed at the Tandjung Sari Hotel in Sanur. That night I met a group of people who were staying in Legian and had to come to Sanur to enjoy a movie night and dinner. They were very friendly, and in the twinkling of an eye, I was invited to stay with Zinski (aka Jogya John) at Nicholas Schwaebe's house on the beach, which was located almost next door to Blue Ocean restaurant in Legian. This had the added attraction of being the hot spot for the "belle monde" and "not so bad" boys of Bali—who were tanned, trim, terrific, fun-loving, intelligent, artistic, dynamic, and adventurous.

We spent the days lunching, sunbathing, swimming, and surfing. Blue Ocean's Australian manager, Malcolm Williams, was always the quintessential laid-back host while fending off those who thought he was Mick Jagger's brother. I met all kinds of black-sheep types who collected antiques and artifacts and those who designed clothes, such as the iconic Paul Ropp. I met the brilliant jeweler Jean-François, founder of Jewels of Nature and also the irrepressible artist Symon who lived in Ubud. I also met Annie and Kiyo, who were taking the world by storm with their Jakpak (which was a colorful patchwork jacket that could be transformed into a bag). Of course, it was always exciting to see what new treasures the tribal art dealers like Zinski, Michael Palmieri, and Perry Kesner had discovered in far-off islands. John de Coney had his own class of madness and was famous for designing and building teak knockdown houses and selling them in America.

Zinski swept me off my feet, and we would take off on various adventures around Bali and other parts of Indonesia. Once, we flew to Lake Toba in Sumatra. In Pulau Tao, our accommodation was a romantic hut on stilts. From our hut we could dive straight into the water, and we paddled our native canoe to secret spots and took long walks to see the architectural wonders—the stone statues and artifacts that abounded. It's one thing to see these wonders in books, but feeling their power in person was undeniable.

By the time we returned to Bali, I was looking forward to living happily ever after with Zinski. However, life had other plans, and after our adventures in other parts of the world, we parted company as friends with many happy memories.

It was my trip to Bali in 1986 that was to have the most profound effect on my life. A few years before, I had become an artist, and I was staying at the Cecak Inn (now the Ibah Hotel) in Tjampuhan. My home studio was a traditional *lumbung* (bamboo hut) by a famous temple and a ridge covered only with *alang-alang* grass overlooking the place where two rivers met. I was a few steps away from a natural spring, with Balinese carvings etched into the surrounding rock. Here I bathed every day.

I heard that there was a "once in a lifetime" cremation ceremony to take place in Denpasar. I donned my antique batik sarong and lacy *kebaya* (women's traditional lace top), took a *bemo* (public transportation minivan) as far as it would take me, then walked to where the ceremony was taking place. Throngs of Balinese in their best traditional dress were a magnificent sight. The temples, high handmade bamboo towers, and cremation bulls were a feast for the eyes. There were so many people, though I knew none, but all the sights, sounds, and smells of festivity were mesmerizing.

Suddenly I heard my name called. I looked up and saw a man I had briefly met in Sydney a few weeks before. He was an artist who had been very kind and even complimentary with his comments and encouragement about my paintings. He was there with a couple of roguish-looking rather handsome friends whom I came to know as Del Negro, an American movie star, and Wini Wowor from Bali, who had appeared in the musical production *Hair* in Paris. I also met the artist Ian Van Wieringen. It was an unforgettable encounter—not just because that day was the beginning of a four-year romance with Van but also because he was to be the father of our daughter, Zen.

I was very grateful to have found three delightful companions who could tell me all about what was happening, take me to the best *warungs* (local food stalls), and know exactly what to order. This was a fun magical day on so many levels.

I went back to Ubud with my new friend Van, and the whirlwind continued unabated. We went to his house in Sayan, which was almost a ruin from neglect because Van had left it untended for two or three years, but some of his art had miraculously survived. He soon moved into my place, which eventuated in my art taking a massive leap forward. Until then, being self-taught, my style was definitely naive. But now the hand of Van made its mark on my canvas, and nothing would be the same again.

Van is a master of the brush, and his peers are the most famous painters in Australia and extremely successful. Van always played his own game and refused to take the path necessary to become rich and famous. However, Madame de Rothschild, probably the richest woman in the world, visiting Van in Sayan while looking at the spectacular view, said, "You should want for nothing more than this," to which he quipped, "That's all very well for you to say!"

Ian Pieter Van Wieringen came from a long line of Dutch painters of the same name. He was born in Holland during the war and then lived in Indonesia in the years of "living dangerously" during the transition from the Dutch to Sukarno's Indonesia, where his father was a diplomat. In the mid-1950s, they left for Sydney, Australia, and Van started his official art career there, having his first show at age eighteen with the talented and soon-to-be-famous John Firth Smith.

Once Van arrived in Bali in the late 1960s, he was hooked on the island and lucky enough to find the quintessential place to live on the Sayan Ridge, in the home where Margaret Mead and Colin McPhee had stayed.

Many others came to live in Bali over the years as neighbors. Next door lived Arthur Karvan, famous for owning the best nightclub in Sydney—Arthur's in Kings Cross. Made Wijaya (aka Michael White) also lived close by. Made was famous for many things as well as being the wicked chronicler of *Stranger in Paradise,* a magazine displaying his deep knowledge of the Balinese culture mixed with local gossip. Musicologist James Murdoch also lived nearby. Shane Sweeny, the artist, used to stay at Van's when he was overseas. Many thought it was his house, but it was Van who was known as King of the Ridge.

Back in the day in Ubud, there were only a couple of phones in the area, so we often had to go to the airport in Kuta to use their phone service. There, one would book a phone call and wait about three hours to get through and then allowed only three minutes to talk (unless you wanted to pay for the next three minutes). To exchange money was also quite an arduous task; sometimes you waited half a day at the bank to collect wads of 10,000-rupiah notes.

There were only a few restaurants, such as the Lotus, where we were lucky enough to buy Rio and Ella Helmi's homemade bread. All the good restaurants were owned by Indonesian and *bule* (foreigner) couples —Lotus Cafe, Murni's Warung, Cafe Wayan, and of course Victor Mason's unforgettable Beggar's Bush, a quasi-English pub. Beggar's Bush was a place for fun and games, and we enjoyed many late nights there accompanied by Victor's legendary jazz collection and copious drinks.

We would take journeys through the rice fields in the dark to some-times get to our friend's home. Sometimes tripping into the rice fields! At filmmaker John Darling's Balinese-style compound located in the rice fields, I experienced my first taste of the fruit durian, an adventure not to be forgotten. John made the fabulous film *Lempad of Bali*—about the Balinese "Picasso" who lived to 117 years old. Van drew Lempad's portrait and also was present at his official departure from this world—a story he tells in a book about Lempad's art and life.

There were many exciting trips to exotic temples for wild ceremo-nies and dancers with Made Wijaya, who of course knew everyone and everything about the events that were going on and had friends wherever he went. His recording of life in Bali in his *Stranger in Paradise* columns and books was a genuine service to historians and great fun for the rest of us—as long as one was not the butt of his acerbic wit. Made had fallouts with almost everyone he met, but somehow he managed to eventually get back into their good graces because he was so clever and funny.

I introduced Made to my dear friend Nyarie Hassall Abbey. Nyarie commissioned him to build her a house in Sanur. She had decided with Made to build several homes on her piece of land, including her own.

The compound was called Villa Bebek and was the real beginning of Made's success as an architect and contractor. Many homes in Bali then were visibly interesting but were almost impossible to live in comfortably. Van and I had lived in several of Made's houses in the past, but Villa Bebek was a real step up. Nyarie came back to Bali to a fully furnished, glorious home. Van and I had a great time living there and painting in the big open upstairs studio while little Zen played in the garden and swam in the pool.

There were many parties with luminaries at Villa Bebek, such as with Chris and Katherine Carlise, Kerry and Ruth Hill, Tim and Annie Street Porter, and Lorne and Lawrence Blair, in between their travels filming *The Ring of Fire*. There were exotic dinners at Batujimbar with Wija and Tate Waworuntu and meetings with all kinds of interesting types who were visiting Bali.

No one who went to Idanna Pucci's Melaspas housewarming ceremony in Sideman will forget that day when Victor Mason fell over the balcony and dropped about twelve feet to the ground below, then got right back up again and had another beer! It was an ideally situated house with expansive views across the rice fields and rivers directly looking at Mt. Agung. It belonged to the Tjokorda of Sideman and had received many famous visitors, such as Charlie Chaplin and the painter Theo Maier.

Bali was starting to expand, and many huge hotels were being built in our area. Van, Zen, and I were living at one of Made Wijaya's "Taman Bebek" homes, overlooking the famous spectacular Sayan view—which is no longer fully there since they plonked the Four Seasons Hotel right in the middle of it.

We managed to live unscathed through the building of the iconic Amandari Hotel in Sayan, whose design was based on a Balinese village by Peter and Carol Muller. Symon was the artist who created the printed screens for the Amandari suites, which all had their own garden wall and pool.

Over the years, I spent many hours with Symon printing and painting in his studio in Tjampuhan, where he lived for twenty-five years. He held many extravagant theatrical events there, particularly at the stage and amphitheater where Buckminster Fuller had left the imprint of his geodesic dome in the floor. It's all a ruin now, since Symon left when his lease expired and went to live full-time at his Art Zoo in Alessari in north Bali. Alessari is an artist's palace—imagine Dali meets Disney. I spent many fascinating times there, also with Symon's biographer Philip Cornwell Smith, who built his own place next door. Sadly, Symon died suddenly just after his seventy-fourth birthday in April 2020, followed by the sudden departure of the glorious talented Italian designer Milo. I shall never forget his parties and the two orangutans that lived with him in his creative paradise in Seminyak until the authorities took the primates away.

The more I write, the more vignettes I fondly remember. Is it any wonder that I chose Bali? Thank you, Bali.

MY ADVICE FOR THE BALI VISITOR ─────────────

Leave your preconceived ideas behind, go with the flow and be grateful to have discovered Bali.

Fantuzzi's
Memory of Bali

FANTUZZI

*Fantuzzi is a global troubadour and ambassador of joy. His charismatic,
sensual energy pulses through music that never fails to get people moving.
A "NewYorican," Fantuzzi's Afro-Caribbean roots and global adventures
showcase his unique presence. Historically, he's regularly spotted all across the
world supporting and collaborating with leading musicians in spiritual and
musical gatherings, often as an MC as well as a star performer.*

I arrived by boat from Java in 1975 for there was no airport. I came
with my tribe. We were called "The Butterfly Family." The minute we
hit the magical island, we felt the vibe. It didn't take long before we had
merged with the expats and progressive Balinese and created a theatrical ceremony/theatre piece.

Bali had never had anything like this, and we had never experienced
anything like this. The Balinese culture is one of the most magical,
colorful cultures I have known, and I had already traveled all over the
world by then.

At that time, Seminyak and Ubud were one. Kuta was nothing.
There was no infrastructure for tourism. The locals were working on
building some kind of a hotel down there. They were begging the hippies to stay a night in their hotel so they could experiment with some of
the more experimental travelers—who were the only ones on the island.

There were no restaurants. There was no transportation to get to Ubud. There was one hotel there at the time.

We created our own "ceremony" that was so powerful that five hundred people showed up. Even the chief of police was in the front row. We had already seen what the Balinese were doing in ceremony, so we incorporated the culture, the *Barong*, and *Rangda* and mixed that in with *Shiva* and *Shakti*. We had just arrived from India not too long ago—and five hundred people had their minds blown.

Word had come that the police were looking for Fantuzzi—the guy who put the ceremony together. Foreigners were not allowed to put on shows with audiences of such a large capacity.

When somebody's looking for you, it's better that you find them first. So I went to the police. Back then the police and the military were the same and operated out of Java.

I walked into a huge room, but there was only one guy behind a desk surrounded by flags and sporting medals on his military jacket.

He was some kind of general, and my Balinese friend had already advised me: "If he asks you, please don't say anything about the ceremony being religious. Just tell him it's all about art."

Just so you know: they've locked people up for a lot less. They thought it was a cover for a military takeover, because if five hundred people were attending, that was enough to execute a coup back in those days.

As I sat in front of the general, every time he asked me why I put on the event, I replied, "For art and love!" The word *love* just blurted from my mouth.

The general couldn't quite make out who I was, but he figured I wasn't dangerous to his position, so he said, "You can leave now. But remember this—you are not to do another one of those unless you invite us first!"

MY ADVICE FOR THE BALI VISITOR ───────────────────

Try exploring the glorious retreats and beaches of the northwest. Visit Tirtagangga—a beautiful place, one of the most exquisite swimming experiences to be had in the mineral-rich volcanic waters of the royal enclosure. Also, check out the small local warungs for genuine Balinese cuisine.

1. Ni Pollok performs the Legong Dance on Sanur Beach. Photo: Kelland Hutchence (1948).
2. 'A glimpse of the beautiful beach' (original quote). Photo: Kelland Hutchence (1948).
3. Adrien-Jean Le Mayeur (far left), his wife Ni Pollok and Kelland Hutchence (center),
with others unknown on Sanur Beach. Photo: Kelland Hutchence (1948).
4. Balinese boy dancing. Photo: Kelland Hutchence (1948).
5. Balinese dancing girls in full costume. Photo: Kelland Hutchence (1948).

6. A Baris dance offered to the gods as part of the Eka Dasa Rudra ceremonies. Photo:
Rio Helmi (1979).

7. Lempad's widow attends a dance offered as part of his funerary rituals. Photo: Rio Helmi (1979).
8. Women quarrying for sand in the river at Mambal. Photo: Rio Helmi (1983).

9. The only bus going from Ubud to Denpasar, usually packed. Photo: Rio Helmi (1979).

10. Batik seller on Jl. Pantai Kuta outside Mandara Homestay. Photo: Chris Hazzard (1972).

11. Veronica with Little Wayan (wife number 3) and her firstborn. Photo: Chris Hazzard (1973).

12. Dr. Lawrence Blair in Pengosekan. Photo: Lawrence Blair (1980).

13. Claudia Karvan being teased about becoming a big girl by her dad, Arthur. Photo: Made Wijaya (1980).

14. Arthur Karvan and Made Wijaya (RIP) hamming it up for camera at Matahari Disco, Hyatt Resort Hotel, Sanur. Photo: Michael Palmieri (1980).

15. Gilbert jamming at a birthday party at Blue Ocean. Photo: Lisbeth (1980).

16. Gilbert playing guitar with Vidal and Joffrey (RIP) in Legian. Photo: Gilbert Garcia (1979).

17. Peter and Made on Pantai Kuta. Photo: Peter Steenbergen (1973).
18. Peter and Made's wedding kiss. Photo: Peter Steenbergen (1974).
19. Made in the original Warung in 1973 with a customer. Photo: Peter Steenbergen (1973).

20. Australian artist Ken Johnson in Ubud. Photo: Ken Johnson (1974).
21. Painting titled *Nutcracker* (1974) by Ken Johnson, depicting village life in Legian.
Photo: Ken Johnson (1974).

22. Rucina with maestro dance teacher I Nyoman Kakul in Batuan. Photo: Barbara Miller (1974).

23. Terry Tarnoff playing outside Puspa Sari losmen in Legian. Photo: Robert Bolden (1974).

24. Waiting for friends to disembark, Ngurah Rai Airport. Photo: Marie Thomas (1973).

25. Peter Thomas and his landlord Pak Rai at the Wisata Beach Inn, Legian. Photo:
Peter Thomas (1984).
26. Carola Vooges and Bruce Carpenter standing in front of Puri Saraswati, the Lotus temple
in Ubud designed by master artist I Gusti Nyoman Lempad. Photo: Unknown (1979).

27. A bungalow in Golden Village, Seminyak. Photo: Ariane Morand (1984).

28. Owner of Golden Village, Agung 'Boss' with his wife and children, Mas (bottom left) in Seminyak. Photo: Unknown (1970).

29. Del Negro (RIP), Van Wieringen, Wini Wowor at a major cremation. Photo: Noelle Simpson (1986).

30. Breakfast at Nick's with Tom Hawkins, Jean Paul, Zinski aka Jogya John, Leigh Lawson, Noelle, Gerald (RIP), Nicholas Schwaebe. Photo: Noelle Simpson (1984).

31. Three posers, John Darling (RIP), Made Wijaya (RIP), Van Wieringen competing for 'who has the best legs.' Photo: Noelle Simpson (1986).

32. Anita received a visit from Papa Wayan every morning. Photo: Ketut Dharma (1975).

33. Mira and Tansen (RIP). Photo: Mira Stannard (1989).

34. Mira and Tansen (RIP) dancing in masks at the Magic, Mastery and Mystery seminar performance at Ubud Palace. Photo: Mira Stannard (1987).

35. Saraswati with Kopling, the tuak maker in his coconut palm fields beside his home on
Jl. Imam Bonjol, North Kuta. Photo: Saraswati Mish (1980).
36. Saraswati at a cockfight with Made from the Kuta Tuak stand which was located behind
Made's Warung. Photo: Saraswati Mish (1980).

37. Victor 'Django Mango' Vidal. Photo: Chris Hazzard (1981).

38. Ken after a morning's harvest of magic mushrooms. Photo: Ken Wheaton (1972).

39. Korti's warung, Korti (left), her mom (far right) on the corner of Jl. Padma and Jl. Legian. Photo: Ken Wheaton (1972).

40. Ken's Balinese family, Bapak Made and Made preparing offerings. Photo: Ken Revdoc (1972).

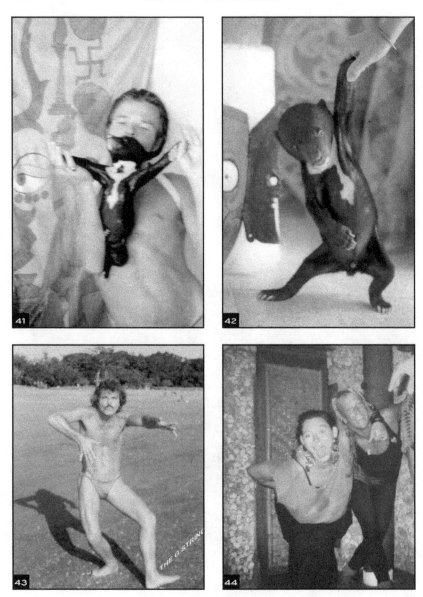

41. Michael and Bubbu Bear, Seminyak. Photo: Michael Palmieri (1979).

42. Bubbu bear was rescued by Michael from the jungle of Borneo after his mother had been killed by poachers. Seminyak. Photo: Michael Palmieri (1979).

43. Michael performing the 'G-string Boogie' in front of the Blue Ocean restaurant, Legian. Photo: Michael Palmieri (1976).

44. Judith and Judy (RIP) having fun at Chez Gado Gado disco in Seminyak. Photo: Pati Marcus (1984).

45. Glenda's Bali wedding day. Klungkung. Photo: D. Ludlum (1982).

46. Glenda's tooth filing, 'just a little bit for tourists.' Photo: M. Rankins (1982).

47. Yanie and first son, Jian, at Yanies Restaurant in Legian. Photo: Nigel Mason (1989).

48. Yanie and Nigel's simple wedding ceremony with family in Legian. Photo: Nigel Mason (1985).

49. The Mason family: Nigel and Yanie with sons, Jian and Shan. Photo: Nigel Mason (1996).

50. Stephanie's woodcarving, *Bodhisattva and the Golden Bird*. Photo: Stephanie Buffington (1982).

51. Wana (RIP) and his employee, Agus, in Kuta. Photo: Karen Anne Field (1979).

52. Wana (RIP) and Soosan happy together in Jatiluwih. Photo: Peter Steenbergen (1983).

53. Lake Batur on a sunny morning. Photo: Peter Croft (1983).

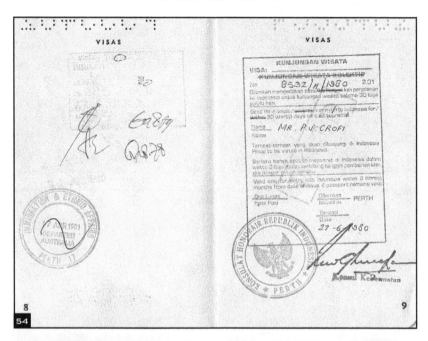

54. A scan from Peter Croft's passport (notice how the Indonesian visa takes up an entire page).
Photo: Peter Croft (1983).

55. My room at the Puri Dalem Hotel. Photo: Peter Croft (1985).

56. Peter and some friends at Cosy Corner restaurant, Kuta. Photo: Peter Croft (1980).

57. Peter's friend Norm haggling in Poppies Lane, Kuta. Photo: Peter Croft (1983).

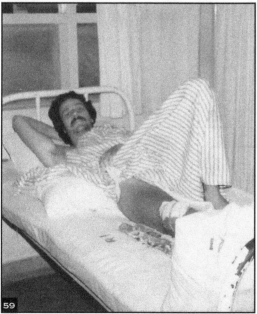

58. Dianne viewing the rice terraces in Bangli with her husband Paul. Photo: Dianne Vincent (1982).

59. Mark Johnson resting in a hospital in Denpasar about 6-7 days after his motorcycle accident. Photo: Mark Griffith (1980).

60. Margrit with her Balinese daughter Iluh (the 'Magic Child'). Photo: Margrit Heldstab (1993).

61. Dem, Rainy, Milan (RIP), Bonnie aka Atta in Legian. Photo: Logi (1974).

62. Marie and Atta at Gordon and Claudia's wedding. Photo: Atta Melvin (1981).

63. Patricia with her son Paul, preparing Wini with a look for the Mr Bali contest. Photo: Patricia Chaparro (1984).

64. Patricia performing with Fantuzzi and friends at Double Six disco in Seminyak. Photo: Unknown (1990).

65. Patricia holding her daughter at a Balinese cremation with a local woman. Photo: Catherine Fourcard (1989).

66. Rachel's Garuda mask, which now hangs in pride of place in her home. Photo: Rachel Lovelock (1988).

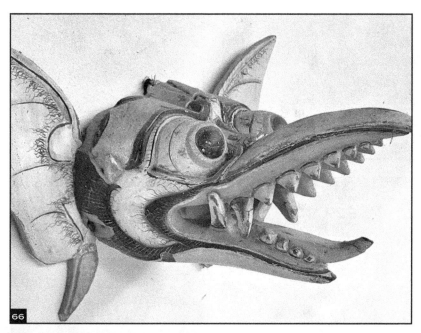

67. Michael's housewarming party for his Legian beach house, built by Symon's craftsmen. Photo: Darvany Deal (1985).

68. Michael at the top of Mt. Abang with his bike. Photo: Brad Grunewald (1985).

69. Negotiating fare from Denpasar to Kuta, with lots of laughs in the process! Photo: Sally Herrero (1982).

70. Playing with local children on Poppies Lane, Kuta. Photo: Sally Herrero (1982).

71. Jalan Legian, outside Twice Pub looking north, 'if only we could turn back time!'
Photo: Sally Herrero (1982).

72. Best snacks at the Swiss Bakery, Jalan Legian. Photo: Sally Herrero (1982).

73. Doris's tropical love mobile. Legian. Photo: Doris Caitak (1984).

74. Easy rider on a Honda, Doris enjoying the breeze and the freedom. Legian.
Photo: Doris Caitak (1984).

75. Doris's bamboo office in paradise in Legian. Photo: Doris Caitak (1984).

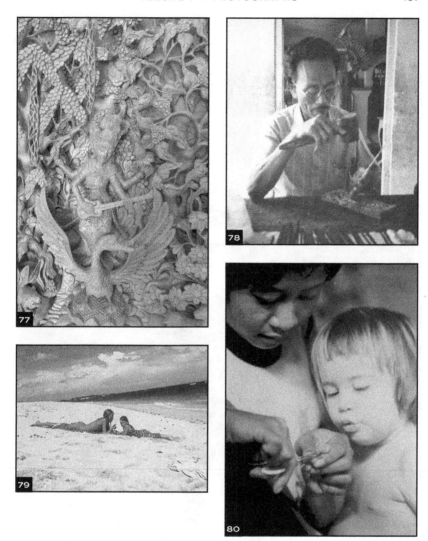

76. Love at sunset while the tribe meets for sunset volleyball in Legian. Photo: Doris Caitak (1984).

77. Woodcarving of Ida Bagus Putu Raka (leaves by Alissa), Batuan. Photo: Alissa Stern (1983).

78. Alissa's woodcarving teacher, master carver Ida Bagus Putu Raka in Batuan. Photo: Alissa Stern (1983).

79. Marie Lasource with daughter Julia in Nusa Dua. Photo: Barbara Hombergen (1987).

80. Nyoman and Marie's daughter, Julia in Seminyak. Photo: Marie Lasource (1985).

81. Alexander; even the monkey thought he had a wig on! Photo: Stephen Miller (1981).
82. Gabriella, Steve (RIP), Ingele and Pablo on their way to visit the shaman in Singaraja.
Photo: Anthony Pablo Gentile (1982).

83. John (RIP) and Diana Darling at the pondok. Photo: Made Wijaya (1981).
84. Ketut Swardana holding his artwork for the cover of this book. Padang Sambian.
Photo: Ni Made Sudiani (2021).

PART III

BALI
1975–1980

If you think you are free,
there's no escape possible.

RAM DASS

The Witches Curse

VICTOR VIDAL PAZ

In memory of the Balinese priest Nyoman Ledin

Victor Vidal Paz likes to introduce himself as Django Mango, especially on his CD covers. Born of a Catalan mother and Spanish father, he has traveled to eighty countries, where he often creates something from his adventures, such as music and filmmaking.

> "We cannot escape fear. We can only transform it into a
> Companion that takes us on all our exciting adventures.
> Take a risk a day—one small or bold stroke that will make
> you feel great once you have done it."
> — SUSAN JEFFERS

The civilized world holds that miracles and spirit powers are an illusion dreamed up by primitive man. The only invisible force that modern man believes in is the air he breathes. Everything he can understand with the aid of reason and survey, on the wings of the intellect, lulls him into a soothing security. And he rejects, like a nuisance, with a blend of arrogance and ignorance, anything that cannot be proven by the axiomatic force of logic. Why? Why? Why?

It is his fear of the unknown. Carl Jung said: "Modern man adores the god of reason and, with the aid of thought, believes he can control nature. This is his greatest and most tragic illusion."

Bali is like a nymph flying ceaselessly in my soul, evoking the most beautiful memories. That island of marvelous fairies, perverse witches, and kind dragons has long been, still is, and will continue to be a haven of rebels that refuse to submit to the dogmas that the system tries to impose on them.

The Balinese have the heart of a warrior, an unbreakable temperament, and a spirit of steel. They will only bow in humility to the god of their devotion. Would you like to know why the Balinese are so staunch in their tradition? Observe carefully the hypnotic force in the sparkling eyes of a *Baris* dancer doing the dance of the warrior—all answers to that question lie in the eyes of that dancing paladin. It is impossible to describe, as ineffable as writing a poem about the fragrance of the rose. The most intense sensations lie beyond the power of the word—perhaps that is why they are so beautiful.

The first question all tourists ask when they arrive in Bali is "Why do the Balinese hold so many ceremonies and offerings?" I would answer: "Because they are infinitely more closely connected to the world of the invisible than we are."

Dear reader, while it may be hard to believe, the following is a true story, which reveals that realities that cannot be proven by intellectual reasoning—yet they do exist.

Nothing in this story is fiction; it is as real as the book in your hands. The most startling part is the ending.

When I arrived in Kuta, Bali, in my early twenties, there was no electricity and no paved roads. The few travelers that went there were searching for solace on its paradisiacal beaches, the refreshing breeze of its tropical waters, the most multi-creative culture in the world, and, above all, the congenial beaming energy of the Balinese.

In the early seventies, the Balinese were not yet tainted by Western stress. Kuta had only one restaurant. Jalan Legian was deserted, and a feeling of relaxation permeated its ambiance.

Every full moon, the *Kris* dance was held along Jalan Pantai, the main street in Kuta, or on the beach, which featured the kris knife—a serpent-shaped knife with magical powers. By merely catching the distant, mesmerizing, harmonious monotony of the *gamelans*, the gongs, and the frenzied counterpoint of the drums in crescendo, the newcomer would realize that he or she was in for an intense experience.

The witch *Rangda*, the Queen of Evil, would appear on stage with her eyes nearly popping out of her mask and two projecting tusks hat made her look like a wild boar.

With white tresses cascading down to her waist, her drooping breasts, and her hands trembling under the weight of her long finger-nails, the harpy strutted about like an incensed monster, lifting up her legs, taking great strides, and making fearsome guttural roars like di-abolical mantras, condensing all the wrath of evil, which would make even the most courageous warrior tremble.

A group of Balinese in a trance, in a fit of collective vengeful fury, would hurl themselves with violent resolve at Rangda, their daggers drawn. Without retreating even one step, the witch would challenge them with her magic powers and, when the threatening blades entered the aura of her magic, like some satanic karmic priestess, she would shake a white handkerchief, a symbol of her evil powers, and turn the daggers against them.

The climax of the ceremony is a dramatic attempt at collective sui-cide. Rolling about on the ground, in this dance, they stab themselves so forcefully that the steel blades bend, but they do not penetrate their flesh because they are protected by *Barong*, the spirit of good, embodied by a mythical dragon resembling the ones that appear in Chinese theatre.

Some fall into such a deep trance that they pass out. The *pemangku* (priest) revives them with holy water and by making them touch the good spirit's beard. The event ends with animal sacrifices to satiate the Queen of Evil's bloodlust.

The Kris dance is the most amazing struggle between good and evil I have ever seen. In the West, God and the Devil are separated by a chasm or an ocean. In the East, the dark and the bright sides of life, the earthly and the heavenly, punishment and reward, form a polarized unity and a dualism in which the two are complementary. One cannot exist without the other.

During one of those animistic rites, I spied a strange blond woman dressed in a long white silk robe. The white gave her an air of purity, but her eyes and lips were those of a consummate witch. She must have been about twenty-five years old. That woman, a blend of angel and witch, had something mysterious and contradictory about her. She seemed to be hypnotized by the witch's mask. A week later, I realized that the witch was a mirror that reflected the dark sorceress lurking in her heart.

The following day, when I was carrying my surfboard along to make love to the most dangerous and fickle of all lovers—waves—I saw her sitting on the sand, her gaze lost in infinity. I went up to her and said, "I'm going to play with the waves. The next time we meet, it will be a pleasure to talk to you."

With her enigmatic light-green eyes like fire emeralds, the woman replied, "I have something important to tell you," and she took her leave with a mysterious smile. It was then that I noticed she had two enormous disturbing fangs.

At dusk the next day, I came across her in a restaurant called Warung Made. I asked if I could join her at her table. She stared intensely at me with a gaze that was both frightening and seductive.

"What did you want to tell me?" I asked.

She replied with devastating self-assurance, "Your father is dead, and you once had a green car with a white roof you used to drive to the snow."

I was dumbfounded. I froze in awe. If someone had pricked me, no blood would have come out. My father had indeed died when I was very young, and in Spain, I had owned a Morris Mini Cooper, and every weekend I used to drive up to the snow to go skiing. Aghast, I thought, *How can that woman know that my father is dead? I have never seen her before.* I would never forget her witch's face, and I'd never mentioned anything so commonplace as the color of my car to anyone.

I felt impotent, disarmed before the stunning power of that strange woman. With obvious nervousness, I said, "Everything you've told me is true... How do you know? Have you been to Spain? Have you talked to someone who knows me?"

"I dreamed it," she replied, "the night I saw you at that strange ceremony with the witch. And I also know what's going to happen to you in the future."

I raised my hand as if to block her energy and countered, somewhat timorously but with firm resolve, "Stop! What I'm interested in is the present. Revealing my future would destroy all the mystery of the unknown."

Everything is uncertain—the only sure thing is death. For some strange reason—possibly due to the magic of her divination and fear—I felt sexually attracted to her.

"I'd like to play the drum for you," I said. "Would you like to come to my shack?"

She got up and, with not the slightest hint of doubt in her eyes, said, "Let's go!"

We went to a bamboo hut I rented in a palm plantation between Kuta and Legian. We walked in silence, both knowing full well why we were heading there.

I played the drum for her, and, setting aside all modesty, she danced like a wounded snake. It was the wildest dance I have ever seen. Trying to make out her sensual forms behind the fine white silk fabric lit by candlelight was a torment for my imagination. The more forcefully I played the drum, the more passionately she swayed. She seemed to be possessed, as if seized by some strange power.

At the height of the excitement, I boldly told her to get undressed. It was more of a command than a request.

A description of the night of pleasure that ensued is beyond the scope of this book. All I can say is that it was one of the wildest experiences in my life. For the first time ever, that woman aroused in me my animal soul.

We arranged to meet the following day before sunset in a small hotel in Jalan Pantai. I knocked on the door but was met by silence. I peered through the window, thinking that she might be resting and saw, in the half-light of the room, a bedside table with an enormous book on it. The book had a black velvet cover and on it lay a butcher's knife.

A hand brushed my shoulder. I turned, startled, and there she was, staring at me with her penetrating witch's eyes, as green as a mamba's.

I felt distinctly uneasy in the presence of that sorceress, and my passion for her turned into aloofness. We went to bed, but I felt cold and confused. Thoughts whirled through my mind like enraged hornets.

That powerful intuition that characterizes women led her to sense my passion had waned and heightened my misgivings. She felt rejected and, staring at me with the expression of a vengeful sow I shall never forget, she pointed at me with her long-nailed index finger, and cursed me with diabolical confidence, saying, "You will die in the sea."

I felt impotent at that cruel abuse of power but, to this day I don't know how, I was bold enough to slap her three times, making her red in the face. Never before or since have I reacted that way—it is a denigrating act of ignorance, which relegates man to the level of an ape. To vindicate myself at the time, I regarded it as legitimate self-defense. Wasting no time, I put on my trousers, grabbed my shirt in one hand— without letting the knife out of my sight, in case she was tempted to use it—and, in a fit of terror, ran out of the room like a dog with its tail between its legs. The owner of the hotel saw me running out, shirt in hand, my zipper open, with a fearful expression on my face, and realized that something odd was transpiring.

I never saw her again, but the memory of that witch is always fresh in my mind. She had power but lacked the wisdom to use it properly, and she had pierced my mind with an invisible dart of diabolical magic.

In those days, prior to the tourist invasion, I used to tie my surfboard to my kayak, paddle out, drop anchor, and, in absolute solitude, ride the waves, those endless nomads of the sea, over the Kuta reef, some five hundred meters from the shore.

What ineffable pleasure—I had all the waves to myself! On days when the sea was rough and the breakers rushed in like enraged five-meter-high monsters, in my mind I could see the witch's eyes and recall her perverse curse: "You will die in the sea! You will die in the sea!" My fears were heightened by the fact that I was alone in the desolate ocean.

I became so haunted by the thought of drowning that I attached two elastic safety systems to my ankle—should one be wrenched off by a wave, I would still have the other one securing me to the surfboard.

Despite being obsessed by the fear of dying, like a warrior of life and death, I continued to make love to the waves every day. Two forces struggled incessantly in my heart—my love of surfing and my fear of drowning. I recall that, as I was alone on the reef, I felt a powerful urge of freedom that led me to surf naked, and I thought that if a wave took my life in its arms, I would leave the world the same way I had entered it.

Ten years later, in Nepal, I told my tabla teacher about the witch's curse. He responded by saying that he was powerless to do anything about it—it was beyond his spiritual grasp, but he advised me to consult a Saddhu from Varanasi who lived in a small temple on the outskirts of Kathmandu. The Saddhu was ninety and, as if he had returned to his beginnings, he lived only on buffalo's milk.

In the evening we set off to visit the Saddhu, who was my tabla teacher's spiritual master. The Saddhu was dark-skinned with white hair falling to his waist and eyes like two moon crystals that reflected all the wisdom of the universe.

My teacher told him about the sorceress's evil spell in Hindi.

The Saddhu lit three sticks of incense and closed his eyes for a long time, as if delving into the depths of his mind. Then he said:

For three hundred days, starting now, you must purify yourself. Follow the way of the superior man. Pay all your debts and eradicate even the slightest shadow of guilt from your mind. On moonless nights you must make an offering to Varuna, the god of the sea, and, at full moon, to Chandra, the moon goddess. And, when you feel cleansed, you must set sail on a dangerous voyage that brings you close to the doors of death. Go with the absolute certainty that you are protected by divine power and will return successfully from your journey. That is the only way you can revoke the curse.

I followed the Saddhu's instructions to the letter and, a year later, started making preparations for a single-handed circumnavigation of Bali in a kayak.

The island's south coast has one of the world's most violent seas and two perilous straits—the Java Strait to the west and the Lombok Strait to the east. The latter has strong currents and devilish whirlpools and is one of the places with the deepest waters on earth. People drown every year in those dangerous waters. The Java Strait straddles two powerful electromagnetic forces—the Agung volcano in Bali and the Rinjani in Lombok. Both volcanoes are over three thousand meters in height.

I performed a ritual cleansing of my kayak and the paddle. The Balinese priest, Nyoman Ledin, tied a sacred white thread around my wrist to protect me. The following day I embarked on my clockwise voyage around the island.

The circumnavigation took twenty-one days, with my paddling some six hours a day and resting seven. It was an intense spiritual adventure during which I struggled with my demons. The Masai of Kenya believe that one must come to terms with one's demons.

Each day I fought a duel with the witch's curse. Her words, "You will die in the sea," resounded in my subconscious like a satanic mantra.

Each pull of the paddle was one step forward to successfully exorcising the curse. I knew that the Saddhu's spiritual vision would not fail and that I was on the way to ridding myself of a burden of evil energy that I had been carrying on my back for fifteen years.

I had many unforgettable experiences on that voyage, which was like a purification rite to the good spirits, but I will limit my exposition to what happened on the last day of the great battle against myself.

That day I thought I was going to lose the war against the witch and that her curse was not just hollow words resonating in my mind but the evil enchantress's victory song. That day I truly thought I would die in the sea.

I left Sanur before sunset and headed for Kuta. I had all the food I needed for the voyage in my kayak. The sea was rough, but with a strong southeaster behind me, I decided to paddle as far as Nusa Dua and stop to eat on a solitary beach. There was a very low tide, and when I got out of the kayak to haul it up the beach, a fire coral shaped like a small nail pierced the vessel.

I ate some food, had a nap in the shade of some rocks, and then set off for Kuta, the place where my great adventure had begun.

It was a full moon, and the waves grew by the moment. Encouraged by the previous leg of my voyage, I paddled fast, confident I would at last arrive safe and sound.

After two hours of paddling, by that time in the open sea, I noticed to my horror that the kayak was taking in water. I tried to use the pump, but it had broken. I was in a critical situation. Within another two hours the kayak would be too full to float. To turn back toward Nusa Dua with such a heavy kayak and a strong headwind and adverse current was physically impossible. And heading to shore was mortal madness because the powerful waves would dash me against the Ula Uatu (today named Uluwatu) cliff face.

To the south lay the infinite open sea, right down to the Antarctic. The only option left was to keep paddling forward, but how was I to make any headway with a kayak full of water and my strength by then gradually abandoning me?

At that stage, I was rounding Ula Uatu, the southernmost tip of Bali where, according to Balinese lore, all the evil forces are ranged. Then I heard the witch's voice inside me: "*You will die in the sea.*" Her macabre voice kept on repeating those words, and their intensity reached such a feverish pitch that I thought I was losing my mind.

Night's dark veil fell over the black sea like the sorceress's magic. The crests of the waves, like liquid mountains, rose higher and higher. The full moon, that witch's ally, rose from behind the gigantic cliffs like a priestess heralding death, and, on the brink of despair, I thought, *This is my last full moon.*

With the kayak full of water from the consistent barrow of waves, being exhausted and trembling with fear, I stopped paddling, raised my arms to the heavens, and entreated Dewa Ruci, the god of Bali, to let me live and to protect me from the accursed witch.

When I had finished praying, I felt as though an invisible arrow of divine magic had pierced my brain. I was invaded by a feeling of absolute assurance that I would arrive safely in Kuta. I cannot recall having ever felt so confident.

Paddling very slowly, completely wiped out, I reached the Kuta reef. Judging by the position of the moon, it must have been around midnight. I had trouble finding a passage across the reef. The kayak capsized after being struck by a wave, then I righted it, placed the paddle in the kayak, and swam toward the beach, pushing the vessel along.

When I set foot on the sand, I was overcome by a feeling of peace and tranquility beyond all description. I looked at my right hand and saw that the white thread the priest, Nyoman Ledin, had tied around my wrist was unraveling and, like a newborn's baptism, despite being in the month of May—the dry season—a fine rain fell over an area of about two hundred meters around me.

Bali Wonderland

SARASWATI MISH

*Saraswati Mish arrived in Bali in 1976, and then resided there from 1989
until 2015. For twenty-six years, Bali was her home, where she immersed
herself in Balinese culture and the expat community and raised her daughter,
Ruby, there. She founded Prasada, a boutique and export company, honoring
Indonesian traditions at its creative heart. Saraswati has been involved in
supporting local orphanages and charities.*

Two things happened in 1975 that led me on that fateful trip.

An older friend of mine took a trip to an island north of Australia.
She fell in love with a prince, and when she returned, full of magical
tales, she offered me a beautiful colorful woven scarf from Sideman in
northeast Bali.

That same year my boss had a group of very bohemian-looking
friends arrive to visit. They had just come from a sailing trip through
Indonesia. I was eighteen, and one of the very cool guys was wearing an
amazing pink shirt with flowers on it. I asked him where he got it. Bali
was his answer, the same place my friend had been.

These two incidents ignited a curiosity and interest to travel to this
little-known island. I managed to secure a flight on an American airline through one of my clients. With an atlas on the dining table one
evening, I was pointing out where my adventure would lead me to my

family. "Bali," my uncle exclaimed. "I was there in World War II. It's wonderful—all the women are topless."

Armed with the knowledge that Balinese women walked around topless, had handsome princes, and made beautiful shirts and scarves, in February 1976—at nineteen years of age and a total travel virgin—I touched down on the island of Bali, beautiful Bali, which would later become my home.

The airport was a large shed-type building. It housed the telephones that travelers used to call internationally. My first memory of Bali is of warm, soft air brushing my cheeks, a walkway strewn with white flowers, and the smell of frangipani mingled with the fragrant clove cigarettes called *kretek.*

After going through Immigration, I ventured outside to face a crowd of young Balinese guys jostling for my attention. I chose Made Lodre, and he took me to his homestay, or *losmen,* in North Kuta.

There were several concrete rooms in a row with a terrace where we could sit and have breakfast or tea, play cards, or laugh away the hours. Breakfast would appear on the bamboo table every morning, comprising of biscuits, bananas, and a thermos of fragrant jasmine tea. From there, I could watch the field of coconut trees beyond the hedged and bamboo fence. I never locked my room and would come home to the girls who worked at the losmen dressed up in my clothes, which they acquired upon my departure.

For a second breakfast or lunch, I would wander over the fields to a place called Lassi Erawati. On one of my walks, I noticed swastikas on a wall and being pretty naïve of worldly affairs got a little concerned thinking of Nazis. I later discovered the swastika in Bali is drawn in the opposite direction of the Nazi version. This local symbol represents *surya* (the sun), prosperity, and good luck.

Lassi Erawati was a great meeting place and served a delicious *bubur injin,* which is black rice pudding topped with grated coconut on top of fruit salad. I immediately loved the food of Bali. The flavors and aromas were, and are, incomparable. There was no electricity apart from a few places at that time, so the smell of kerosene cookers and lamps wafted through the air with all the other aromas of food, flowers, incense, and kretek.

In the afternoons, I would ride my bicycle through the maze of small pathways or wander down to the beach. The ice cream cart would come in the afternoon as would various other cycling vendors.

I recall riding by bicycle down the main road to what is now Seminyak. There were old ladies walking topless along the road and smoke willowing out from small fires burning off leaves and rubbish. In those days, all rubbish was organic. Take-away food was served in banana leaves and tasted *so* good. Seminyak was like the end of the world.

Just before sunset, there was a soccer game in the field in front of the losmen. They were always fun and filled the air with laughter, flirting, and meetups.

A young boy, Ketut, who was a relative of someone in the losmen, played there each afternoon. He was a huge Muhammad Ali fan, and I nicknamed him Muhammad Bali, as he looked a little like the great boxer. He was going to school but had no shoes, so one afternoon I took a *bemo* (public transportation minivan) into Denpasar with Ketut to the Bata store in Jl. Gajah Mada and purchased him his first pair of shoes. It was a big moment for him, and he wore those sneakers with a grin from ear to ear.

Evening entertainment consisted of eating in local restaurants or going to the cinema. One cinema in Kuta was open air and played Kung Fu movies, and there was another one in Jl. Gajah Mada Denpasar, which also aired Kung Fu movies. I think those violent movies were all that was offered. In later years, we would entertain ourselves by lying exhilarated at the end of the runway as the jets flew over us.

The kerosene lamps would be turned on after sunset, and the flickering light would create a charm of days gone by all throughout Bali.

Our bathing ritual consisted of bucketing cold water out of a tub and pouring it over ourselves. Still, many houses use this system today.

Later in the '80s, I would frequent the local *tuak* bar. Tuak is a wine made from the sap of the coconut flower. The bar was a great pre-dinner meeting spot for travelers. We would sit around with the local men drinking tuak from bamboo vessels before venturing on into the evening. I became friends with the tuak maker, Wayan Kopling, and his friend. Wayan took me to his village to see the distillery, and I watched him climb the coconut tree to retrieve the nectar from the flowers. We rode on the motorbike, and I carried huge buckets of tuak on the back.

The fields were on Jl. Iman Bonjol, which is now a bustling thoroughfare from Kuta to Denpasar. His small son received one of the first facial surgeries in Bali from Dr. David in Adelaide. That charity still exists today, now called Yayasan Senyum (The Smile Foundation).

We would go with his friends to cockfighting matches, where much gambling occurred, and food stalls serving turtle sate and other treats abounded. I never liked the cockfighting, but the atmosphere was electric and colorful.

Trips to Ubud, Singaraja, and through the mountain were my entrance into a magical land. I traveled alone for the most part and don't ever recall feeling afraid. On several occasions at night, I stumbled upon *wayang kulit* performances (shadow puppets). With the whole village watching and screeches of laughter, these were some of the most beautiful pieces of theatre I have ever witnessed. Behind the screen were men with a myriad of delicately hand-cut leather shadow puppets whose shadows were projected onto a screen using small oil lamps. The puppeteers in that magical light was a work of art in itself. The children's faces and laughter of the crowd would lift my heart. There is nothing quite like it.

On one trip to Singaraja, I stayed in a small losmen on the edge of town, which had the most incredible library of books about Bali. I spent many hours reading and drawing. One night I was drawing, and an image appeared on the page. I traced it and drew what was presented to me. It was a butterfly with a woman's body, not extraordinary, but it was magical and mystical how it presented itself. Many mystical things happened in Bali. I dreamt of a snake, then walked outside and found a snake at my feet. The sense of connectedness to realms beyond was always there.

Kuta at that time was a maze of small tracks meandering through the villages and around the coconut fields. The main road was dirt, and the only real transportation methods were bemo, bicycles, and the odd Holden car. I don't recall many motorbikes, though there were some, and I did go on jaunts around the island on them—unlike today, where they are the main mode of transport.

The bemos were the local transport system all over the island. They were small, low utility vans with a hard cover over the back and bench seats along either side. Inside was a world of undiscovered localism. Upon hopping in the bemo, you would discover you were sharing it with. There were chickens, market produce, and chatting locals who were often smoking. Hanging off the back would be a local lad shouting out the route and picking up passengers. I took those bemos all over the island, including Ubud and as far as Singaraja. My days were filled with discovery. The trip to Denpasar was forty Indonesian rupiah from my losmen. One US dollar was around seven hundred rupiah.

Not long after arriving in Bali, I met a guy from Sydney staying in the losmen next door. Robert was making clothes in Bali and sending them back to Australia. He was also building an outrigger canoe in a small village on the other side of the airport called Kedonganan.

One day, he told me about a fishing village and the family he stayed with and said he thought I would really enjoy it. Thus began my introduction to village life in Bali. I rode my bicycle out past the airport and the enormous banyan tree and spent endless days in the fishing village, staying with the fisherman and his wife and kids. Made had two wives, and they would cook together, but one wife lived up the path and would come down during the day. The boys, who were under ten years old had Krishna-style haircuts—shaven heads with a strip of hair on the top. They played in the dusty courtyard accompanied by the dog named Blog. Then there was Ka (grandpa), who had no teeth. I worked on the family outrigger fishing boat in the field, shaving the bamboo balancing bars and painting the boat. I was in the field alone with Ka as he wove baskets. Every now and then, he would holler out a word in raspy Indonesian and point to an object: *pohon* (tree), *matahari* (sun), *bawa* (the ground). These words were my introduction to the Indonesian language, and his voice is ever etched into my being. I hear his raspy, low, toothless voice to this day.

The days were filled with simplicity and fun. Our showers were from a small ceramic pot with a cork in it perched on a wall in the field. The pot was filled from the well, where we would bring up the cold water in buckets. It was quite an art to get wet, lather up, then rinse off before the ceramic pot ran out of water. The toilet was in the bushes, wherever you could find privacy.

In the evening, the most delicious dinners were served. These consisted of mainly fish, vegetables, and rice, often in a broth. They were cooked in the tiny kitchen on a wood fire. To this day, fish ball coconut soup is one of my favorite Balinese dishes. It's not served in restaurants, so you need to get a local to cook it for you or learn the recipe, which is a bit ad hoc.

In the evenings, we would sit with Made as he contemplated going out on his nightly fishing trip. Robert told me Made was fearful of the ocean.

In the morning after sunrise, while Made slept, I would go to the beach with the kids and Blog, and stack tiny fish neatly on a rack, ready to go to the market.

The local kids would all sit around and talk about me and laugh hysterically. They had a habit of poking my bronzed skin until there was a white patch when they removed their finger. I was poked every morning happily. My life in the village was one of the loveliest times I can remember. The Balinese kindness and generosity, their willingness to laugh, and their openness touched my heart so profoundly. That was the beginning of my love affair with Bali.

The magic of Bali, in those days, was palpable. I recall feeling the heartbeat of the earth pulsating. I witnessed a girl go mad from magic. Magic could go either way. Luckily, I didn't encounter any of the darker sides of it at that time, as I doubt I would have been equipped to handle it. Robert brought the girl who had gone "mad" from the island's energy, to the village. Whether it was black magic, or she couldn't handle the energy, or took a mushroom trip that went bad, I'm not certain, but she was taken to a local *dukun* or shaman.

Over the years, I witnessed many people flip out in Bali. The energy is strong, and when ridden for a high or used the wrong way. you can find yourself on the other side of a happy experience. The Balinese have great respect for this energy, and their temple ceremonies pay respect to both sides of the light and dark. The *poleng* black-and-white-checkered flag seen in front of temples is a recognition of both the light and the dark.

With that energy comes an environment of incredible creativity. I don't know of anywhere in the world where such creativity abounds. Balinese are some of the most creative and artistic people in the world. Being an artist and designer, this was an entry into a world of possibilities and led me to develop and discover many talents within myself that I would never have otherwise. I am forever grateful to Bali for this.

The days of 1976 in Bali are a blurred memory of adventure. Trips in the back of bemos all over the island. Kind and welcoming people with infectious smiles. I had never before been told by strangers I was beautiful, but this occurred several times a day. My mother told me later I was never the same after my first trip to Bali. It was like having a long-distance lover who knows you better than anyone and can see deeply inside your soul.

I traveled back and forward to Bali for many years, watching the changes and at times feeling despondent about the influx of the outside world into Bali and its effects. Over the years, I ventured deeper into Balinese culture, even having a tooth filing with my Balinese family, who kindly adopted me.

I eventually moved to Bali to raise my daughter, and Bali is her home.

Regardless of what has happened in Bali through tourism, the magic is always there if you are open and curious.

Bali is known as the Island of the Gods. I always feel there is a portal to the divine in Bali.

Bali is my true love.

MY ADVICE FOR THE BALI VISITOR ————————————————

I would encourage anyone traveling to Bali to embrace the local culture. Learn a few words, try the food, go to the local markets and smell the flowers, buy directly from local producers, interact with locals and venture off the beaten path. The Balinese are the most welcoming people you could meet. They will love you all the more for trying and teach you to laugh at yourself when you make mistakes.

Those Bali
Wild Times

JANE HAWKINS

Jane Hawkins has been a teacher, clothing designer, CEO, retail consultant, leader of her own personal development retreats, and founder of a residential community. Jane has climbed Mt. Kenya, Mt. Kilimanjaro, and the Himalayas and followed spiritual yatras to Mt. Kailash and Gangotri Glacier, the source of the Ganges. She and her husband Peter reside in Bali with two wonderful sons, Morgan and Jamie, and their exceptional cat, Joki.

When I was twenty-five, though I was born in Kenya of British descent and educated in Kenya and Britain (I received a master's in educational psychology), I found myself in New York City designing jewelry. One day while on a sales mission to Henry Bendels, the shi-shi boutique department store on the Upper East Side, I saw a piece of fabric on the arm of a man as he walked by. Fascinated by the shimmer and intrinsic "energy" that the cloth held, I followed after the man, whom I later came to know as Gabriel (the angel, of course!). I stopped him, asked about the cloth, and sat him down in a café for further investigation of this wonderful metallic-shot ikat. It turned out to be designed by Milo and made in Bali.

Bali—who had ever heard of Bali in those days? Certainly not from the distant planet of New York City, halfway around the world. Determined to find out more about this far-off place, two weeks later (in

1976), I jumped on a plane, following the mystical trail of this cloth. I had no address for Milo—who needed an address in Bali in those days? Every expat was known by village telegraph. I simply knew he could be found in the village of Seminyak! There was no international airport in Bali—just a single runway, one small building, and a few passengers who had transit through Jakarta.

Carrying my Samsonite suitcase and wearing high heels, I had no idea what was in store as I found my way to Seminyak Village, to wait, in a hammock in the garden, for Milo. Falling into business for the next twenty years, we pioneered the clothing industry in Bali with CV Merta Jaya (owned by Simon and Anita Haryantho) and Aurora, Zelinde, Suzie, and Noelle ("Milo's Angels"). The Balinese are a yes people, and nothing ever was impossible or too difficult to manage. With this wonderful attitude and much laughter and lightness of spirit, we managed to overcome those early difficulties within the garment field.

I rented a small house in Petitenget Village, and perhaps because of my African upbringing, I never heeded the cries of alarm from my Balinese friends. "No! No! It is too far from Kuta, too many spirits, not possible for a woman alone!" Petitenget means magic box (in Balinese), and, boy, was I to have some interactions with magic and spirits.

In those days, there was only a small track to the Petitenget Temple— through the rice fields and a long way to go around by bicycle on this track—so we would walk on the beach (a good two kilometers) to Legian village in order to pick up a *bemo*—a public minivan with plastic seats, a *kretek*-smoking (clove cigarette) driver, usually broken and dirty windows stuffed with newspaper, and twelve passengers carrying baskets of fruit and vegetables, chickens, and other things, all crammed into eight spaces.

In those days, cars and motorbikes were very rare, and we all got around in bemos. Needless to say, we mostly walked in and out of Petitenget. With no internet or telephone, one would set off in the morning and just follow the day as it progressed. A totally marvelous way to live, allowing the co-creative Spirit of the Universe to determine your day, allowing oneself to follow one's intuition rather than preset plans.

One night after a party in Kuta, Aurora—a friend, who, with Giorgo, had built a house in Petitenget in the late 70s—and I were walking home after midnight along the beach in front of the Petitenget Temple. To our consternation, we saw, up on the high-tide mark, a man standing completely still, with extended arms, holding two luminous deep-green orbs in each hand and wearing a black top hat five times the size of his head. Hardly able to contain our fear, we agreed to scurry home as fast as we could, hugging the seashore and not paying any attention to this spectacle. The next day, I went to the temple to consult with the priest, and he told me that this was a classic case of a man practicing black magic.

In that same temple, on Melasti Day, a group of friends would go to the temple after midnight, when the villagers would take part in sacred ceremonies. We saw many unusual happenings. Melasti is a Hindu Balinese purification ceremony and ritual, which, according to the Balinese calendar, is held several days prior to the Nyepi holy day. Melasti was meant as the ritual to cleanse the world from all the filth of sin and bad karma through the symbolic act of acquiring the Tirta Amerta, "the water of life."

One time we were six people together, and as we came out of the temple in unison, we all began to run down the long temple steps. At the bottom, catching our breath, we all had had the same sensation of a big black birdlike creature fastening its claws onto our shoulders. Just as we were getting over this shock, we saw six to eight Balinese men, fully dressed in ceremonial garb, gliding six feet above the ground in front of us and disappearing toward the beach. All six of us saw the same thing; this was not an individual hallucination!

The Petitenget villagers had always told me to avoid the bamboo grove in front of my house—this was a circular grove about twenty by thirty meters—which held many naughty spirits (*Tuyul* in Balinese) who lived in the forests (according to myth, they especially love bamboo forests). These Tuyul loved to play tricks on humans.

One day, walking home in a hurry and without thinking or being cautious, I mindlessly walked into the bamboo grove. After about ten minutes, I realized I was still walking in the grove while I should have been through it and well home by then. I stopped and began walking in a diagonal direction, thinking I had taken a wrong turn, and again after five minutes, I stopped and began walking in another direction. Again, five minutes later, I realized I was lost! How could I be?

By this time, I was sweating and beginning to panic, and the mosquitoes were hot on my sweaty, fearful body. I fell to the ground, crying, lost in my own fear and panic. After about ten minutes of this nauseating panic, I thought the only way to get out was to pray, so I did this reverently—which, thankfully, eventually brought me back to sanity. I stood up, and in two minutes, walked straight out of the grove.

One night my now-ex-husband, Tom, decided to go body surfing on the beach in front of our house in Petitenget. The house had a two-story boxlike configuration, with a small bedroom and verandah upstairs over the lower kitchen, bathroom, and living room. There was no electricity in the village in 1977, and we lived with oil lamps and gas stoves. I was upset (actually fuming!) that he had gone body surfing on this notoriously dangerous beach at night.

As I sat spewing my anger, the oil lamp hurtled (on its own accord) across the floor upstairs, over the edge of the verandah, and dropped next to my feet. Alarmed, I looked up and saw Tom's head gliding across the garden toward me. I instantly stood and walked toward the head, and as I approached, it disappeared. I continued walking across the garden and down the path to the beach, meeting Tom halfway. He had blood streaming down his face. He had been knocked over by a wave backwash, hit his head on the sand, and knocked temporality unconscious. Luckily, he then managed to get up on the beach, where he went cold again for a short period. Perhaps during that momentary unconsciousness, his spirit had floated out over the garden, heading home.

Spirits and magic were not the only experiences in Petitenget. The gardener at my rented house was arguably the first punk Balinese! He had a Mohawk hairstyle dyed turquoise and pink and piercings in his ears and nose. He came from the Tabanan area, where the village people in the '70s worked for food and coffee (there was little money in circulation). During the '70s, Bali had little electricity in the village areas.

I remember seeing Claude riding a bike, bringing the first electric pole to Kuta. There was certainly no internet, no telephone, no police, no government agencies, no income tax, few schools, and generally no modern world as we know it. So how Gede came to punk is a mystery.

Gede would go out on a Saturday night to the Kuta clubs, coming home with a different Western girl every weekend. He lived in a small house at the back of the garden and would pull his bed out into the middle of the garden to "while away" the hours until the early morning. I then would have to decide how to handle this spectacle in my garden, and since it was a rented house with a fixed gardener, it was always a conundrum! Needless to say, I always managed to rent a hotel or stay with a friend on a Saturday night!

The village situated just to the north of Petitenget was Umalas (or "U-maling," as it was colloquially known—*maling* being Indonesian for thief). The head of the biggest thieving gang in Umalas lived next to my rented house in Petitenget, and for this reason, I never had any trouble at my house. However, one night while I was house-sitting at Aurora and Giorgio's house, I had an encounter with this head thief. For some unknown reason, I chose to sleep downstairs in the living room with an open window over my head. I woke in the night, aware of someone in the garden. As I was taught from many safaris with wild animals around, I stayed completely still, lying with my eyes open and staring up at the open window. As predicted, a face appeared through the open window—who else but the head thief!

He was so shocked at seeing me that he gasped and ran away as fast as he could. From then on, he never could look me in the eyes, and we Westerners living in Petitenget never had a robbery!

There was never a dull moment with this abundance of magic and spirit in those early days, but as Bali entered the modern world and has become increasingly "concretized," those experiences have become less and less frequent or normal.

Finding My Home
and Mushrooms

KEN WHEATON

Ken Wheaton "found his paradise" and spent most of the '70s in Bali. He lived and studied yoga with the Iyengar family in Pune, India, in '73 and '74 and went trekking to Jomsom and Mt. Everest during those same winters. Ken spent the '79 and '80 winters living in a yurt in Aspen and learning to ski. From the beginning of the '90's, he taught at both Chuo and Tama Art University in Japan. He spent summers rediscovering the United States and riding his Harley to Sturgis and around the West. He retired about three years ago and is waiting to see what the future holds in store.

It was morning in Gilimanuk. All night long from Surabaya I rode on a funky rehabbed American high school bus if I remember (it's been fifty years).

I'm in Bali! I thought.

I had just made the crossing from Java overnight, sleeping on some local grandmother's shoulder, who was returning home. I knew nothing except I was headed for paradise. This was well before Lonely Planet and the *Hitchhiker's Guide to Southeast Asia* (thank the gods).

I'd come down from Bangkok by train to Penang, then caught a Pelni boat to Medan and from Medan to Djakarta. Then I traveled across Java by train and the last leg to Bali by bus from Surabaya.

I awoke, bleary-eyed and confused and having no idea where I was or what I was doing. I only knew that I was headed for "Paradise."

As the bus jangled me awake, I looked out the fogged-over windows to see these amazing compounds on the side of the road. I'd seen in my travels the most amazing places, but this was something entirely different. My "Bali experience" started here. I cannot explain what I felt upon seeing these compounds. Balinese ladies walked along the roadside with completely straight postures carrying water bottles or piles of offerings on their heads. I was on another planet. I understood why people had told me, "stepping on Bali is like stepping into a tab of acid." It was in an indescribable place. I'd been looking for salvation/paradise, and it looked like maybe I'd found it.

The bus dropped me off in Denpasar, and I got a *bemo* (local public minivan transportation) to Kuta Beach. I'd heard of this place in an old *Washington Post* article. The bemo dropped me on the gang just after Jalan Pantai. It was the ice juice/monkey juice corner. A young beauty, Ketut, took me to her dad's place, and they gave me a room that cost me less than one US dollar a night. In those days a US dollar converted to 412 rupiah. *Tjap Tjai* (fried noodles with vegetables) was 35 rupiah, and *nasi goreng* (fried rice) was 25 or 35 rupiah. We stayed and ate for less than a US dollar or two a night, and everyone was happy.

At the head of the gang, where the bemo first dropped me and before young Ketut found me, I thought I was going to be dropped off at a beach. Kuta Beach, right? Instead, I was on the Denpasar airport road, holding my bag, in front of the only *es jus* (cold juice) shop that existed in those days. Perhaps one traveler was sitting there, and my first culture shock was to see a large bell jar full of grain alcohol with a monkey fetus in it. They would dip a shot from it and sell the drinks like that, replenishing the alcohol as needed. I soon learned it was a meeting place to find out who was in town at the time. I would later meet many new travelers there. Most new arrivals like me got dropped off there by the bemos coming from Denpasar. This was before "Bemo Corner" and before Jalan Legian became an often traveled road.

I lived with a Balinese family—parents and two daughters who took me in and treated me as one of the family. That was the custom at the time. The first day I walked down to the beach, every Balinese greeted me like family. I was in heaven, not believing the world I had stumbled upon. I watched the first of many sunsets, sitting with the dozen or more Westerners dressed in sarongs, if anything, and I was lost in the most beautiful world I had ever seen. Every face had a beautiful wide smile plastered across it. The Westerners were either Aussies starting their journey overland to Europe or others nearing the end of their journey. Travelers reaching the end of their stay and finances went to Timor for the USD 80.00 Merpati flight to Darwin, where they planned to pick fruit or whatever and earn enough money to come back.

Everyone would sit and trade travel advice and talk about their incredible adventures. A few, like me, had "found it"—we felt we were home. I was where I wanted to spend the rest of my young life.

There were no motorbikes and very few bicycles. We walked everywhere, and life was spent either at Dayu's or Jenik's (the two main restaurants at the time) or down at the beach. Sunset was when all the Westerners met daily. I'd spend the rest of my time either sitting, eating or wandering around Kuta, meeting the different Balinese who lived there. I would explore paths through what at that time was jungle, rice fields, or palms. All I could do was rave about what a magical place I'd stumbled upon. I can still remember one day sitting in Dayu's restaurant, going on and on talking, and an Aussie lady said, "It's good to hear a raver." I have no memory of what I was saying, but I must have been crazed by the magic of paradise, Bali.

I stayed on in Kuta for around six weeks, floating in bliss and not believing what I'd stumbled upon. I knew nothing of Bali. I was not your average traveler. I was truly a soul in search of paradise. But reality reared its ugly head, and my money was running out. I had only enough to survive on and a ticket from Delhi to New York, which was soon to expire. So I vowed I would return, trusting in fate that I would find a way. I headed back overland and made it to Delhi. I had only my ticket back to the States, my few belongings in my US mailman's bag, and my clothes, which were pajama pants and a vest made from an American bedsheet. I had to sell my last roll of film to pay the airport tax out of

India. I got on the flight, and my girlfriend in the US arranged a ticket for me from New York to Washington DC. That was what they called at the time a "commuter flight," and businessmen in suits would buy their tickets from the stewardesses as they came down the aisle. Here I was, this spaced-out dark-brown-tanned dude in pajama pants and a vest, headed home, and all these people were helping me and treating me as if some hospital had just discharged me. But nothing mattered. I'd found paradise and was headed back there—whatever it would take.

I arrived in DC, met my lady, and stayed long enough to put some money together and to convince her that I'd "found it." We rented out our place (I lost my *Norton Atlas* that I'd left in the basement) and sold pretty much everything else of value, and we took off, each with a mail-man's bag full of all our earthly possessions. We headed for Europe, took a charter flight to Singapore, and then boat, train, and ferry again to Bali.

We skipped Kuta and moved up to Legian Kelod, where we lived on Jalan Padma, the only place available in those days. We raised ducks and cooked food that we bought from the local market. Our kitchen comprised a wok and a kerosene stove. Life was good. Our friends were mostly Balinese. Wayan Sadi, who worked for the owner of our losmen, took care of us. We'd send him to Kuta for bananas at night after hitting the bong. He'd go smiling. Twenty years later, when I came back with a new wife, he had married, opened a shop, and was about to open a los-men. He reminded me that years ago when he had nothing, I'd bought his family a pig. I'd forgotten, but he never did. I was about to learn that I had a family and a loving connection with the people of Banjar Legian Kelod and Legian Kaja. All of these people years later still considered me family.

I lived in Bali before the party scene. My people were the Balinese. Dul and Broken Leg Michael and later the De Coneys settled in, but Bali was yet to become a destination. Maybe half a dozen surfboards were around.

One of the first things you heard about Bali, as early as 1970, were the "mushroom omelets" that were served in only a handful of restaurants in the early days. The Garden Restaurant comes to mind. Bali was famous even in the early days for magic mushroom omelets. They were even on the menus in some restaurants, and everyone had heard the story of the family that goes for breakfast and Dad orders the mushroom omelet. (In those days, there was only one type of mushroom omelet on the menu, and the Balinese figured everyone understood, even if the word *magic* wasn't noted). So Dad has the omelet, and when things get a bit strange a little while later, he becomes quite distressed until someone explains to him, "You've been dosed—it's a treat. Enjoy your day." And when he understands what's going on, his Bali experience becomes a bit more alive and a bit more special.

After moving to and living for a while in Legian Kaja, I learned from the Balinese (who didn't partake) where to find these mushrooms and what season, weather, and time of day is best to gather the finest. So I began to gather and cook with magic mushrooms. I looked at it as becoming one with the island. I'd spent many hours tripping through jungle and rice fields surrounded by undulating green, which were the loving arms of my paradise. Down at the beach was different—mostly pink, with the beach rising and falling beneath my stretched-out body.

I would giggle with the gods as the sunset shimmered and carried me away.

But rather than go to a restaurant and eat an omelet, made for and paid for with cash, I was "Mr. Natural." After a good rain, I'd wake before sunrise and wander over to the cow pasture between my place and what would later become the De Coneys' homestead. The morning was already magical. Balinese cows looked like gentle deer. As I wandered around them, exchanging glances with their amazing huge brown eyes, I'd go from cow pad to cow pad picking the mushrooms that had grown that morning out of the cow dung. I was early in order to beat the competition from the Balinese restaurateurs.

As I picked the mushrooms, of course, I would munch on one or two (or three), and as I worked, the grass got greener, the cows really did look like deer, and the palm trees overhead danced under a distant rising sun. I'd wander home with my morning's bounty to be made into soup, added to scrambled eggs, or whatever. Then I would float down to the beach, jump into the purple surf, and come back up to lie on the beach for an amazingly magical morning.

This was not a daily habit of mine, but I partook enough to build a special bond with the island. Mushrooms became a part of a new culture we were building. They later became a motif in rings I designed.

MY ADVICE FOR THE BALI VISITOR ─────────────────

Have a magic mushroom omelet and walk along the beach at sunset, through the rice fields during harvest or along jungle trails. Lie on your back at the foot of the volcano of your choice and enjoy your day in the navel of the universe.

Seminyak in the 1970s

MICHAEL PALMIERI

Michael Palmieri is an American explorer and a California surfer who headed south to Mexico in the early years of the Vietnam War to dodge the draft and ended up on the hippie trail, bouncing from Mexico to Europe to India to Nepal to Afghanistan before alighting in the paradise of prelapsarian Bali. Once there, he began exploring the most remote parts of Indonesia, specializing on the Dayak tribes of Borneo, acquiring pieces of tribal art that now reside in museums and private collections around the world.

In the quiet little village of Seminyak in 1976, there were only two houses lived in by foreigners: Italian designer Milo's and ours. There was no electricity or running water, no sounds of car or bike engines, and most of the roads and pathways in Seminyak were made of earth. There were no spas, boutiques, Western restaurants, clubs, or bars. No telephones and no villas. Seminyak abounded in a green sea of rice fields, and the only sounds to be heard were that of nature and *legong* music while the Balinese went about their daily life.

My wife, Fatima, and I were strolling down the beach in 1976 when we noticed a lovely thatch-covered beachfront house made from white coral, totally abandoned. This house was meant to be the manager/owner's house for the Hotel Kayu Aya, also abandoned. Today it's called the Oberoi Hotel.

One of the Agung family members gave us this house, and in return, he asked if we could ask our hippie friends from Goa, India, to stay in the abandoned hotel, which was overrun by jungle vegetation. There was no electricity—only a generator they used to pump water up from the well but not enough to fill the Olympic-size pool. We filled the hotel, charging from five to ten dollars a day, and rocked out by night on magic mushrooms and other heavenly delights with good friends and great parties.

We rescued a sweet little honey bear from the jungles of Borneo. His mother had been killed by poachers. We called him "Bubbu Bear." We brought Bubbu Bear with us back to Bali, which caused major confusion with the Balinese because there were no bears in Bali. The Balinese called Bubbu Bear a "Monkey Dog." Well, Bubbu Bear got really big really fast, then one day he escaped from our little grass shack in Legian, next door to Sunset cottage. Bubbu Bear went directly into the beachfront restaurant's kitchen in search of food. The Balinese staff laughed and said, "*manis sekali*" ("He's so sweet"). They then tried to pick him up. Big mistake! Bubbu Bear did what most bears do when threatened: he stood up on his back feet, making him around one meter tall! Bubbu Bear opened his sharp toothy mouth and let out a high shrieking primeval scream, scaring the shit out of the Balinese staff, who immediately ran for their lives. Well, Bubbu Bear totally ripped up the kitchen in search of food.

The following day, the animal services folks came by and arrested poor little Bubbu Bear. The next day the capture of Bubbu Bear appeared on the front page of the Bali newspapers. The only problem was the editor got two stories mixed up. A foreigner had been arrested for a small quantity of ganja, and Bubbu Bear also got busted on the same day, so the headlines read: "Ganja Bear Arrested in Legian."

Another memory was our encounter with the estimable Baba Ram Dass, one of the founding fathers of the LSD culture. It was around 1976 in Legian Kaja, Bali. Fatima invited Baba Ram Dass over for dinner, and afterward, we wandered over to one of Bali's first and only clubs called Rum Jungle. That night Rum Jungle was really swinging. Baba

Ram Dass said, "I have something special to share with all your tribe." He then pulled out some LSD crystal and said, "This is my gift to all of you." He put a large crystal on a plate, and Max pulled out his giant Buck knife and began chopping fine lines. The only problem was he should've made one hundred lines and instead made only around twenty or so. People started floating over to our table, and Max offered them a line. Within a very short while, those who'd taken the LSD went into a state of trance. The energy level shot up 1,000 percent. "The show must go on," and it did. RIP Richard Alpert Ph.D. (also known as Baba Ram Dass).

Adventures
in Adat

STUART ROME

Stuart Rome is an American photographer whose interests in anthropology led to projects photographing antiquities in Latin America and Asia as well as recording remnants of those expressions found in the rituals of trance. This documentary work led to landscape photographs of forests as a manifestation of pantheistic energy.

It must have been around 1978 when I started coming to Bali, making a home to come back to from travels throughout the archipelago while working on a book project.

Bali was a place to recharge after difficult travel, and it was a place where I made a community for myself.

Early on, I was introduced to a Balinese family in Mas (a village south of Ubud) who made me feel welcome and treated me as part of their home. The head of the family was Ida Bagus Sutarjara, a renowned mask carver and dancer whose father was perhaps the original Mas mask carver and boyhood friend of the man who would be known as the Ratu Pedanda of Dawan.

I was introduced to this elderly gentleman for a *malukhat* cleansing and to bless my work when I had newly arrived, after which we sat in his *bali gede* (outdoor post), smoking cigarettes while my new family spoke in Balinese, which, along with Indonesian, I didn't understand.

So, I did what photographers do and looked at my surroundings. Up on the wall was an insect-attacked old photograph of Ratu Pedanda as a young man, and it looked to me to be in the style of Henri Cartier Bresson—perhaps from the '40s.

Over the years, Ida Bagus Sutarja's son, Ari, and I became more like brothers, and we traveled together, sometimes circling Bali, sometimes to other islands. Still, we always visited Ratu Pedanda before our trips. I started to go regularly for malukhat in the mornings. It was said that Ratu Pedanda spoke no Indonesian, but after his students, followers, and supplicants left his compound, he would tell us tales from his youth in Indonesian so I might understand. And he began sending Ari and me on missions to find odd materials to fashion ceremonial talismans— things like a particular Australian coin for a specific year, a stone of a particular color, shape, and size...

To this day, I am not sure if we did this for him or if it was his way of cementing the bond of friendship between Ari and me. Still, they led to wonderful adventures that at certain times of the year were celebrated with sharing a durian from the shady garden in Dawan.

MY ADVICE FOR THE BALI VISITOR ———————

For first time visitors, know the island's adat *(customs) and* hormat *(respect) before arriving. It's a sign of respect to know how to dress when entering temples; never to wave at a Balinese with your left hand or show or point towards them the bottom of your feet. Showing respect will grant a visitor a much closer and vivid experience of a brilliant culture.*

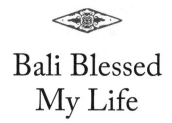

Bali Blessed
My Life

JUDITH OLAH

Judith Olah was born in Hungary. She has been a kindergarten teacher, head waiter, buyer and manager for a retail store, wholesaler of vintage clothing, garment wholesaler, designer and manufacturer of clothes from Bali, and retail store owner from 1982 to 1990 in Sweden and from 1996 to the present in Hudson, Montreal. Judith is a mother to a wonderful twenty-two-year-old son and currently living in Quebec, Montreal, Canada.

It was 1979, the second week of January when I first set my feet on the beautiful island of Bali.

I was coming from Singapore and landed in Bali at five p.m. and meet up with fellow traveling friends Lazlo and Eva Britt.

I had been traveling for four months and spent most of my money in Malaysia and Singapore. I had many friends there and loved both places. I enjoyed spending a long time in one place—living there, breathing the culture, getting to know people, and really feeling that I had been there. I am not much for visiting as many places as possible just to say I have been there too.

For a person like me, who lived most of my childhood in a very strict society, coming to Bali was like a paradise I never even thought was possible.

I was born in Budapest, Hungary, just a year before the big revolution in 1956, and Stalin was in power. In Hungary, we had no TV. I had never seen an orange or a banana. There was no ocean—no shrimp or fish or other seafood. We could never travel. We had no news from anywhere in the outside world except Russia.

For years I had heard so much about how amazing and special Bali was. All my friends kept telling me, "You have to go!"

Finally, I was here. I got in a taxi at the airport and gave the driver the address I had. It was a small *losmen* (homestay) that was somewhere on Legian Beach. The taxi driver had no idea where it was, so he let me out in the middle of Jalan Padma (a street along Legian Beach). At this point, the sun had gone down, and it was pitch black. Just to welcome me, it also started raining in a way I had never seen before; buckets were falling all at once. My bags and I were soaking wet within two minutes. It probably took a good forty-five minutes to finally find the cute little losmen off Jalan Padma on a little path, with a flashlight, helped a very nice Balinese boy.

Suddenly we stopped in the dark, yet nearby I saw three little houses with kerosene lamps and candles, with chairs outside, and there they were—my two traveling friends, Lazlo and Eva Britt, sitting and listening to music.

"Oh, wow, you are wet! We never thought you'd make it," they said as I approached. I was so relieved to find them.

The next day, in the glorious, wonderful sunshine, I started exploring my surroundings. The first day I learned and felt that there was a kind of atmosphere, some magnetic energy, a sort of gravity that pulled you in. The beautiful paths with small stones on the side, the cows in the distance, the people, the powerful ocean. Jalan Padma was full of people coming and going, tourists, and the Balinese. There were lots of cute shops and little restaurants. Yet behind all the buildings, there were only rice fields or gardens. On Legian Street down toward Kuta there were small restaurants and shops selling the most inviting colorful clothing and jewelry and all kinds of knick-knacks.

In front of almost every house, there was a temple made of stone and beautifully carved. The foot of each temple was covered with black-and-white-checkered fabric, like a skirt. Small steps lead up to a place to set offerings. There, one would find small woven leaf baskets filled with different colored flowers and rice and sometimes pink rice. I learned these were the offerings of the day, made for the gods and spirits. These offerings could also be found on the ground in front of a house, a shop, or a restaurant entrance.

The Balinese say prayers to make the gods happy and ask them to keep their families, their island, and the world forever blessed and harmonious. Prayers are repeated and offerings are made, every day, every morning and every night, forever and ever...

Every day I saw women preparing little baskets and other decorations for ceremonies or just everyday offerings. This custom made me very happy and comfortable. I felt protected and safe.

I also learned that night and day are very different in Bali, especially in those days, when we had no electricity. Most Balinese went to bed very soon after sundown, as they believed that there could be bad spirits coming out in the dark. Without a flashlight, one was lost.

I must admit I have always been a bit scared in the dark, so the day electricity arrived, I actually welcomed it.

Unfortunately, my time in Bali began running out. I had only two weeks left before I had to return to Sweden. I also had spent most of my money and had to be very careful with my spending, which drove me crazy.

Never have I ever been anywhere where I wanted to buy so many things. Before I left, I did make a few purchases. I bought a beautiful straw bag, which I could use as a backpack. I also had to choose one from all the hundreds of amazing gold lurex striped fabrics, to make a pair of pants. I couldn't resist buying a silver ring, and a silver bracelet with two dragon heads hooked into each other. I still have them. I added to my purchases a beautifully carved box for my little things, a painting for my parents, and a wood carving of a Balinese man, which is still hanging on my wall, forty years later.

During those two short weeks, I fell totally in love with the island of Bali. The stunning rice fields and nature in such breathtaking harmony.

The magnificent ocean and the beach, where Balinese women would hang out all day, selling clothing and sarongs and offering the best massage one could get, for only three dollars. When I rented a house in later years, a local woman named Nyoman came to give me a massage every morning. What a wonderful way of waking up and starting the day. Other Balinese women who worked in the houses around me would also join me for a morning coffee and a little chat. I loved listening to them, even though I did not understand what they were saying.

I learned about the Balinese—how they are very simple yet complex and proud and strong people. I found them to be most intelligent and good-hearted. Always ready to be a part of life, living fully and with responsibility.

We say that religion and politics should not go together, but the Balinese have mastered a marriage between the two.

Their whole existence and everything in their life is tied to the rules of their religious beliefs. Their society is made up of many strict rules. Some people do not like rules and think they take away their freedom, but nature, the earth and the universe have rules. The sun comes up every day, and the earth rotates. There's a secure feeling in knowing what to expect.

I also think that the strict social structure of the Balinese makes them strong and gives the feeling of connection to life and everything around them.

When people do not have to dwell on the "how" and "what" and "why," they can develop and feed their creativity and create beautiful things and life, which then just gives strength and happiness.

 Rules in Bali are there to make the spirits and gods pleased and to have a happy life. The purpose is to create balance, stay together, and respect one another and the spirit world.

The Balinese people have many, many ceremonies, and most of them are about purification that provides a person with "spiritual energy." One needs spiritual energy to be able to exist peacefully and stay productive in this challenging world.

For example: to respect the items that you buy new, one has to make offerings to the spirit of the new fridge, or bicycle, or motorbike—whatever is purchased. This keeps you thankful and humbled.

Every question about life, living, why, and how, the Balinese people already have an answer along with a smile. These people have a connection to everything, to one another and the purpose of life.

Maybe one could say that of many other tribes and people on earth, but I have never met people who are so totally dedicated and fully believe in their religion and live it every minute.

Most Balinese have never left their island and are still amazingly intelligent.

The people of Bali were extremely poor before the tourists arrived. They subsisted on farming and fishing. They did not own much. They lived in very simple houses and used banana leaves and coconut shells for plates. Their food was also very basic. White rice with vegetables and chicken or fish—whatever was available on a given day.

I find that the Balinese connect on a level of one's soul. Even when you just meet a very annoying saleswoman on the beach, there is something beautiful there. I say annoying because she seriously nags you to buy something, and she will not go away.

I knew I would come back here again and many more times in my life. I stopped being obsessed over the fact that I had only two weeks in Bali and very little money, and I started to enjoy everything, already planning to return as soon as I could.

In those two weeks, I found friends that I knew from Spain, places to stay with lovely gardens, and the beautiful quiet beach in Legian a bit further away from all the tourists in Kuta. I went around the island and to Ubud and Singaraja. I went swimming in the ocean at night at Lovina Beach amid plankton that glows in the dark.

One day we rode a motorbike to Ubud. We were not traveling very fast, maybe forty kilometers an hour, and I remember thinking we were going too fast. I wanted to go slower to experience the hundred shades of green as we passed the rice fields.

I sensed that in the future, lots of unexpected and life-changing events would occur. Bali was like entering another universe—one full of kindness, adventures, beauty, and new friends, with endless possibilities for creating and working. Bali was feeding and bringing out the best parts of me.

I returned often and stayed at least four months each time; the longest was almost a year. There were times I left Bali for two months and returned as soon as I could for another six months, which was all my business visa allowed. If you overstayed your visa, you could get in serious trouble.

I met the two most important men in my life in Bali. The first one was an Australian man from Perth. Through him and with him, my whole working life took shape.

I designed my first clothing collection and started our wholesale and retail business with a small store in Stockholm. I learned all about batik and fabrics, wood carvings, and silver jewelry.

In Bali I met so many incredible, creative people and made lifelong friends. The Balinese I worked with or had interactions with left me with enormous happiness and love in my heart and soul. The creative Western and local people who worked in Bali designing clothing, jewelry, furniture, wood carvings, batik, and fabrics gave me a feeling of amazement and satisfaction.

I brought my Balinese dog back to Sweden as I refused to leave her behind. A man named Alex gave me the puppy and made me promise that I would never abandon her, like other people who came and stayed four months, got a dog, and then left Bali and their dog behind. I looked him in the eye and promised. Alex died three weeks later of a heart attack. I knew when I returned to Sweden, I would have to take Billie. my dog, with me.

I had all the necessary papers for her departure from Indonesia, but there was no vacancy in the quarantine center in Sweden. So I smuggled her to Germany. A German girl helped me in Frankfurt. I had met her on the beach in Bali, and luckily for me, she was on my flight, and she had a pet store in Frankfurt. She gave me a leash and collar and some dog Valium.

We traveled by train from Frankfurt to Stockholm. Billie slept through the Customs inspection in a big bag. I was so worried because the Customs agent was searching the train with a big German shepherd dog. I thought, This is it. They are going to find me. But all went well; the dog was looking for drugs and not dogs.

Everything was perfect.

Billie loved her long walks. Here she was—a Bali dog from Legian in a city far, far away from the beach in front of the Blue Ocean restaurant.

One morning the doorbell rang. I opened the door to three big, tall men who had come to arrest me. as they somehow found out from an anonymous source about the dog.

They kept me all day, questioning me why, where, and how I had this dog.

They kept my Billie for four months in quarantine. I had to pay five hundred dollars to keep them from euthanizing her.

We went to court and court again, and the prosecutor argued that I should serve prison time. Crazy!

At that point, the judge said, "That will not be necessary." Then he turned to me with very kind eyes and a smile and said, "I hope you will get your dog back very soon."

The TV news channels and the newspapers were full of articles about the story. I was scared to even go out for a couple of days.

After four long months of being quarantined, Billie the Legian Bali dog finally came home to me.

The second important man in my life I had met on the beach outside Sunset Beach in Bali. This handsome Canadian traveler became my husband and the father of our son.

I packed up my life in Sweden and moved to Montreal.

Thank you, Bali.

I kept coming back again and again to Bali. There was the beach, the surf, lots of great food, fruit drinks, parties, and new people to meet. I met people from almost every country.

We took trips around the island and up to Lake Batur and swam in the hot springs that were part of the lake.

Every time I came back. there was something new going on, even if

I had been gone only three months—new jewelry designs, a new restaurant with live music, a new club on the beach for dancing, and the best cheese puffs I ever had.

There was Mr. Bambang and his batik store Libra. His fabrics were works of art—multicolored animal prints that are the mainstream prints today. Not many people know their origin.

Beaded shoes and bags and all the beaded clothing.

All the gorgeous ikat blankets were made into fabulous clothing.

Always new sterling silver jewelry. Bali is famous for its very special silver beads and intricate designs.

The amazing houses people built.

The legendary Jakpak jacket that turned into a bag and a pillow. Followed by the Jakpak dress that also could be worn as a skirt.

Interior decoration, furniture, blankets.

Paintings and art.

I could go on and on...

To describe Bali and its depth accurately would take many more pages and much more knowledge than I have.

MY ADVICE FOR THE BALI VISITOR ———————————————

Don't leave the island without going to the original Made's Warung restaurant in Kuta!

My Balinese Wedding, Klungkung July 1982

GLENDA RAKA

Glenda Raka first visited Bali in 1979 after tossing up between a holiday in Fiji or Bali. Because her parents had said it was a must to visit, she chose Bali and changed the direction of her life profoundly. She fell in love with the island and a Balinese man whom she met three days before going home. They have been married for nineteen years, living the first nine years in Australia and the next ten in Bali. She feels enriched by her experience of Bali. Glenda is forever grateful for their two beautiful children, who are living bridges between the two cultures and wholly embraced by her extended Balinese family.

We met at Kuta Beach at sunset in June 1979 at the end of Jalan Pantai—the road that led straight onto the sand at that time, where the Balinese guys played Frisbee on the beach—and I was suitably impressed. We knew we loved each other in three days.

We exchanged letters every week until November 1980, when he was able to come to Australia to be with me, and we had a Western wedding in Melbourne, Australia.

In July 1982, the day had finally arrived for our Balinese Hindu ceremony. It was a warm day, although the climate of Klungkung is slightly tempered, being elevated on the slopes of Mt. Agung, the highest mountain in Bali. Being a typical *desa* (village) in Bali, there was a humble bathroom, but water was not easily obtained. Water for the bathroom had to be carried by family members in a plastic bucket on their heads from a well a few hundred meters up the hill.

To prepare for my marriage, it was decided that I would be taken a little way down the main road to where clean, clear water was in plentiful supply in the open-air channel on the edge of the rice fields. The Balinese are quite adept at this, as they never expose the full naked body when bathing in a river or rice field but discreetly keep parts covered at all times.

So, duly refreshed, I was taken back to the ancestral house. Prior to the actual marriage ceremony, I also chose to have my teeth filed, as I hadn't grown up in Bali. A few family members who had not undergone this joined me. The actual filings are spat into a young coconut, and this is buried at the family temple. Because I am a Westerner, my teeth were only filed mildly, and my front teeth actually became more even because of it. This was quite an emotional experience, and my sisters-in-law shed some tears.

Marriage always happens at the groom's house, as the wife comes under his family ancestral umbrella, and I also chose to take on the Balinese Hindu faith. As part of the ceremony, I was given the Hindu name Jero Puspawati. *Jero*, because I was elevated in status for being married to a man of caste, and *Puspa*, meaning flower. *Wati* is the feminine form.

My hair was styled in a ponytail with a real hair extension extending almost to my waist. My fringe was trimmed with a razor blade to form a very short frame to my forehead and kept in place with pig fat instead of hairspray. Beautiful gold-leaf flowers and leaves were placed in my hair, along with fragrant fresh flowers. I was dressed by many aunties and cousins in a gold brocade sarong that made me feel like a princess.

On that day, I also underwent my *Otonan*, which are rites of passage usually performed on Balinese babies at 210-day intervals. So I was all caught up.

The actual marriage was presided over by a Brahman priest (*pedanda*) who sat on a raised platform, chanting and ringing a sacred bell, and we were doused by him with fragrant holy water. Throughout the ceremony, a local Balinese *gamelan* orchestra played, and hours had been spent by the extended family preparing the intricate offerings and delicious food.

I loved every moment and am eternally grateful for this enriching experience.

MY ADVICE FOR THE BALI VISITOR

Make sure you go far enough away from the busy areas into the Balinese villages to experience the verdant green of the rice fields.

Massage and Mysticism in Bali

JUDY SLATTUM

*Judy Slattum came first to Bali in 1979. In 1986, after resigning from acade-
mia in the USA, she created Danu Enterprises educational tour company
joined by her partner Made Surya. In 1993 Judy wrote* Balinese Masks, *the
first and only book in English on the subject, published by Chronicle Books
(later by Periplus). Judy and Made Surya live between Lod Tunduh Ubud
and Santa Cruz, CA.*

I first visited Bali in September 1978 while on sabbatical from the
California college where I taught theatre. Motivated to research and
study mask dance, I set off on my maiden sojourn, two days out of a cast,
my right leg having been broken in three places due to an auto accident
four months earlier. By the time I completed the eighteen-hour Merpati
Nusantara flight from LA, my leg had swollen to resemble a sausage and
was essentially numb to the world. I picked up a cane a friend had lent
me, and as I limped through the plane's exit hatch, a blast of tropical air
enveloped me.

After hobbling through Customs, I emerged into a throng of palm
trees and taxi drivers who were all vying for my attention. I ended up
in the wide-bodied Chevy of Nyoman Sunata, who, within my first ten
minutes in his cab, asked in broken English if I wanted to see the "holy
man." From my research I knew he meant one of Bali's famous healers.

I marveled at my luck in making such a quick contact with the country's mystic interior.

I had read about the massage men—expert practitioners who could reset bones, heal diseases, and provide chiropractic services to locals and the few savvy visitors with the right connections. My leg, stubbornly L-shaped from months of incarceration in plaster, needed instant therapy. Furthermore, my bone doctor had informed me that I would not be able to convolute my head under my ankle again, a yoga position I had mastered and grown quite vain about.

Nyoman agreed, for a hefty fee, to pick me up in two days and transport me to the home and workplace of the "holy man." I was required to wear traditional Balinese temple garb consisting of a sarong and a sash, with my shoulders covered, and to bring an offering of rice, incense, flowers, and palm leaf, all available at the local market, with the equivalent of three dollars in rupiah concealed inside the offering.

The auspicious day arrived and we took off in my pricey cab; I was sweating profusely in the constricting garments. The holy man lived in a small family compound across from a big electrical plant and worked on a raised platform, and patients lined up below. The walls around were decorated with coy Javanese pinup girls. In the back room kids watched cartoons on TV. My romantic notions of a holy man's esoteric environment were immediately challenged.

The holy man, who resembled a fat, happy Buddha, beckoned me. A wad of betel nut protruded from his cheek, staining his tongue and gums bright red and his teeth black. He was in the spotlight as assembled patients watched and applauded his every move. The holy man dipped a hand tipped with fantastically long fingernails into a bowl of oil.

Grinning at those that watched, he casually told jokes while kneading my inflexible knee joint, swinging it back and forth. Without warning he popped it, creating the sound of cracking walnuts. Panic and sweat-drenched my body. The holy man laughed at me, and the entire room joined in. I slunk off the platform humiliated but with two inches more movement in my joint.

After subjecting myself to several more treatments by the holy man over the next two weeks, my leg became strong enough to leave the flat beach lands and venture to Ubud, Bali's "cultural center," an area of hilly rice fields rimmed by volcanoes.

Soon after arriving, I heard of a skilled local massage man—Pak Gading. His technique was learned from his father and not sent from heaven like the holy man's. It was gentler, less humiliating, and equally effective. By the time my three-month stay was finished, my heel could touch the back of my knee. In gratitude, I gave Gading my most prized possession: my rain poncho (such ponchos were not for sale then in Bali).

Australian surfers had already discovered the superior waves at Kuta Beach and claimed the sleepy fishing village as their own mecca by the time I arrived, but cow pastures still framed the thatch-roofed family compounds where budget tourists could bunk down with the locals for a paltry USD 1.50 a night, breakfast included (usually tea and a banana). At five p.m. visitors and locals alike sauntered down to the wide sandy beach, watching the sun melt into the Indian Ocean, while the clouds created vivid crimson mandala-like patterns in the sky.

By day, the beach was crowded with topless sun-worshippers, serviced by villagers bundled up in long-sleeved shirts, sarongs, and broad-brimmed hats, peddling pineapples, bikinis, Coca-Cola, and massages.

The massage women were part of an old custom in Bali—every family includes at least one skilled masseuse who has been trained by another family member. This is consistent with the Balinese belief that massage is an essential healing tool to be sought out with regularity.

During my stay in Kuta, I decided to explore an alternative to the holy man's abrupt massage technique and so began the bargaining process with one of the first persistently cheerful masseuses who approached my beach mat.

The woman told me her name was Putri, which translates as something akin to "beautiful young woman", and offered me a beach massage for USD 4.00 (although later experience revealed one could bargain down to as little as USD 1.25). But the cut-rate massage lasted only about twenty minutes and was cursory at best. In other words, you got what you paid for.

While Putri toiled away in the hot sun, I asked her why she was swathed in such voluminous clothing in the sweltering tropical climate. "Balinese no like black skin," she informed me. "Mean you poor, must work outside. If inside, skin more beautiful, like king."

Although Putri's strong, experienced fingers were skillfully kneading my leg muscles in long, strong strokes, some drawbacks were becoming apparent. It was almost impossible on the windy beach not to find some sand sticking to one's skin, and the slightly rancid coconut oil (nothing left to waste!) favorite by the beach masseuses glued the granules to my skin. This, combined with Putri's heavy calluses, amounted to being massaged with number 2 sandpaper.

I begged Putri to cease, requesting instead we conclude the massage at my beachfront bungalow, at Hotel Yasa Samudra, (now the Hard Rock).

Putri frowned. "If in hotel, cost more."

"Why?" I asked.

"Hotel boy ask me for commission," she replied. I sighed, paid Putri, and wondered if it was too tacky to ask to inspect the hand of any future masseuses I might engage.

Indonesia was then considered a developing nation at that time, and the average yearly income was only five hundred dollars. Everyone worked, and, as many have noted, Balinese women especially seem to work hard. I am certain that all the women performing beach massage also had homes to care for and gardens to till and probably helped in the labor-intensive harvests of the rice fields that consumed the bulk of Balinese land mass.

Massage, whether by healers or everyday practitioners, is still something I seek out when in Bali and for which the Balinese are rightfully famous.

MY ADVICE FOR THE BALI VISITOR ———————

It is still possible to visit authentic Balinese healers, but there are dishonest opportunists looking to profit from tourist's dollars. Beware of "healers" who promote themselves as such with ads or websites, who work at hotels (rather than at home), or practice western style methods such as fortune-telling, palm reading, tarot, etc. All of these are against the ethics of the tradition.

The Natural State

STEPHANIE BUFFINGTON

Stephanie Buffington has been an author, TV producer, and fashion designer. She first came to Bali in 1980, and her love of Bali has brought her back just about every year since. She now travels the world with her company Tribal Music Tours and, when home in Los Angeles, facilitates Rhythmic Prayer circles at the Sacred Rhythm Lodge.

What is it about the jungle that I crave? Is it Mother Nature's shimmering cloak in shades of chartreuse? Is it the sound of distant gongs and the flocks of stark white ducks waddling along the road? Such beauty seemed to mesmerize me that day as I pumped my push-bike through the rice fields. I love to ride my bike down the back tracks of Bali, where everything is alive and vibrating. Perhaps all that lush and fertile life is what gives the Balinese an animistic perspective and belief that all living things are sacred. Somehow the glorious embrace of such natural beauty awakened my sense of animism too. I could see the One animating force within everything, oozing and pulsing with life... and I was part of it. It felt holy.

Maybe that's why Bali is called the navel of the world, and maybe that's why Bali is my favorite place on earth.

That morning sun gave the swaying banana leaves an electric glow above me. Soft punches of perfumed air enveloped me as I peddled along the narrow trail. I was in utter bliss.

I only had to pull over twice. First, when a swarm of monkeys came up from the ravine to my right. Suddenly I was surrounded by a furry flurry in a hurry. I froze in place and watched a wooly grey tsunami wash over the road, bumping into the bike in a frenzy. It was over in minutes. This happened every morning after the piles of rice balls, cakes, and fruit were left as offerings at the local temples and shrines.

An irresistible urge to follow a blaring loudspeaker into the center of a small village was the next stop. At the center of every village is a *pondok*—a large covered pavilion with a marble floor and an altar at one end. It is the community meeting hall.

Traditional *gamelan* music crackled through the well-worn speakers. About twenty tiny young girls wrapped tightly in colorful sarongs, swayed and held poses at the command of the dance master. The girls held their arms akimbo, elbows up, while fluttering small fans in each hand. At the same time, their heads slid from side to side as if detached from the neck and being pulled by an invisible string.

Like a synchronized flutter of delicate butterflies, they swooped in perfect form as the old man called out instructions. I sat spellbound and invisible to them. Hours or minutes, for how long, I couldn't say.

I did make it to the woodcarver's village of Mas, even with the spontaneous diversions. I found the shop where my friend Ketut was waiting, with still a few hours of sunlight left. Ketut was very kind to introduce me to the patriarch of the village. He was a bandy-legged, shirtless, nut-colored man with an ornately carved walking stick. His name was Wayan, and this was his workshop and storefront. He looked even more ancient than all the old antique pieces that filled every inch of space there.

The men exchanged riotous greetings and shuffled along behind me as I made a beeline to a dusty back corner of the gallery shop. I was not sure what I wanted, but I knew that what I was looking for would find me.

I love mythic religious deities and icons of the Hindu epic *The Mahabrata*. These tales used symbols and metaphors to teach life's transcendental lessons.

Then I saw it—a noble face rising out from behind several stacked works of art in front of it. It was the embellished crowned head of Lord Shiva, looking more like a Buddha with black eyes that followed me. In fact, it reminded me of my own beloved guru I had met in India when he was a child. Finally free from the pile, I saw the crowned figure was standing upon three skulls. That symbolized the three *gunas* or obstacles to enlightenment: spiritual ego, inertia, and action. This was definitely the piece for me.

Quickly I had my treasure wrapped up and strapped to the back of my bike, and I was off before sunset. Riding my bike in the darkness of a black moonless night could be a very different experience. One I wasn't up for.

I could tell what time it was not just because the sun sets and rises at six every day on the equator but because of the earthy, sweet smell of evening fires and the amped-up hum of the insect kingdom. And every evening, for as long as anyone could remember, a siege of white herons would silently wing across the pink sky. Their long necks were gracefully crooked into hieroglyphs as they made their way back to the same village every night. I rode alongside them in the magenta twilight, as my homestay bungalow was just a kilometer from their village. We headed home together.

Birds in nature have always been a personal totem or signifier, a way Spirit makes itself known to me. Reminding me, "Behold, I am always with you."

I thought about my beloved teacher's last talk. It was about a bird that became so used to its gilded cage, so comfortable, that it did not realize the door to the cage was wide open, and, more significantly, it forgot that it could fly! I felt like that bird, sometimes forgetting I really was free and that I was born to fly. This story was fresh and meaningful to me that day.

I'd been staying in the same bamboo house off and on for many years. It was humble by Western standards, but it had an electric generator to run the ceiling fan, and the bamboo only creaked and moaned under the torrents of the monsoon season. I shared it with a family of pokey green geckos. The Balinese considered my little dragons as lucky.

I brought in my precious package and carefully placed it on the bed before stepping into the adjacent open-air bathroom. A stone wall surrounded the tile floor, shower, and toilet, but it was open to the sky and all the critters that lived in the neighboring tropical forest. As I approached the sink to turn the spigot and finally wash my sweat-streaked face, I looked up to see a bright-green parrot with a yellow beak perched contentedly atop the mirror. Not more than three feet from me, it showed no fear.

"Well, hello," I said as it quizzically bobbed its head. I had seen lizards, baby snakes, and bugs as big as matchboxes out there but never any other creature.

"Okay, okay. Please stay right there," I implored my new friend as I dashed to get my camera just ten feet away.

Back at the sink the cocky green bird was still there, so I lifted my camera to my eye and tilted back to focus on him. Unexpectedly, he fluttered down onto my extended arm, holding the camera. Bobbing up and down, he sidestepped his way up my arm to sit on my shoulder and nuzzled his yellow beak into my neck and hair. Transfixed in that position, I was able to click a photo of our reflection together caught for a moment in the mirror. The instant I moved to set the camera down, my new feathered friend flew away.

I was gleeful that Nature had so lovingly expressed its presence in such a delightful way. A way that nobody would believe just to hear about it, but I had proof. I had the precious photo.

Now it was time to unpack my woodcarving and really have a good look at it. I cut the string and unfolded the newspaper wrappings to let out my magnificent celestial deity, freeing him to dance upon the three skulls. The wise and serene face was not Hindu or Buddhist but a mystical fusion of both, just like the Balinese themselves. Nonetheless, to me, it resembled my beloved teacher in exquisite ceremonial dress. As I looked more closely, I saw what I hadn't seen before in the shop. My beautiful adorned deity was holding a golden bird tenderly against his heart!

I couldn't help but weep right then and there. The significance and the meaning was completely clear. Oh yes, my beloved indeed held me close always.

MY ADVICE FOR THE BALI VISITOR ────────────────

Make a trip to Gunung Kawi and see the hidden caves dating back to the 11th century and before. It is magical to say the least. Be sure and be there before 8 a.m. as it has become quite touristic.

PART IV

BALI
1980–1985

That is all there is to life—beauty.
You find that and you have found everything.

CHARLIE CHAPLIN

Against All Odds

Nigel Mason

Nigel Mason arrived in Bali in 1980, fell in love with a local girl named Yanie, and opened a small restaurant that was named after her. They went on to kick-start Ubud's adventure industry in 1989 when they opened the first white-water rafting company, followed by rescuing critically endangered Sumatran elephants—and making chocolates, among other things—all under the heading of Mason Adventures.

It all started in 1980, when I came to Bali for the first time and checked into a small back-lane *losmen* named Kortis in Legian. Little did I know then that this small one-thousand-rupiah-a-night homestay with just six rooms was owned by the uncle of the Balinese girl that I would later meet in the same lane at a small bamboo local shop named Lisa's, owned by her older sister.

I had left Melbourne, Australia, to travel to Bali on a whim to escape a broken marriage and a career in retail that had become unbearable to me. At the age of thirty-seven this was a big step, as I had arrived with little money and no real picture of what I wanted to do. But I instantly fell in love with the island and decided to stay a while longer, which was to turn into what is now at seventy-six years old, a lifetime.

Made Karyanie (Yanie) and I first met at Yanie's older sister, Lisa's, shop in what is now known as Garlic Lane. However, back in the early

'80s it was purely a sand track, no more than two meters wide. I was standing with Lisa when I first saw Yanie and it was love at first sight, even though it was more than a year later before we finally got together. She rode up to her sister's shop on a blue Vespa, long hair flowing behind her, a face like an angel and as beautiful a girl as I had ever seen. Lisa introduced her sister to me, and Yanie politely said hello—and as quickly as she had arrived, she was gone on her way.

Yanie was just twenty-one years old and was studying English part time at a university and was also the secretary to the manager at Bali Intan Cottages on Jalan Melasti, where she also ran a small gift shop with her family inside the hotel foyer. She was very bright, very intelligent, with an inquisitive mind, and was most definitely the most beautiful girl in Legian. Her family home was close to Lisa's shop and only a fifteen-minute walk to the Intan Hotel.

A year after that first meeting, we met once again, this time at a youth club meeting where I had been taken to by her cousin, Made Robert, the son of the Kortis Losmen family, where I was still staying two years later. During those two years, I had been buying and selling art to take back and sell in Australia and had also been trying to put together an investment in Lombok. Both these ventures failed miserably, and I was now down to my last couple of hundred dollars and had been living on street food for the past two years to save on expenses.

That second meeting was love at first sight all over again, but this time I plucked up the courage to ask Yanie to come and have dinner with me. However, this was easier said than done, as it was definitely not acceptable for Western men to date Balinese girls and was frowned on by the village. However, Yanie's family also ran a small losmen, where many backpackers stayed, and had no objections to their now twenty-two-year-old daughter going out with an Australian. Over the next week or so I would visit Yanie either at her family house or at the Intan Hotel.

Our first dinner date was a week after that second meeting, at the newly opened Nusa Dua Beach Hotel, far out of sight of the prying village eyes and gossip. To even consider this first date, Yanie had imposed two rules: 1. I had to find a friend for her younger sister so that she could chaperone us. 2. We all go on two separate bikes. So I organized a guest staying also at Kortis to come on the back of his bike, to meet up with Yanie and her sister Nyoman halfway to Nusa Dua near the airport. Here Yanie hopped on the back of my bike and her sister onto the back of the other bike, driven by the other guy I brought along. We then rode off to the Nusa Dua Beach Hotel for a sumptuous meal.

That meal at the hotel that night cost more than my budget for two weeks; however, it turned out to be the best investment of my life. Two years later we were married, and starting out in a life together that was to be filled with drama, comedy, and challenges that saw us build a small business and later a small adventure empire that is now legendary on the island—Mason Adventures—and raised two handsome boys, who both work in the family business.

The wedding to start with was our first challenge, as at that time everyone was completely against it. Yanie's Filipino boss at the Intan Cottages was very much against the relationship to start with and within only a few months of us getting together, stood Yanie down for two weeks with no pay to force her to end our new friendship. Yanie, being very stubborn, refused to give in and instead resigned from her job permanently. As only she and her older brother were bringing money into the family, this was a big step and didn't go down well with one of Yanie's younger sisters, who told me to stop seeing her sister so that she could get her job back. She never did, and that's now history.

I was now running out of money fast, so Yanie suggested that her other uncle who had a derelict house in Legian, that was in the lane down to the graveyard, was for rent. So we borrowed five million rupiah from her brother for a five-year lease and moved into the broken-down small grass-roofed house that sat on two hundred square meters of land. I then set about restoring the building to make it habitable and later to turn it into a small bar and later a restaurant that I named "Yanie's" after my beautiful new love.

We had been living together for two years when we finally decided to get married. This again was easier said than done. The village youth club were completely against it, as Yanie was the most eligible and gorgeous girl in Legian, and I was looked on as an old man who was seventeen years older than Yanie and also a divorcee.

The head of the village, convinced by this youth club, introduced a new law to try and block the wedding. This law stated that no inter-religious marriages were allowed in Legian. I immediately said, "No problem. I will change to Hindu." But this again was not easy. The rule had been thrown at us the last minute, only a day before our wedding (which had been divined as a good luck day for a wedding according to the Hindu calendar). However, Yanie's father arranged for me to go through a lifetime of Hindu ceremonies in just one day with the family quickly rallying to plan all the many offerings that were required for the ceremonies. The night before I was "christened" by a Brahman priest in Denpasar. The next morning I went through all the other Hindu ceremonies to legitimize us before we were finally wed late in the afternoon in a small and simple ceremony by the village *mangku* (priest) at Yanie's family home. That week we also had a small wedding at the Australian Consulate with just two witnesses, performed by the consul himself, with a borrowed ring and a dress that Yanie had sewn herself the day before. But disaster was to strike yet again, before we were even married two weeks.

Back in the '80s, the immigration department at that time was known among expats as P. T. Imigrasi, which meant that foreigners were often blacklisted and had to leave the country unless they could buy themselves off the blacklist. It was almost a "coming of age" in Bali to be blacklisted and then buy yourself off to stay longer, and numerous foreigners' businesses on the island were targets of this corruption. Not a huge problem for most expats if they had some money, but Yanie and I were in debt to everyone back in 1984 and weren't nearly able to come up with the money required.

It all started one morning when Immigration arrived at the newly opened Yanie's Restaurant demanding us to come with them to the office of the Kantor Kanwil Kehakiman, the local branch of the Minister of Justice, where I was informed that I had two days to pack up and leave the country and never return. No reason was given and no amount of protest could change the decision. So, two days later, I was put on a plane back to Australia alone, as Yanie had no passport and no money to join me.

For the next year and a half I came and went in and out of Indonesia illegally, hiding away while in Bali and getting caught and deported numerous times. As time progressed I had more and more trouble getting into Bali and staying, as after a few times caught, I was soon a marked man, and if I was seen while hiding at Yanie's I was quickly reported, arrested by Immigration, and deported once again. Over that year and a half, I had to avoid the Bali airport and instead fly to Jakarta, then come two days by bus to arrive at night in Bali and sneak into Yanie's through the jungle at the back. Later I even changed my name in Australia and came on a new passport with a new name spelt "Naaijel Meisen," instead of Nigel Mason, to confuse the computers at the airport. I had disguises and often changed my hair color or the shape of my beard. However, each time I would get caught and thrown off the island once again. Sometimes I got away with it for a month or so; sometimes I was caught within just days after arriving.

Yanie finally managed to get a passport. However, by then we were living on very little. On Yanie's first trip to visit my family in Australia, we could only afford a flight to Perth and then a bus trip from one side of Australia to the other on our small budget. For us to fly to Perth, I had to first bus it to Jakarta, catch the plane to Perth from there, to be joined on the flight in Bali by Yanie, so that we could travel to Perth together. On the way back we had to do the reverse, as I was still black-listed and banned from Indonesia. Finally, through Yanie's constant complaints and visits to the Minister of Justice, nearly two years later my blacklist was canceled.

In the years after that we worked hard to turn Yanie's Bar and Restaurant into a Bali icon for the after-disco crowd. We had live music and Bali's first Western-style hamburgers and later catering to become the only place known to have good Australian-style food that didn't taste like it was cooked in peanut oil. By the end of the '80s, we had completely paid back everyone who had helped finance us and saved enough money to start the first Original Bali Doll Company in 1987. Two years later we opened Bali's first rafting operation. It had steps in and out of the river and a whole superb infrastructure uniquely different from anything Bali had ever seen before, catering to hundreds of people every week.

But yet again, we were smashed by the corrupt system and a greedy opposition that had sprung up and were jealous of our success. Behind closed doors a deal was done with another company and the government, to get our business off the Ayung River. We were closed down at gunpoint in 1994 by a team of government-led police and officials, who boarded up our business, then known as Bali Adventure Rafting, for almost three years. This was completely illegal, and it took some years to fight this, depleting our money and putting us into massive debt, yet again.

After finally reopening in late 1996 to a now crowded river, we followed that by starting a completely new venture a year later: the Elephant Safari Park, with Indonesian elephants rescued from certain death in Sumatra. Now the company was renamed Bali Adventure Tours, with mountain cycling, trekking, and later helicopter tours added to our portfolio. The Elephant Safari Park added a hotel and spa and a large restaurant, as well as a gift shop in Kuta, all on borrowed money from the bank.

The two Bali bombs yet again smashed our company, and it took some years to recover from it, as again we had to borrow money to survive. But over the years since, we have built a huge new rafting operation from scratch and continued to extend the Elephant Park to make it one of Bali's most well-known attractions and the first rescue park in Asia to be awarded a gold certification in animal welfare from the Asian Captive Elephant Standards organization.

The original Yanie's Restaurant was finally closed after fifteen years in 1999 when a disagreement with the uncle's family failed to renew the lease. However, by this time we had sold our shops in Kuta and were doing all our business in the Ubud area. Our latest business,

Mason Chocolates, was formed near the elephant park in 2017 together with another restaurant and a Jungle Buggies operation. While the COVID-19 scare was on in early 2020, we struggled on to complete a second, larger chocolate factory in Ubud, while at the same time building a 150-seat theatre at the Mason Elephant Park.

The company now known as Mason Adventures, was closed for the most part of 2020 and continues to be today in 2022 due to the global Covid pandemic and the complete absence of international visitors to Bali, but we as a family, struggled through these bad times, once again going through all of our savings. The elephants we look after have always been the main priority to keep alive, especially now during these hard years, which has completely used all of our funds.

Hopefully this latest chapter of our lives will be yet just another hurdle to look back on as the world looks toward brighter times.

MY ADVICE FOR THE BALI VISITOR

Having lived in Bali for forty years, my message to anyone contemplating a visit is to book a flight as soon as you can, as this island is unique in its climate, culture and charisma and you will fall in love with it, just as I did.

Jasi's Little Lie

SOOSAN SURYAWAN

Soosan Suryawan was born in Massachusetts, USA, and began painting at the age of five. She received her bachelor of arts degree from Rhode Island School of Design. Upon graduating, she left for Bali at the age of twenty-one and fell in love with the culture and with Wana Suryawan. They were blessed with three children.

It was 1980 when I arrived in Peliatan, the village of artistic painters. I lived at a modest homestay owned by a traditional painter named Ketut Madra. I had a one-room bamboo bungalow with an open veranda. In those days, there was no running water, but Ketut was fortunate to have a well on his property. Usually, it was the Balinese women who climbed down the steep river gorges to fetch buckets of water for their daily needs. Bare-breasted with colorful sarongs wrapped around their waists, they gracefully managed this task, often with a baby slung on one hip.

My days were filled with painting and long walks from village to village. At night I'd follow the distant sounds of chanting and *gamelan* music to the temple ceremonies. It was there that one experienced the multidimensional world of Balinese culture.

Another interesting facet of life at the time was the collaboration between local master craftsmen and artistic foreigners. Among them were two of my first expat friends, Ella Helmi and Linda Garland.

They had discovered a spring-fed swimming pool in Gianyar called Bukit Jati and invited me to join them. As we neared Puri Gianyar, they pointed to a small gold-jewelry shop. "That's where the gorgeous Mr. Mahogany's family home is." They kept going on about him until I asked who this guy was. They burst into praise about his extensive knowledge of music, how gorgeous he was, what an amazing martial artist he was, and what a perfectly defined body he had. And they said he was the best DJ on the island. They went on to explain how he owned Kuta's best music cassette shop called Mahogany, which was a hub for "Kuta Cowboys"—a subculture of exotic bare-chested sarong-clad, longhaired Balinese males who were intermingling with foreign girls in bikinis from all over the world. Linda, Ella, and I began a routine of going to the spring-fed swimming pool in Gianyar, and they never missed an opportunity to point out the gold shop and comment on the divine Mr. Mahogany.

Ketut Jasi, owner of Beggar's Bush in Campuan, was another close friend at the time. It was the most popular nightspot in the area for locals and expats to mingle. Jasi told me of the upcoming all-white dress code full moon party at Beggar's Bush with music by Mahogany, sponsored by Pak Tari, a Jakarta man living in Sayan.

On the day of the full moon party, Brazilian Hugo came to my place and found me mopey because I didn't have a white dress. He quickly scanned my room, grabbed a roll of unpainted canvas, and proceeded to fashion it into a fabulous dress that fit like a glove. Mr. Mahogany lived up to his reputation and had everyone dancing nonstop to music from around the world. It was one of the best parties I'd ever been to.

Not long after, Jasi asked me if I wanted to create another full moon party at Beggar's Bush. She would provide the venue, and I would provide the people. I said yes, but only if Mr. Mahogany was playing the music. I made flyers saying "FULL MOON PARTY AT BEGGAR'S BUSH FEATURING MAHOGANY DJ" to be handed out if he agreed to do it. Jasi and I went to Kuta together, and I saw her enter the cassette shop, but I was busy doing something down the road. When we met up, she said the owner said he'd do it. Only then did I hand out flyers and invite friends from all over the island.

A few days before the event, I ran into Agung Boss, the owner of Golden Village in Seminyak. He said, "Wana is *not* doing your party."

I was not aware that Mr. Mahogany's name was Wana. I tried to explain. "The guy from Mahogany is."

Agung Boss replied, "That *is* Wana; he owns Mahogany."

I sat there kind of dazed, when Malcolm and Donna (managers of Blue Ocean restaurant) said, "We're seeing him tonight in Sanur at a disco; he's really nice," and they offered to give me a lift so I could discuss the situation with him. Thus began perhaps the strangest twenty-four hours of my life.

~

On the way to Sanur, Malcolm's jeep broke down. It took hours to fix, but eventually, we made it to the club. Someone, by way of introduction, stated that I was the one having the full moon party at Beggar's Bush.

Wana asked, "Who dared use my name on a flyer without asking me?"

Confused, I said, "It was me, but only after my friend Ketut Jasi said she'd gone to your shop and asked you, and you said yes."

He asked me what day that was. When I told him, he said he wasn't in the shop that day because he went home for a ceremony in Gianyar. I was dumbfounded and told him I was sorry and confused. I pleaded for him to reconsider.

He was polite, said he believed me but had no desire to do the party. I asked him to sleep on it, and we made a date to meet in his shop the following day to see if he'd changed his mind. I left the disco and headed to Legian on a bemo to stay with a "friend" who had invited me to spend the night. On that ride, someone pickpocketed *all* my money, and a crazy Italian lady who was shivering asked to borrow my cashmere sweater. The next time the bemo stopped, she jumped off and ran away with it. When I arrived, my friend threw me the keys to her house, saying she was meeting a man for a date, and took off. I was alone and sleepless, without money or a sweater, and feeling a bit dejected.

The next morning, I put myself together and found the lavender-colored Mahogany shop. Wana greeted me from across the counter and politely reiterated that he was *not* playing music for my party "on principle." I told him that I had been robbed, didn't even have bemo money to get back to Ubud—never mind the funds to go around the island to cancel the event. We sat staring at each other for a while, and then he kindly offered to take me everywhere to uninvite everyone and to take me home to Ubud afterward.

So off we went in his silver VW Safari convertible, which was airbrushed with surfing monkeys. After many stops, Wana asked if I minded making one more at his father's gold shop in Gianyar (the shop I'd passed so many times on the way to the pool). As we emerged from the car, I could feel the whole village thinking, "Ohhh, who is he bringing home *this time*?" I remember feeling indignant and telling them in my head I wasn't one of his girls. I went in and met his father, and after a short visit, we continued on to our final destination, my *lumbung* (bamboo bungalow) up a steep flight of stairs just before the Campuan Bridge.

I was so exhausted that I told Wana I needed to lie down and asked him if he'd like to rest too. He mistook this as a come-on and began to fall into role, but I told him that I meant to rest. He lay down next to me and went into a deep meditation. When we awoke, I asked him if he wanted to take a *mandi* (bath) in the spring at the bottom of the river gorge. There was a place for women and men to bathe separately. His face lit up, and he said he'd love to.

The crystal-clear water bursting from their underground source rejuvenated both of us completely. He took me to dinner at Warung Ibu Oka next to the palace of Ubud. Just before he left, he kissed me on the lips and told me he would be happy if I visited him at his shop.

As charming as he was, I decided I wasn't going be one of the girls hanging around Mahogany shop. A few weeks had passed when I told Ella the story and how it ended in a kiss and an invite to visit. I remember Ella saying, "Wait—Mr. Mahogany kissed you, invited you to visit, and you never went? Are you crazy?" It made me rethink it, and I headed over there a few days later. As I entered his shop and saw him, I heard a voice in my head that said, "If you don't marry him, you're not who you think you are and should never take yourself seriously again."

Later, Wana told me that when we visited his dad's gold shop in Gianyar, he saw a sign over my head with the words "SHE WILL BE YOUR WIFE." We were both surprised, as he was living the carefree "love as long as the visa lasts" life, and I was twenty-two years old and hadn't thought of settling down. A few days into my visit, he asked me to try on a gorgeous Balinese antique gold ring with a star sapphire. It fit as if it were made for me. He observed this, then took it back without saying a word. We became inseparable, and after two weeks, he told me about the ring I'd tried on. He'd been saving it for nine years, believing that when he met his future wife, it would fit her perfectly. A few days later, he said we should make a baby, and I agreed. Two months later, I was pregnant with Putu, and three months after that, we were married. Somewhere during that time, he slipped the ring on my finger.

Wana and I had three children. After Putu, came Nava and Bayu. Wana continued to DJ at all the private parties and was the one to make Gado Gado and Double Six nightclubs take off. He never again refused anyone who asked him to DJ an event. I was the only one who had received a flat-out refusal. That party didn't happen, but we did, and that event lasted almost two decades until his sudden passing in 1999.

In retrospect, I will say I'm so grateful for Jasi's little lie. It delivered me to destiny's door. And I walked through it gladly. Thank you, Jasi.

MY ADVICE FOR THE BALI VISITOR ————————————————

Go to Laughing Buddha Lounge for the best live music (Koko and the Cooltones play covers like Led Zeppelin and Pink Floyd, sounding just like the original bands, and their guitarist, Agung, is world-class). Also, venture to Sayuri's and Bali Bohemia for open-mic nights, where expats and locals showcase their talents.

The Bali Boys
From 7

PETER CROFT

Peter Croft was born in Sydney in 1947 but has been a West Aussie since 1950. He worked in a job he loved at TVW Channel 7 in Perth from 1966 to early retirement in 1999 and has made two marvelous trips to Bali with work friends in 1980 and 1983, then solo in 1985, 1989, and 1990.

I first visited Bali in July 1980.

Yes, we needed a visa then.

I was never a surfer or bar hopper. A pool, a good book, and my camera were all I wanted. And things to photograph—and there was no shortage of that. Bali must be the most photogenic place in Asia. Other countries like Thailand and Malaysia have their charms, but Bali stands apart. Add in the marvelously friendly people, and it's a winning combination.

Being only three and a half hours from Perth, it's become the default holiday destination for West Aussies. I still have friends there and not only Balinese—but also Germans, Dutch, and Russian friends. My Austrian lady friend lives there for the climate too, but this damned virus is a curse.

I worked as a technician at a commercial TV station in Perth, Western Australia. Three other guys who were operators—they threaded the machines and played the videotapes and films to air, and I fixed the machines they broke—asked if I'd like to go with them to Bali. "Oooowwwwaaargh yeah," I said, so we set the dates and bought our tickets. We would have just booked a package with a local travel agent as there was no such thing as the internet, but it was for three weeks, staying at the Kuta Seaview Cottages on Jalan Pantai Kuta, in those days literally on the beach. You stepped out of the hotel and walked across a few meters of sand, and you were on the beach.

Unfortunately, it's a traffic-jammed road now with thousands of motorbikes angle-parked against a "tsunami proof" wall, rumored to have been donated by the Japanese government. The name Seaview is no longer applicable.

It was the first time to Bali for all of us. QANTAS ran 747 Jumbos from Perth to Bali then, with free drinks included, so we willingly submitted ourselves to this three-and-a-half-hour ordeal.

I was thirty-three, and we were all about the same age. I traveled with Dexter, so named by his father—a US serviceman in WWII stationed in Perth, who married a local lady and had three sons. Unfortunately, Dexter has passed away, but he was a life-of-the-party kind of guy, full of jokes, and everything was a laugh.

Next was Norm. a quiet-spoken guy but also a good man to have along. The third man was Shane. If you remember Christopher Reeve as Superman, you'd be close to what Shane looked like. A chick magnet, in other words.

I'd been to Singapore a few times, but this was my first time in Indonesia. Like a good boy, I read the *Lonely Planet* guidebook, and in talking about dress, it said, "Some of the better restaurants might require a light jacket." So, totally naively, I took trousers, shoes, and a sports coat. Hah. What a joke. They never left the wardrobe.

The Seaview was a pretty mid-level hotel then, maybe what we'd call three-star now, but it had a pool, and the bar was open all day and evening. I can even remember the names of the staff: Wayan, Made, Nyoman, and Ketut. How about that? And another Wayan, and another Made, another Nyoman and Ketut. I've always particularly liked Ketut as a name. I think it's cute, but if I were a Balinese guy I don't think I'd like it so much. One of my Balinese mates is Ketut, but he now goes by the name of Yudhi.

Luckily, most of the staff had other names, such as Willy. We thought Willy was a little bit crazy, but a mine of information and a good laugh.

I liked Sutri at the hotel. She was gorgeous but married with *anak-anak* (children).

I had hair then. John was the manager of the bar and smarter than the average bear.

We had a couple of rooms at the back of the hotel, and one of my best memories was showering out by the pool in the pool showers—just screen walls, no roof, with the morning sun on my shoulders. That's a Bali *mandi* for you. Lovely.

At first, we ate at the hotel, but after a day or two, we started to explore other options. The Seaview adjoined Gang Poppies I, and so we walked (slowly) along it toward Jalan Legian, looking for cassette shops, T-shirt shops, and restaurants. We left Perth a bit wound up, as our jobs were quite stressful, but after a few days, we realized that the stress melted away if we just slowed ourselves and our walking pace down.

Being July, the weather was beautiful, so melting wasn't too much of a problem. I've been plenty of times in the wet season around Christmas since then, and I'm quite happy in the heat, especially since I like the afternoon thunderstorms and rain.

Once we reached Jalan Legian, if we turned right, we were at Bemo Corner. Across the intersection with Jl. Pantai Kuta and fifty meters down Jl. Buni Sari was the Cosy Corner Restaurant. What a find! Once we'd sampled the food, we ate there almost every night.

The owner told us that he'd been trained at the Bali Beach Hotel, Sanur, which was probably the only five-star hotel at the time (except for the Oberoi in Legian, I guess). Of course they all said that, but we were happy to accept his word, as the food was proof of it. I especially remember having a starter, a main course, and a Bintang *besar* (large) for AUD 2.00. Can't complain about that. The money went far then.

In talking to the owner, we heard that good refrigeration was a problem for him, so we got all enthusiastic and started plans to get him a good fridge. We thought we'd ship a second-hand one from Perth, but, like all starry-eyed plans, it never left the wharf. Knowing what I know now, we could probably have bought him one in Denpasar.

This was where I introduced Dexter to the music of Michael Franks—you know: *Burchfield Nines*, *Tiger in the Rain*. If you're younger than fifty you probably wouldn't know him, but Dexter thought it was cool music. So do I, still.

Next on the agenda was a motorbike rental. Luckily I'd learned on a scooter in Perth, so I had a license and could bring an international driving permit, present it at a *kantor polisi* (police office), pay the fee, and I didn't have to take a Bali test. Even so, although I'd ridden a scooter, it had been a while. And I hadn't actually ridden a motorbike, as such.

The other guys knew the ropes, though, and once I got the hang of it, it was some of the best times I've ever had. I was a keen photographer, so once I learned to put my camera bag on the front, secured to the handlebars, I was away. No helmets then, remember? That meant I could ride around slowly, see a shot, quickly stop astride the bike, pull my camera out, and take my shots, unrestricted by helmet or laws.

Once I got used to this, I was away nearly every day, on my own, so I could concentrate just on photo opportunities.

I ended up with vibration wrists and hands in the evenings, but what the hell.

The camera on the first trip was a Konica Autoreflex T3, body number 586755, with a 50mm Hexanon lens number 7627303. Yeah, I'm a real nerd, but the reason I remember this is I bought this camera on my first trip overseas to Europe in 1974, and theft was always on my mind. So I memorized the numbers. No problem. And once they're in there, they're in there.

In fact, it came in very handy later, after this trip, because Dexter bought that camera and lens from me back in Perth. About six months later, he said, "You don't happen to have a record of the serial numbers, do you? I've been burgled, and it's been stolen, and I need them for the insurance." So right there and then at work, I was able to reel those numbers off to him. Hah!

Anyway, I clearly remember riding the bike up Poppies, across Bemo Corner, and onto the road to Sanur. There was almost no development then—just a narrow road heading east through rice paddies and coconut groves with grazing cattle. No bypass, no shops, just paddies on the left and mangroves on the right.

I distinctly remember the sweeping turn over to Sanur (I didn't exactly know where I was), where it went north.

There were just *kampungs* (villages), small houses, and coconut palms. I do remember a small, very new *toko* (shop), painted red and white like a Circle K. Jalan Danau Tamblingan must have been there, but it was very narrow (still is!) and undeveloped. I don't think I went on from there much because it seemed so empty. How different it was compared to today!

Once I'd got my motorbike legs, I made longer trips and rode from Kuta, via Sanur, Ubud, and straight on "up the hill" to Kintamani on the rim of Gunung Batur and Lake Batur.

Of course, this was shot on film—three shots combined and a "tobacco" filter used, as was fashionable at the time.

I rode my motorbike down the winding road to the lakeshore.

This was 1980, and it was still very much kampungs and *losmens* (homestays). For some reason, I've always had a wish to visit Trunyan, but I haven't managed it yet. There was something about the name, the lights across the lake at night, and the stories of a different Bali there. Maybe one day.

A thunderstorm came in only about thirty minutes after the glorious sunshine.

Then it was the ride back, probably via Bangli, Gianyar, Sanur, and finally to Kuta. I can't remember whether it was 1980 or 1983, but forest fires in Borneo meant a smoke haze over Bali—not good for our health but great for sunsets.

One thing I've never forgotten about the ride back was stopping for a durry drag (I was a smoker then) on a pretty new concrete bridge at the top of Sanur. I was reminded of a line of that Joni Mitchell song, "They paved paradise and put up a parking lot."

I went down to the little creek under the bridge to sit and saw women toiling away, carrying baskets of rubble from the stream up to the road. One of the young women, very pretty despite her job, smiled and shyly said, "San' an' stones." I was charmed!

I used to get back to the Seaview Hotel with my hands buzzing and trembling from the vibration of the handlebars. It was all I could do to hold my beer.

I would be pretty tired but recovered quickly, ready for a good meal, either in the hotel or down the road. There was a good restaurant about where the Pizza Hut (ugh) is now on Jalan Pantai Kuta and another one on the corner where the Hard Rock Cafe is now.

There were the musical instruments for a *gamelan* orchestra in the bar. I've always liked Balinese music, and I used to take the hammers and try to pick out tunes on the xylophone. Completely amateurishly, of course, but Ketut came over and helped me out.

I also remember having great laughs because I thought I was doing the right thing by saying "*Selamat Jalan*" when I was going out. "No, no, if *you* are leaving, *we* say selamat jalan. You say *selamat tinggal*." OK, got that. Never forgotten. *Jalan* means "going." *Tinggal* means "staying."

We had great times in the hotel bar.

On the first trip in 1980, Dexter became infatuated with one of the waitresses at the Seaview: Nyoman. She responded to the attentions of this rich Westerner, of course, and they went out on dates a couple of times. I don't have a photo, but I can still remember Nyoman being all dolled up for her date in her beautiful brown dress, which probably cost her a week's wages.

But in my mind, I was saying, "Nyoman, *warning, warning*—don't fall for him. He's just going to return to Perth, and you'll be left high and dry," which is exactly what happened. I hope she wasn't too hurt, as she was so vulnerable.

On the '83 trip, I had a couple of incidents that are not such good memories. I was sharing a room with Dexter, and being a bit security conscious, I used to sleep with my wallet inside my pillowcase. One morning I woke about eight a.m. and went for my shower by the pool.

When I came back, Dexter was still asleep, but my bed had been made by the room boys. Of course, my wallet was gone from the pillow.

I went to the hotel desk, but they didn't do anything, although I got plenty of concerned looks. Around midday, I went to the Kuta police station and made a report. I was so naive that I assured the policeman that I didn't think the room boys would do it. Ho ho! Nothing came of it except that I had a piece of paper that I could use to claim on my travel insurance. I did make a claim, and the result was... nothing. They wouldn't cover cash, and the rest of it was just a leather wallet, an Amex card, a bank card, and a few pieces of paper. Worthless.

Back at the hotel, I told the bar staff about it, and they asked how much was in the wallet. I told them it was AUD 70.00 and about Rp 490,000 at the time. Their eyes became saucers, jaws dropped! That was a couple of months' wages for them. Yet I could spend AUD 40.00 at the bar in one night. It made me think.

We were lucky because just prior to this trip, Indonesia devalued its currency from 4,000 to 7,000 rupiah to the Australian dollar.

The other incident was both hilariously funny and a bit scary at the same time. We were out exploring Legian, which was just a *kampung* (village) then, riding our bikes along narrow dirt roads.

The road next to a village was separated by a drainage canal containing all sorts of matter, as you know. It became narrower and muddier, and in an effort to avoid the mud, I rode up onto the grass verge next to the canal. I was forced to slow and was losing my balance, so I put my left leg down, and there was nothing there. Over I went, into the muddy water. It wasn't deep, but the villagers and their kids saw me and thought this was a riot. It was, but not so much for me.

I was soon out of the water and back on my bike, but I'd sustained a small scratch on my left ankle. I left it until we got back to the hotel some hours later, and I cleaned it, thinking, *She'll be right, mate.* The next morning, my left leg was inflamed and burning, and I felt a bulbous swelling in my left groin. Uh-oh.

I asked about a doctor and was recommended to a Western doctor who practiced at the Oberoi in Legian. There was nothing for it but to hop on the bike and find him. It was just straight-up Legian Road in those days—keep going and hope to reach your destination. No GPS, no mobile phones.

Sure enough, the Oberoi was easily found (I remember it being in a coconut grove), and I was able to see the doctor. He prescribed an antibiotic, but I had to find an *apotek* (pharmacy) to get it. It was two days until we were scheduled to fly home, and I was feeling pretty sick and anxious. There was nothing to worry about, though—it all healed up in the end.

Another strong memory is from the '80 trip. We decided one night that we wanted good satay and so on someone's recommendation, and probably a bit full of bravado, rode to Denpasar to get it.

Having eaten well, we headed back to Kuta along a narrow road in the dark. I got separated, and suddenly the bike started sputtering and stopped. Uh-oh. I was probably standing there wondering what to do, when a Balinese guy on his motorcycle pulled up. He diagnosed "no fuel syndrome" and indicated I should get on the back of his bike. He took me to a service station and told the attendant I needed a fuel can. He filled it up, I paid, and he took me back to my bike. He filled it for me, and I'm sure I thanked him profusely. I'm sure I also gave him some money in gratitude, but being a bit the worse for wear, I can't remember that bit. But what a great thing for him to do.

My next trip was solo, in 1986, when I stayed at the Puri Dalem Hotel on Jalan Hang Tuah, Sanur. It's still there, on the landward side of the bypass and close enough to the beach that I could walk down there at dawn to see Gunung Agung appear through the mist.

The hotel was quite traditional with bungalows and woven-mat walls. I remember reading just before going that raspberry cordial was a good water purifier, so I took a big bottle or two and added vodka for good measure.

Once again, I rented a motorbike and took off; still, no helmet needed. The traffic was nowhere near as bad as it is now.

I remember walking down Jl. Danau Tamblingan from the north (although I didn't know where I was then) and buying a painting in a small shop. Dammit, I didn't really want it, but I got into a haggling match and couldn't walk away. That boring painting sat rolled up in my cupboard at home for the next twenty years before I finally ditched it. It wasn't much—maybe AUD 15.00, but you know what it was like, trying to resist the sellers.

The next trip was in 1989 (three-year intervals, for some reason) when I went with a friend to Bali as the starting point for a trip through Java, east to west, by public transport. We stayed at a hotel near the airport, maybe the Kartika Plaza, for a few days while arranging our bus tickets. The hotel put on dance performances in the foyer.

We caught a bus from Kuta that took us to Gilimanuk and then on to the ferry to Banyuwangi, and that's a whole new story detailed in my book *Java, the Other Side of Bali*.

MY ADVICE FOR THE BALI VISITOR ───────────────────

It can be amusing to read the menus in restaurants and signs with their quaint misspellings: "Chicken Gordon Blue" (Cordon Bleu), "Wrestling" (Riesling), "curry-gency" (currency), for example.

The Motorcycle Accident in Bali

MARK JOHNSON

Mark Johnson has been a collector, dealer, and researcher of Asian tribal art and culture since the mid-1970s. He has traveled to many remote areas of Asia, including Afghanistan, the northwest frontier of Pakistan, Nagaland (Burma), Mindanao (Philippines), and Borneo (Malaysia/Indonesia). He recently published a book on Borneo art: The Kayanic Tradition, Kayanic Dayak Art from Borneo, Volume I: Guardian Sculptures. *Volume II is due for publication by the end of 2020. Johnson is a native of Southern California and currently lives in Los Angeles.*

SPRING 1980

After a long evening of socializing in Kuta Beach with a group of expats that I randomly fell in with, I talked a young woman from England into coming back to my rented house in Seminyak. I offered her my helmet, but she declined and I put it back on my head. We hopped on my motorcycle and headed down the road. At that time, the area west of Kuta was mostly unoccupied by the shops, restaurants, and bars that you see today. A long stretch between Legian and Seminyak was essentially dark and deserted.

En route, we were involved in an accident. I never saw what happened, and my last memory was seeing a lone horse cart with a single candle for illumination. My next memory was waking up in the hospital in Denpasar, lying on a gurney with my knee broken, skin torn open, and bones exposed. In the room, I recall seeing a body of a young Indonesian man on another gurney, the young woman from England sitting nearby, and my travel partner and roommate, Mark Griffith, as well as a doctor and other medical staff.

Based on others' recollections of the events, a couple of Australian tourists had been walking along the road and observed the accident. They reported that a second motorcycle with a driver and rider (no helmets) and no headlight, was racing down the road from the other direction. It seemed that rider approached the horse cart from behind, then suddenly swerved to avoid a collision, but unfortunately, it put him in direct line of impact with me—more specifically, my right knee, which was sticking out from the right side of the motorcycle. This would explain why I never saw the other rider—because he had no headlight and came around from behind the horse cart too quickly for me to register his approach.

According to these Australian tourists, the impact threw me off the end of the bike, and I landed on my head. If not for the helmet, I would have likely been killed—or at least more severely injured, with massive head injuries. The young woman was bumped up and off the bike, but landed safely on her bum, suffering virtually no injuries. The driver of the other motorcycle was thrown from his bike, hitting his head, and was killed instantly. His passenger was also thrown but survived, it seemed, with relatively minor injuries.

The two tourists were able to flag down a truck, pile us all in the back, and take us to the hospital. They also took the time to file a police report of the accident before leaving Bali and heading back to Australia. I never found out the names of these two tourists.

The Indonesian owner of the motorcycle I had rented happened by coincidence to ride by the scene of the accident soon afterward, noticed his damaged motorcycle and then rode immediately to the house I rented to notify my friend Mark. This is why he was at the hospital when I regained consciousness.

While I was still semi-awake, the doctor at the hospital told me that their facilities were not able to handle my type of injury and that I would need to leave as soon as possible to get to another larger and more modern hospital. He also noted that he was trained at John Hopkins, and in theory could have performed surgery but had hepatitis and was not able to operate. After that point, I passed out and basically was unconscious for about four or five days.

After a few days of drifting in and out of consciousness, I finally was able to grasp my situation. I was lying in a hospital bed in a community room. I was still wearing the same clothes (shorts and a T-shirt) from the day of the accident. I had not yet been to a toilet, and my bed sheets and clothes were soiled. I hadn't eaten and was suddenly aware of the pain in my knee. The doctor had wrapped my leg in a full cast. Mark had been coming by regularly and was now able to convey the situation to me.

I needed to leave and get to another hospital ASAP. But I was not yet able to do so because I was essentially under arrest because of the death of the young local Indonesian man. The authorities had confiscated my passport, which happened to have been with me, so I couldn't leave without their permission. The police had come by several times to interview me, but I was either already unconscious or passed out while they asked questions. The US consulate officer had also tried to interview me but with the same result.

Later that day I was finally able to talk to the police and give them my story, which frankly didn't amount to much, as I never saw the other motorcycle and could remember almost no details. The consular official confirmed that I would need to go to a hearing or trial for the other driver's death before they could release me to leave the country. He was trying to arrange that as quickly as possible. I was able to eat some food, which at the hospital was a broth with some vegetables. Luckily Mark brought me food and antibiotics (but no pain pills), which were not available at the hospital. The hospital staff finally cleaned my sheets and, to some degree, me.

About nine days after the accident, I had a court date (thanks to the consular official, I presume) and was literally carried into the courtroom on a stretcher, still wearing the same clothes I had worn in the accident, with my leg in a cast and my face bruised. I was assigned a translator, not a defense attorney, and listened while the judge and prosecutor discussed my case. That is when I first heard the Australians' report to the police, which indicated that I was the victim and had not caused the accident. Some other testimony was revealed that this young man had been drinking that evening (not sure where that came from). A relative of the deceased man—an uncle, I believe—testified that the family knew the man was troubled and accepted it was his fault. He declared that they had no problem with my innocence and understood the need for me to leave the country for proper medical care.

Finally, the judge was told that I was in possession of a valid Balinese driver's license. This was a fluke, as I had rented motorcycles many times on previous trips but never bothered with the regulation to have a local license. The vast majority of tourists never follow this rule, and the authorities rarely, if ever, enforced it and were more than willing to accept a bribe if it ever came to light. As a lark, I had decided to do it this time. The judge was quite impressed and found me not guilty without contrary testimony, returned my passport, and allowed me to leave the country.

I was carried back to the hospital and the next day taken to the airport. To digress for a moment, Mark had been in communication with my family back in the US, and it had been arranged for me to get a first-class ticket from Bali, via Singapore, to Los Angeles, as I would need the extra seat due to the leg cast. Originally the airlines had insisted I buy a row of seats and be accompanied by a nurse for the trip home, but that would have cost an insane amount of money. They finally relented and let me go solo in one first-class seat.

I was brought by wheelchair to the airport and flew to Singapore, mostly babbling to anyone who would listen to my story. I was kind of out of it and did a lot of babbling, repeating over and over parts of the events I could recall. I had to spend a night in a hotel in Singapore before catching the next flight to LA. When I got in the room, it was the first time I saw myself in the mirror in about ten days. My face was scratched all over, my hair was a tangled filthy mess, my clothes torn, and I had lost a lot of weight. I couldn't walk with the full leg cast, and every movement sent stabs of intense pain through my knee joint, but I crawled up to the bathtub, filled it with water, and tried to bathe. I dipped my head into the tub, and it immediately went brown from the clumps of dirt that were still in my hair from the day of the accident! I did my best to wash, changed my clothes (finally), and went to bed. The next day, I caught the flight to LA.

On arrival in LA, I was taken to my home in Laguna Beach. Arrangements were made to see a knee specialist at Hoag Hospital in Newport Beach the next day. By the time I was in a modern hospital, it had been fourteen days since the accident. The doctor removed the cast, which had been plastered to my leg with no bandages in between. The area around my knee was swollen and full of green pus.

The doctor was aghast, to say the least, and told me that the infection was so bad, he would likely have to amputate from just above the knee! I freaked out and begged him to come up with another solution. His only alternative was to put me on a major regimen of antibiotics for a full week, hoping that would kill the infection.

After a week, it did (barely), and he operated, mostly to remove the broken pieces of kneecap and put things back together as best as possible. The intent was to save the leg and get me healthy again, assuming that I would return in a few months for a second operation to replace the kneecap and restore as much mobility as possible. However, I was not insured, and basically, I had to spend every last bit of money I had to cover this part. I did get insurance after this accident, but, with this as a preexisting condition, I was never able to afford the second part of the operation.

Some interesting insights: I did not own a motorcycle helmet. An American acquaintance living in Bali at the time (nicknamed Easy) saw me that morning and, for reasons that are not clear to anyone, insisted I borrow and wear his helmet that day. I did wear it all day and even offered it to the young lady I was taking back to my house in Seminyak.

She declined, and I still had it on during the accident. Had Easy not loaned me his helmet or if the young woman had taken it from me, I would have almost certainly died from head injuries, as it was reported that I landed hard on my head and the helmet was knocked off and flew fifty feet into the bush. At the very least, I would have had severe head injuries. I ran into Easy in Bali about twenty-five years after the accident (he had moved away and was living in India for most of the time in between) and he did not recall loaning me the helmet or why he would have done so. Mysterious forces were at work that day.

The local man who had rented me the motorcycle knew the family of the deceased. I did not know that until much later, but it was he who convinced the family to send a representative (the uncle) to the court proceedings, who told the judge to allow me to leave quickly to get proper medical care. This part was extremely fortunate for me. In some circumstances, especially if the family is Hindu (and most Balinese are), they may have demanded that the court fine me heavily or try to extort money from me to help cover the funeral expenses, even if it was not my fault. Another bit of luck for me was this family was Muslim, and they had already quickly buried the young man in a simple ceremony (as is customary in Islam).

I also had a lot of support, not all known to me at the time. Besides having my good friend Mark on hand, who provided food and medicine that the hospital was not capable of, he coordinated with my family in the US to arrange for the flight out of Bali to LA. He also worked with the consular official to communicate with my family and the airlines. Without his help, this situation could have been much worse. In addition, some savvy friends in the US, who heard about the accident, had decided to plan for the worse. It would not have been unheard of for me to be found guilty or have some problem with the family or other red-tape issues that could have kept me in Bali for longer than my health would have allowed. It was clear I needed to get out ASAP and get to a good hospital. They had actually hired a pilot and extraction team to fly from Darwin, Australia, directly to Bali, pull me out of the hospital, and spirit me away back to Darwin so I could get safe medical care in time.

Because the court decision went my way and I was allowed to leave immediately afterward, that plan was scuttled at the last minute.

Finally, I had some bizarre experiences in the hospital. At one point, the man who had survived riding on the other motorcycle, and was also in the same hospital, came over to chat with me and express his regret. He was all messed up and had some severe injuries to his face, including swelling that made him look monstrous to me in my half comatose state.

In the bed a few feet away from me was a young boy who had been severely burned in a cooking fire. I happened to be awake and watched as his mother came to see him for the first time. She freaked out and, in a desperate move—I assume to put him out of his misery—jumped on his bed and tried to strangle him to death. A couple of nurses were nearby and leaped on her back and pulled her off her son before she could harm him. I later saw her being interviewed by the police but never found out what happened to her or the boy (he was taken away to another part of the hospital after the incident).

Medically, I was never able to go back for the final surgery that would have possibly corrected the injury. Forty years later, I am still missing a kneecap on my right leg and walk with a slight limp. I have problems going up and down stairs and can no longer do any kind of sport that would require quickness and agility. I continue to suffer from neck and lower back injuries, but I have learned to live with it. It took more than a year for me to be able to walk and drive normally (relatively speaking).

About a year and a half after the accident, I decided it was time to return to Bali and get back to business. I certainly needed to get back on the horse, so to speak. I'll admit I was kind of nervous about returning to the "scene of the crime," as I just didn't know what was going to happen once I got back there. I had also decided I should avoid motorcycles for a while.

I arrived in Bali, checked into a hotel in the Kuta area, and walked out onto the street. Literally, within seconds, I heard someone call out my name! Running up the street was the man who had rented me the ill-fated motorcycle. "Mr. Mark, Mr. Mark, I am so happy to see you!

I have a big problem since you left, and we need to go to the house of the dead boy right now!"

As it turned out, because this man had negotiated with the family to have a representative (the uncle) come to the courthouse, that family had assumed he was working more or less as an official go-between. Although the family had not requested a settlement in court over the death of their son and knew it was not my fault, they still expected some kind of ritual compensation. A small cash payment would have been acceptable, a 100,000 rupiah note (about USD 60.00 at that time). The family believed that he had received this compensation from me before I left Bali after the accident and, for some reason, did not give it to them. There had been bad blood between these two families since that time over this disputed USD 60.00. He needed me to go see the family, make sure they knew he had never been given this money, and then pay them this amount to end the dispute. Interesting to note, as it seems so easy to do this in the West, that in a year and a half, this man could not come up with USD 60.00 on his own to solve this problem.

So within an hour of arriving in Bali, I was on the back of a motorcycle driving out to the home of the dead boy's family (near Denpasar). We arrived unannounced at the family home, and I was introduced to the father, mother, and siblings of the man killed in the accident. My Indonesian was okay in those days, and I could follow most of the conversation but often needed an intermediary to translate the details. I told them that I had no idea about the compensation and was only aware of it once I arrived. I thanked them for helping me at the courthouse and told them how sorry I was over the death of their son. I then pulled out the 100,000 rupiah note and gave it to the father. Everyone started crying and hugging, and it all seemed good.

Then, just as we were wrapping things up, the mother suddenly declared that I was going to be adopted by the family as their new son to take the place of their deceased child! I hardly knew what to say, and frankly, I was so out of sorts from the whole experience I quickly agreed, exchanged contact info, had more hugs, and then we left again, on motorcycle, back to my hotel.

I did stay in touch with the family via mail for a few years until the father died. I was sent a letter from a "cousin" with a photo of "Pak" lying on a bed with the family praying around his body. After that I decided that was enough and never contacted them again, nor have I ever visited with the family the times I was back in Bali.

There was very little good that came out of this experience other than a good story, but with one possible exception. In a mystical way, this accident may have given me some edge in doing the business of buying and selling ritual objects from Indonesia. Traditionally, ritual objects were sanctified, often with a blood sacrifice—perhaps by killing a chicken or pig (in the old days, that may have been a slave). When removing these objects for sale, it is not uncommon for villagers to perform another ritual sacrifice or bloodletting to de-sanctify the piece so it can be spiritually removed. I feel that my accident was a blanket blood sacrifice to the ancestral spirits of Indonesia, thus giving me some leeway and protection when bringing out these artifacts. In fact, I have had very few problems over the forty years since this accident, and I do have the feeling that I have been protected as I went about my business, either with the luck of finding good objects or the ability to get them out and safely to the US.

MY ADVICE FOR THE BALI VISITOR

When I first traveled to Asia in the mid-1970s, Bali was on my list of places to visit. As I worked my way down the Malay Peninsula from Thailand to Singapore, other travelers constantly told me that Bali was already ruined by tourism and had lost all of its charm. Well, I went anyway, and of course, it was a magical place, and an island that I returned to regularly for decades to come. It still is a magical island, and ignore those who will tell you that it was better "in the good old days." Go anyway and find your own magic.

Reeling Back the Years

DIANNE VINCENT

Dianne Vincent lives in Balmain, Sydney, Australia. She worked at the Australian Broadcasting Corporation, the CPSU (the trade union for the public sector) and other Australian Government agencies. Now retired, she loves travel, yoga, bike-riding, film, museums and galleries. She and her husband have an adult daughter who loves Bali too.

For almost forty years, I return again and again. This is how it all begins—my Bali longing.

"Hello, madam. What your program today? Where you going? Where your husband?" It's my first morning in Bali, my first in an Asian country, and only my second time out of Australia. I'm a small-town girl but soon learned this is how conversations start in Bali.

We arrived late in the darkness the night before. It's been a rough ride from the airport dropping other tourists along the way in dusty Kuta, the bus wrenching itself up narrow dirt tracks, to private little places protected from view by carved stone entrances and lush gardens.

And then to our small family-run hotel in genteel old world Sanur, with bungalows up to the beach. The heat and the tropical dampness descend like a cloak as we step from the bus. The huge frangipani trees with pink flowers are a wonder. The bougainvillea and the hibiscus on another scale. The elegant Dutch colonial furniture, all hand-carved, is new to me, and I can't wait to see it in daylight. Stone sculptures of Hindu deities line the path to our bungalow. Insects hum, and frogs croak all along the way. But best of all is the stillness and the sound of the sea at night.

On waking, I peek through the curtains. Yes, it's all still there from the night before but now saturated in golden light. There are roosters making a racket and strange birds singing, not in the raucous way of Australian birds but with restraint.

We eat tropical fruits for breakfast in a bamboo pavilion, open at the sides but wide enough to protect from a downpour, attended by dignified older waiters in traditional Balinese dress. They are patient and worldly and adept at handling the demands of guests, whatever their nationality or personality.

Two elderly *gamelan* players, one of whom is blind, sit cross-legged on the floor, gently playing in the background. Our waiter points out a couple of geckos on the bungalow ceiling, explaining it's good luck if they make their distinctive "gecko" sound seven times. He tells us not to be alarmed if we see any of these sweet and entertaining creatures in our room.

Although it's only our first day, a wiry older gentleman, the marketing manager, convinces us to attend the "semi-compulsory" gala dinner that night. It's an extravagant buffet with watermelons carved as demons, complete with a *Legong* performance. Later I discover that when he's not organizing gala dinners or socializing with guests, he's often sound asleep, sitting upright in his car in front of the hotel. Whenever he sees me he calls out, "I like your skin. It's like milk." To which I respond, "I like *your* skin. It's like coffee!" He tells me he had a holiday in Sydney once but will never return, as it was far too cold, even in summer.

Night came heavily and early in those days, when there were hardly any cars or motorbikes and little lighting. The days roll by blissfully— we swim and explore on a motorbike in the tropical sun. We have two weeks, and we quickly feel we never want to leave. Without noticing, we adapt to the Balinese way of going with the light—early to bed, early to rise. Up in time to observe the soothing ritual of early morning sweeping. In the Balinese way, it is more a meditation than a chore.

We eat club sandwiches with strange bread for lunch on the beach. There's not much Western food, with Kentucky *Ayam Goreng* (fried chicken) one of the only fast-food places around. We decide we prefer the local dishes of *sate* perfectly smoked over hot coals on the beach and *ikan pepes*—fish marinated in a spicy paste wrapped in banana leaves— washed down with Bintang beer or *arak* (traditional alcoholic beverage).

There is little wine, and no minibars unless you are in an expensive hotel, so my husband had packed a Rosemount Traminer Riesling from home to satisfy any cravings. Using an old wire coat hanger, he cunningly hooks it up to the air conditioner to cool.

I'm getting used to Balinese whimsy and the unexpected poetic observations from strangers. By the time a young man lounging in the street calls out to me, "You have a beautiful frangipani behind your ear. It is a symbol of your respect" to the great amusement of his friends, I burst out laughing too.

A Bali smell follows us everywhere on our road trips and attaches itself to our belongings. Months later, we open our suitcases to a nostalgic blast—a not unpleasant mix of incense, coconut oil, and other mystery ingredients, possibly Gudang Garam, the ubiquitous clove cigarettes.

On one of our day trips, we head down to Nusa Dua and find nothing there except for a magnificent beach, three young boys eager to practice English, and a sign announcing a major new development.

Leaving at dawn one day for the long trip to Kintamani, we arrive early at Murni's Warung, next to the Tjampuhan bridge in Ubud, then on just one level. It is one of the few places open for breakfast in this quiet village, and we relish our first taste of black rice pudding looking out over the dramatic ravine. On we go via Bangli's terraced rice paddies with the back roads to ourselves all the way, the peace shattered only by children rushing out of their houses yelling "hello!" at the top of their lungs when they see us coming. Returning at dusk with thousands of insects buzzing around our faces, we pass the local *banjar* (village council) and hear the magical gamelan orchestra in rehearsal.

On these trips, we are in awe of the skill and creativity we see in everyday life. We learn that the Balinese are all artists in some way—carvers of wood or stone, painters, jewelry makers, dancers, musicians, gardeners, or flower arrangers. We make slow progress, stopping and starting whenever something catches our eye, from exquisite offerings to the gods to traditional carved doors.

Back then, my favorite holiday outfit was a pink playsuit, which was cool and comfortable in the heat. I didn't give a thought to appropriate attire or cultural sensitivities—or helmets or sunblock. Like so many tourists before me, I ended up with the inevitable burn on the leg from the exhaust pipe of the motorbike.

Almost forty years later, more sedately dressed, I'm still returning. Still getting that Bali longing. Still needing my Bali fix, as there is nowhere else in the world with the same artistry, beauty, and charming people. These days as we wander around, we are no longer offered the "honeymoon" price but a "second honeymoon" price. I take off to yoga and language classes, perhaps the Ubud Readers and Writers Festival next time, with other femmes d'une certain âge.

On our most recent trip, Kadek, the daughter of our old friend Made from the village of Peliatan, near Ubud, comes to collect us. Always beaming, she is laughing almost hysterically when we meet her, introducing a young man from her village with whom she has grown up. He is at once shy, excited, and amused to be collecting tourists from the airport. She teases him that he is an *anak kampung*—just a simple village child—who hasn't even been to the airport! He takes it all in good spirits.

At twenty-one, Kadek has scraped up enough money from driving to fly to Singapore, against her parents' wishes. She is a multilingual dynamo who has the usual Balinese mastery of all things craft and practical. Like other young Balinese who make a living using the world's latest apps, she has left the world of the anak kampung far behind, as I have too. But it is in Bali that I feel most like my youthful self.

MY ADVICE FOR THE BALI VISITOR ───────────

Dine at the elegant beachfront restaurant at the Tandjung Sari Hotel in Sanur, established in 1962. Soak up the glamorous history of one of Bali's first boutique hotels. Marvel at the spectacular gorge setting of Murni's Warung, one of Ubud's first restaurants.

A Magic Child

MARGRIT HELDSTAB

Margrit Heldstab was born in Zürich, Switzerland. She visited Bali for the first time in 1980 and was immediately fascinated by the Balinese culture and its people. She's grateful to return to Bali twice a year for two months for her jewelry business, which enables her to visit her Balinese family and learn Bahasa.

Once upon a time in Bali, in 1980, when the dogs still were lying on the streets at night and when we still could enjoy the way between Seminyak and Kerobokan by bicycle, there were a few memories that stayed with me.

One night my security guard was sleeping soundly in his *pos* (station) outside my house while it was raining cats and dogs. A flood was approaching through the rice fields toward my house. I woke him up in a panic with the question, "What shall we do if it continues to pour like this and we can't escape?" He answered casually as if nothing was happening: "*Mudah-mudahan tidak*," which means "Hopefully not."

Another time my Balinese friends were drinking beer while waiting for me at my house, while I went to play cards in the house of my Balinese family. When I returned and asked them if they had been drinking, they lied and said they hadn't drunk (even though I could smell it). After a long discussion with my friend Nengah, who was an expert in Balinese tradition and etiquette, I understood that in Bali, it is not polite to enjoy yourself before the host of the party arrives and that it is always better to tell a lie than to be impolite.

In those days, my Balinese "sister" Nyoman suffered from a few miscarriages, usually in her third trimester. It had happened again, and I was sad and felt sorry for her. I asked my Balinese friends what would happen if she never could have children. They said that her husband could have a second wife, or they could take a child from a sister or brother who already had many children. As I couldn't have children myself, I was quite bewildered by this answer.

Before I returned back to my homeland, Switzerland, I told Nyoman encouragingly, "When I come back to Bali in four months, you will have a big stomach. I will meditate and pray for this!" As Nyoman is a "believer," she probably was not as stressed as in previous times, but, amazingly, when I came back, she was pregnant.

I brought her from Europe a Body Shop cream that was supposed to be good for the belly's skin, but Nyoman was convinced that the cream helped her to keep the child. When I said that this was only an ordinary cream, she answered, "No, no! I gave it to other women who had the same problem, and they kept their baby too!"

Well, the Balinese might call it magic.

In our world, we call it a placebo.

When Nyoman's little girl was born, she put the baby in my arms and told me, "This is also your daughter!" She named her Iluh.

I felt humbled and overjoyed with this heartfelt gesture.

This feeling of parenthood my partner Martin and I have still today. Iluh is already a mother herself and is working after her studies in a five-star hotel in Bali. She has visited us in Switzerland three times. Our magical child!

MY ADVICE FOR THE BALI VISITOR ——————————

I suggest being open to the friendly Balinese people. Travel to the east of the island. There you can find "Bali asli," which means the "original" or "true" Bali.

Down the Rum Jungle Road

ATTA MELVIN

Atta Melvin is a former stewardess for United Airlines, which gave her a love of travel. She has lived in and often worked as a volunteer in Nepal, Mexico, and Bali, Indonesia, where she resides today. She has also lived in Osho's ashram in Pune, India, worked on the commercial fishing boat Salty Dog *out of Sausalito, and performed in many theatrical productions with the Theatre FireFly in Bali. She is an active adventurer and even spent time in a women's prison in Australia. She loves life!*

Back up to 1980, I returned to Bali to fill an order of rayon jersey shirts in Sannyas colors for Osho's Commune and fell more and more in love with this magical island. Now, electricity was being installed, and roads were being paved. Westerners were moving in with their ideas of not yet luxury but creature comforts, buying small refrigerators and better than kapok mattresses. Motorbikes were becoming the norm, but still, mostly *bemos* (public transport vans) got us around. Binters were big. They were 145 Kawasaki's with leg guards and *the* thing to be seen on, for men and macho women (which we all were, in our twenties). The best features on those Binters were the electric starters. I drove a Honda GL PRO, a bit smaller, but a really nice bike, sadly with no electric starter. Kick-starting that thing for many years surely contributed to me needing a hip replacement.

Because I knew the language, I found work as an agent for garment producers who returned to their countries and needed me to check on orders and ship them. The agreement I had with my husband about our son was that he would spend summers with me in Bali. Somehow, he never spent more than three weeks with me.

"Oh, he wants to go to Space Camp," I was told. Or, "We are coming too, and he will return with us after two weeks." There was a lot of heartache for me around this. I would design my whole year around these visits. I would save up USD 2000.00 and invest in the latest hip clothes from the talented designers of the day. I'd send it as accompanied baggage, clear it on the other end in America, put it in the trunk of my old car, and go around selling to the trendy boutiques in San Francisco.

Many stores were happy to buy ready stock. I would turn my USD 2000.00 into USD 6000.00, buy my son and myself round-trip tickets to Bali, and still have USD 3000.00 to make a rental contract for my thatched-roof house for the year. This worked nicely for several years.

In the eighties, we had no TVs or videos. We had to make our own entertainment. We were becoming a fun community of surfers and groovers from all over the world. The hippie trail in those days was Bali, Ibiza, and Goa, following the seasons, and some of us stayed in Bali all year. The beach in front of Blue Ocean is where we met every day. Guys and girls wore only G-strings, and no one cared. We played paddleball and Frisbee all day long. Local women sold us massages and fruit. There were no umbrellas or lounge chairs.

Here on the beach is where we found out where the party was, or who was going to which of the two discos. We smoked a lot of dope and we danced a lot. Often we had costume parties. We loved those! The best ones were held at Nicholas's house, or Tabetha's or Double Six. I remember the themes: "Dress as Fruits and Vegetables," "Jungle Fever," "Red" parties, "Lust in Space," and "Dress as the Opposite Sex" were just some of them.

We also had many performances. Having no other entertainment, we held our own shows at the disco Double Six. Dance teachers, like Lasensua or Fantuzzi, would come to town and collect us dancers to learn and rehearse some calypso or African dance number. Then we would make our own costumes and perform for everyone on Saturday night, just for the fun of it! Some other shows we did were *The History of the World in Five Acts*, with an erupting volcano, and *After the Holocaust*, with our costumes made from" junk," and my nine-year-old son riding on tall Rodney's shoulders in the end as the New Hope.

House parties were big, and no one ever bothered us then—except the police did bust us for erupting the volcano with "fountain" fireworks. The house was too close to the Kayu Aya Hotel, so they called the police. A lot of us were on acid that night and didn't care because we had finished our show, and it was just so much fun!

Jane Fonda had introduced aerobics to the world, and it reached us in Bali. We girls would gather at someone's house and sweat away. We moved on to use the disco spaces at sunset for our aerobics. We did these things just for fun. No one thought to charge for these classes. Later, though, I was hired by the Hyatt Hotel in Sanur to teach twice a week for USD 50.00. After a year, it was "Aqua Aerobics with Atta," which was more fun because the husbands would join in at the pool, which is really where vacationing people wanted to be.

Another fun night was "Bali Mock Stars 1987." We all chose who we wanted to be, rehearsed and costumed, made a banner and put it on the side of the bus, and went to Made's Warung and the other nightspots and performed, lip-synching. We were Tina Turner, Madonna, Whitney Houston, Kiss, Rickie Lee Jones, Robert Plant, and a few more. The crowd loved it as much as we did! Leo was behind that one and the many "Girls' Night Out" events we organized. On Thursdays, we would dress up and visit the pubs with themes like "Aussie Girls' Night Out," "Pregnant Girls' Night Out," and "Lingerie and Dangerous." They were mad and hilarious!

MY ADVICE FOR THE BALI VISITOR ─────────────────

Go to Amed for a nice getaway and stay at Good Karma Bungalows where the legendary Baba is still laughing and joking. It's right on the beach, with great snorkeling out front.

The Island That Changed My Life

PATRICIA CHAPARRO

Patricia Chaparro is an artist born in Bogota, Colombia. She has tra-veled throughout her life and lived in Italy, France, and Indonesia and now currently resides in Asheville, North Carolina, USA. Her work is a fascinating amalgamation of South American, Asian, and European cultures and is especially inspired by her many years living in Bali, Indonesia. Her paintings have been exhibited and appreciated around the globe, from cites in the United States to Brazil, Colombia, and Indonesia.

It was 1981 when I came to Bali for the first time.

I was living in Paris, married to a very nice Parisian guy. I was twenty-six years old—an age when you question yourself about existence. I was the wife of a well-to-do man, but I felt I was a nobody and was lost.

I needed to change my life, so I decided to make a trip overseas to find myself. I didn't know where in the world to choose my future destination.

I went to a travel agency in Paris. The lady at the counter handed me a world map. I said to myself that I would go wherever my finger landed on the map. I closed my eyes and moved my finger around the paper, then stopped.

Bali! At that moment it was not very clear to me where this island was. I bought the whole package: a ticket together with accommodation in a five-star hotel in Sanur. After leaving Paris and transiting in Abu Dhabi, Bangkok, Singapore, and Jakarta, finally, I arrived in Denpasar.

Everything was so dark. I arrived late in the evening, so I couldn't see the beauty surrounding me outside.

There was no electricity on the island yet, only in my hotel in Sanur. I was not too impressed with the hotel. It could have been any hotel on Miami Beach. So, the day after, I took a *bemo*, the local transport at that time.

As I looked around me from inside the bemo, I was mesmerized with the sights I saw—the beautiful Balinese in their colorful sarongs, and the rice fields were so green!

Eventually, I arrived at Kuta Beach. I lay down on the sand, looking at all the surfers catching waves, soaking in my new environment. Suddenly a Balinese guy approached me and asked me if I wanted him to show me Bali. He seemed charming enough, so I accepted the offer.

After a long afternoon of sightseeing, later that night he took me to a typical Balinese restaurant that was known to serve psychedelic mushrooms in their meals. He asked for two soups. He only consumed half his bowl. Me, being very naïve, ate my whole bowl of soup.

While we were walking on the streets of Kuta for some time, this crazy feeling started to come over me. The mushrooms were kicking in. Everything seemed to be coming at me in full force. The Garuda statues, the Asiatic faces, nature, even the incense smells were driving me crazy, and it was too much for me to handle.

Trying to escape, I took a taxi to my five-star hotel. Yet even being in safe surroundings in my room was a nightmare. I couldn't stop hallucinating, and I was desperate for some kind of normalcy to return. I wanted this trip to stop!

I called the front desk and told them I needed a doctor. A few minutes later, the doctor knocked on my door. He raised his eyebrows with a look that said, "Another stupid tourist." He obviously had encountered other tourists who experiment with mushrooms for the first time. He gave me an injection that put me to sleep for the next twenty-four hours.

That was my first day in Bali. Everything that had happened was so disorientating that my first reaction was to go back to Paris to my husband and son, to my safe and comfortable surroundings. I did all the procedures to change my ticket, and after so many phone calls with the airline company, I was rescheduled to leave in two days. I decided to go to Kuta to buy last-minute souvenirs to take back to my family.

While I was in a small *toko* or shop, suddenly a beautiful longhaired Venezuelan walked in, smiled at me, and said "*Oye catira de donde eres?*" He told me his name was Jack. I was so happy to hear a familiar voice. After chitchatting for a few minutes, explaining to him about my situation, he said to me, "You can't leave Bali without knowing it. Come, let me show you."

Jack seated me on the back of his motorcycle and took me to Seminyak. After traveling the small back roads and sandy lanes, we arrived at a restaurant on the beach called Blue Ocean. There I saw a different kind of crowd, the most beautiful people amid an atmosphere of freedom. The hippie vibe seduced me immediately. It was a place that felt like home. I could relax. Everyone I met felt like family, without even knowing them. I started to feel at ease, especially through the Balinese masseuse whose loving hands helped me to surrender to where I was.

That day, I met Perry, a guy from NY who loved traveling to India and Ibiza to collect original ethnic objects. I also met Razame, an eccentric taxi driver also from New York, and Regina, a beautiful German lady. And also Maria, a Brazilian woman married to John, another amazing and creative guy who worked in New York with Vidal Sassoon. All these free people lived a life in great contrast to my bourgeois life in Paris.

So I finally understood the reason I came to Bali.

I called my husband and told him that I was going to stay the forty-five days I'd originally planned.

I didn't know that was the beginning of my nine-year Bali experience.

MY ADVICE FOR THE BALI VISITOR ———————————

Go to any small beach warungs *in Southern Bali and ask for 'Bulung' (Seaweed and Coconut Salad). This delicious dish is usually made adding peanuts and chili.*

Pulau Dewata – Island of the Gods

HELENA DARSANA

Helena Darsana was born in Melbourne, Australia. She moved to Bali with her mother in 1980, married a Balinese from Ubud in 1996, took on Indonesian citizenship the same year, gave birth to her daughter in 1998, and still lives in Bali to this present day.

Bali is my home. Living almost forty years on this magical tropical island, I could not imagine having spent my existence anywhere else. I have ticked the most valued boxes. I married a Balinese man, took on Indonesian citizenship, and mothered a beautiful daughter. I have had the most incredible time here, and, as this book of chronicles displays, the decade of the '80s was definitely the most exceptional, colorful, and lively period to mention.

I first arrived here in January 1980 to visit my mother. My mother had been coming to Bali since the '70s. My brothers were here exploring the islands of awe and had encouraged Mum to come over and see the exotic archipelago of Indonesia. My mother, being such a high-spirited adventurer, naturally fell in love with the island of the gods—Bali. She then made a monumental life-changing decision and decided to uproot her life in Australia, come to Indonesia, and purchase some land out of town from Kuta Beach, through the rice fields, down a small dirt road, and close to a deserted beach.

She then planned the building of a very beautifully designed lo-
cal-style "boutique hotel" with thatched roofing, bamboo *bedeg* walls,
open-style garden bathrooms, and spectacular gardens, fish ponds, and a
huge swimming pool, adding her own creative influences.

It was a very well-known hallmark on the island, as was my mother with her large colorful personality and her tremendous love of the
people and life on the island. Although life then was so interesting and
novel, it was also very challenging, especially for Mum, an older Western
woman, to be living and finding a foothold in what was then still a very
undeveloped, rather primitive place in many ways. However, with her
tenacious character, she forged ahead to create a fascinating and alluring
lifestyle for herself here in Bali.

Those were definitely the best years for her; life was abundant in joy,
laughter, love of the Balinese people, and the manifestation of a dream
in building an idyllic tropical haven of accommodation for travelers and
friends alike.

Unfortunately and very sadly, it all came to an abrupt end. Just four
years into the making, enduring many obstacles, hard work, and mile-
stones, the beautiful property she had created was shattered and burnt to
the ground in one deranged night. Within an instant, my mother's life
changed... yet nothing would ever burn out her zest for life and her love
of people around her. She went on and tried her best to keep life going
on here in her beloved Bali, but it was never to be the same again after
that fateful night when she lost everything.

This is an acknowledgment to you, Mum. You were definitely one of
the pioneers in Bali to have encouraged others to come and experience
this fascinating, exotic island. In just one short story, here is a minuet
minute of countless adventures of early Bali days: trekking dirt roads on
motorbikes, savoring the Balinese foods, learning of the mystical traditions, dancing in cyclones at full moon parties, and psychedelic trips on
the broad white sandy beaches, watching mesmerizing sunsets...

Ahh, Bali was a life's education within itself.

This is a memoir in honor of Bali and the outstanding beauty she
holds to this day and to my mother for being the amazing person she

was. Full of such fortitude in the search for a stupendous, exhilarating life, she brought all those she loved around her to also share in some of her fun-filled journey.

Thank you, Mum. If it wasn't for you, I may never have come here at all. I may never have known there was a very different path of life for me, here in my home in Bali, the Island of the Gods.

MY ADVICE FOR THE BALI VISITOR ————————————————

Go to Menjangan Island, north of Lovina, for beautiful snorkeling.

Mushrooms
and Mountains

MICHAEL DIFFENDERFFER

*Michael Diffenderffer has been an entrepreneur all his life, ran his own
contracting and trading business in Saudi Arabia, sailed on a teakwood sail-
boat from Bali to Australia, motorcycled from Saudi Arabia to Switzerland,
recorded Tibetan music in India for Nonesuch Records, owned a champion
race horse in England, developed real estate in Europe, was CEO of a cargo
airline in Hawaii, dabbled in making ethanol out of garbage in NYC, and
sold mass-produced oleo-graphed paintings all over Europe. He currently
lives in Underhill Center, Vermont, with his beautiful wife Emily, two
daughters and son, in a restored 1840s farmhouse on the river. They are soon
opening a cafe and co-op workspace.*

The first time I went to Bali in the early '80s was when a friend that
I knew in Saudi Arabia (where I was living at the time) told me I would
enjoy spending some time there. He told me to look up a friend of his
named Jean Salundra, who had a Mexican restaurant called TJ's in Kuta
Beach. I became friends with her and her son. They called me "Big Bird"
because of my funny hair and tall, hunching posture.

I stayed a couple of months and loved the beautiful terraced rice
paddies and mountains surrounded by surf-able golden beaches. Happy
and creative people lived simply and joyfully in the midst of rampant vi-
brancy, ethos, and culture that clanged through your heart by the sound

of *gamelans* (a xylophone-like instrument that the Balinese people play) everywhere you went. Everyone seemed to be celebrating of all aspects of life. The Balinese were always making offerings to literally everything that existed under the sun and all the drama that comes with it. Art was a way of life for all Balinese.

There was also a lot of partying going on of the Western genre. One night I was at a party at the beach, and a girl I had never met lent me her motorcycle and told me to go to Norm's Restaurant and order a magic mushroom milkshake. They had small, medium, or large sizes. When asked what size I wanted, I replied, "I will have a double large."

The man behind the counter replied, "OK, President Reagan."

Within moments after drinking it, I was overcome with extreme laughter. My journey back to the beach on the motorcycle was miraculously successful and included a stop at a nightclub where I was literally hanging upside down from the ceiling rafters, still laughing hysterically. By the time I got back to the beach party, most people had moved on, and I was having trouble forming an intelligible word. I left the motorcycle there, where I hoped the owner would find it and tried to make it back to Poppies Cottages, where I was staying.

I was lying on the bed thinking, *This will wear off sooner or later,* when a huge barong-like dragon head as big as the ceiling with fangs came out of the ceiling and snarled inches from my face. Needless to say, the journey continued with an exit stage left, where I met a good Samaritan on the beach who invited me to smoke a few joints and come back from the nether. Daybreak found me lying with a woman who had aggressively pursued me with an invitation to come and lie down at her house. She requested I take off all my clothes; it was more than obvious that her brother was trying to steal my wallet. I think my calm attitude, smile, and taunting laughter scared them out of it. I probably looked like Jack Nicholson in *The Shining.*

I remember staying with someone named Lilian, who made leather belts in Legian. When it was time to go back to Saudi a couple of months later, I realized I had lost my passport at her house. Bali did not want me to leave, and the feeling was mutual.

VOLUME I • PART IV

I vowed to go back to Saudi and shake some money out of that place, then come back to live in Bali.

I succeeded in my quest and found a niche in Saudi, where I employed four hundred people that I paid in cash out of a suitcase every two weeks. I also won USD 100,000.00 on a horse race in England. So with all of that tucked away with the Swiss bankers, I arrived back in Bali to live forever... or so I thought.

After spending some time with my girlfriend for a few months, she had to leave and go back to work in England. I stayed on in Bali and discovered more of the freedom to be the unabashed lust puppet I was.

I explored so many beautiful things, like learning the Baris warrior dance from an old man named Kompiang in Ubud. I met an artist named Symon who said he had a friend named Brad who would let me build a house on his land on the beach in Legian for USD 3,000.00. He had a couple of his guys build a simple structure with two silkscreened wings and a triangular tower in the middle that you could swing up into via monkey bars. Brad arrived one day not knowing a thing about it but did not seem to mind that I had built a house on his land. We later became partners in the land, which was located between American and Australian neighbors named Dem, Nicholas, Roger, and Sandy. Brad was a gold smuggler in Hong Kong and later landed in jail for a few years in Belgium for smuggling hash from Amsterdam all over Europe. So I did not see much of him in Bali after that. One of the things he turned me on to was mountain biking, and one of his friends brought me a stump-jumper.

One of the times Brad was in Bali, I convinced him that I was sure there was a trail going along the ridge down the other side of Mount Abang, which is across from the volcano bordering Lake Batur. I had been up there before and had noticed what looked like a trail going down the other side. Brad and I hiked up there one afternoon with our mountain bikes. I tied a sarong around the middle bar and carried my bike hanging from my head. When we got up there, we found the trail that I thought would take us down the ridge, but it ended in dense brush after a few hundred yards.

A huge violent storm appeared out of nowhere. It got very dark, and we climbed back up the ridge to the top, leaving our bikes in the brush. Our teeth were chattering with the cold, and we were soaked to the bone. We repositioned a little temple that was at the top to try to take shelter from the wind. It didn't do much of anything to relieve what was soon becoming hypothermia.

By this time, pitch-black night had arrived. We decided to slide down the trail in the mud just by feeling our way down because we couldn't see. After a couple of hours, the rain stopped, and we had made it a few hundred yards down the muddy trail. Brad had a paperback book and some matches in his backpack. We managed to light the book on fire and lie in the ditch curled around it, which brought some temporary warmth, and we spooned as best as non-gay males can do until sunrise. We walked back to the summit and went down the other side and got our bikes, took them back up to the top, and slid down the steep muddy trail for hours until the trail flattened out enough to ride down the last part. We had mud and scrapes all over us, and it had almost been worth the experience to see the expressions of some people who were hanging out by the trailhead. They must've wondered, what type of people are these that jump down mountains on bikes? For a moment, we looked like warriors instead of the fools we were.

There are so many other tales to tell of mountains, waterfalls, mystic kung fu experiences, sailing adventures, and a not-so-happy ending to my time in Bali when I mistakenly believed that my kung fu sense could help my mentally ill sister with Chinese medicine. Maybe I'll save those stories for another time.

The four years I spent in Bali were a rich chapter in my life that I will always be thankful for.

MY ADVICE FOR THE BALI VISITOR ——————————

Climb up Mt. Agung on a full moon night and stay up there and watch the sunrise. While you are at the top, try singing a favorite song at the top of your lungs and listen for the echo.

The Winged Messenger

RACHEL LOVELOCK

Rachel Lovelock is a freelance writer originally from England. When she first visited Bali in 1982, the island's magic captured her heart, but it wasn't until 1998 that she returned and knew within five days that she wanted to stay. Bali has been her full-time home ever since.

I first became aware of the winged messenger when I visited Bali in 1982. He is a prominent figure in the ancient Hindu culture, and his name is Garuda. Believed to represent the sun's rays, he is the devourer of serpents and the king of birds; books describe him as "mythological." Legendary, yes. Fabulous, yes. But this guy is no myth in my book. Half-human and half-bird, he is the vehicle-mount of the god Vishnu and the "go-between" between the worlds. What a great name for an airline. I always used to think it was a special compliment to the tiny Hindu island of Bali that the Republic of Indonesia chose Garuda as its national emblem as well as naming its flag-carrier airline after this character. Actually, the symbolism goes back way before the invention of jet engines, to the sixteenth century, when Islam first arrived in Indonesia and adopted some of the traditional ornaments for its own use.

It was probably because I flew to Bali with Garuda Airlines that my interest was first aroused all those years ago. I remember seeing wooden statues and stone carvings of the mystical Garuda perched on a pedestal, and later when I returned to England, I wished that I had purchased some memento of him to take home with me.

Ten months later, while browsing through the Oxfam Christmas gift catalog, full of handicrafts from Bali, India, Thailand, and South America, I saw him again. I could have sworn he flew out of the page at me. Mail-order Christmas gifts for my friends forgotten; I just knew that I had to have the hand-carved wooden Garuda mask. The price was only five pounds, but somehow it was so important to me, I would have paid a lot more.

Well, two weeks later he arrived. No, he didn't fly; he just landed on my doorstep, packed soundly in shredded paper and polystyrene chips in a large cardboard box delivered by Parcel Express. I hung him up in my hallway, where there was an imposing archway, positioning him in the center on the apex. All my visitors noticed him as soon as they stepped into my house with his long beak, prominent pink tongue, sharp teeth, big ears, and bulging eyes.

"Arghh. What's that?" people used to ask.

"Oh, that's Garuda." I would reply. "He's from Bali. He's a protector, and he brings good luck."

After a particularly difficult period in my life, one of my friends commented, "Well, he didn't bring you much luck, did he?" At the time I did wonder, but now I believe he helped me through the hard times and gave me the strength to prepare for what was coming next. I believe the winged messenger between the worlds—in my case, the contrasting worlds of England and Bali—had a plan for me. He didn't want me to stagnate in a small town in England. Instead, he wanted to take me back home to Bali with him so that I would have the opportunity to embrace some of the many alternatives that this life has to offer.

It took the winged messenger many years to deliver his message—to coax and cajole me, convince and prepare me, but after that, it was easy. Allow me to explain.

The set of circumstances leading up to my new life was unprecedented. I had always wanted to live and work overseas, but the time had never been right, and then suddenly, the time was just so very, very right;

everything was pointing to and leading me in a very precise direction. I knew I wanted to travel, but I had no plans to sell my house, and then abruptly, it seemed to be the most obvious way forward. I had to sever my ties—no point in doing it halfheartedly. I had to be fully committed, but I still had no idea where I wanted to go.

Yet, following a series of bizarre "coincidences," everything just very simply slotted into place. I received an unanticipated offer of a "golden handshake" from my longstanding job. I sold my house, despite pessimistic predictions from the estate agents about its lack of marketability. I received a couple of unexpected telephone calls. I got swept up in a great wave of unyielding energy, jumped at an unsubstantiated offer of work, and found myself bound for a faraway tropical island.

I had put all my furniture, and Garuda, into storage. So in the end, he didn't come with me; instead, he sent me on ahead of him, alone. I left my mystical, magical guardian in a storage warehouse, but I never forgot him. I was poignantly reminded of him nearly every day in Bali; Garuda was all around me.

A year later, I returned to England to sell my furniture. Although my flimsy job hadn't proved to be fruitful, I had no doubts that I wanted to stay and live in Bali. I carefully retrieved Garuda from his cardboard box in the warehouse, and together we flew back to our island abode.

Inferior jobs gave way to something good, and my new life in my new world came together. My protector has long held pride of place in my Balinese house; my visitors notice him as soon as they walk in, but nobody squeals, "Arghh. What's that?" His face is far too familiar here and, for me, an enduring reminder of how Bali came to be my home.

MY ADVICE FOR THE BALI VISITOR ————————————

Visit Negara in West Bali to catch the Makepung bull races, which take place every other Sunday morning from August to November. Each race comprises two pairs of Bali's most handsome water buffaloes festooned with silks and strings of bells, running against each other at speeds of up to sixty kilometers per hour along an erratic two kilometer track. Thrilling, spectacular, and highly entertaining with a distinct lack of tourists and safety measures.

It Was a Sunday Morning

SALLY HERRERO

Sally Herrero grew up on the mid-north coast of NSW, Australia. An avid traveler, over the years, Sally has enjoyed paella in Spain, walked the stairs of the Eiffel Tower, island-hopped through Thailand, cooked a tagine in Morocco, and received a rice blessing in a Balinese ceremony from a village priest. Not even a terrible bout of food poisoning and a hair-raising plane ride on a twenty-seat aircraft has dampened her enthusiasm for traveling. She resides in a coastal abode, and her bottles of sand from the many beaches she has trekked take pride in her living room.

It was a Sunday morning, November 1982. I was having a sleep-in after a night out with friends.

My friend came over and woke me up with a piece of the Sunday travel section of the newspaper advertising "Bali Sunset Club"—one week's accommodation, return flights, two meals a day for AUD 450.00.

"Come on, Sal! Let's go!"

I was eighteen, but my parents allowed me to go as my friend was also my distant cousin. We had grown up together. He would look after me.

The next thing I knew, Anthony and I were on the Garuda bird to Denpasar. We had no travel insurance, no credit card, no mobile phone, and AUD 400.00 spending money between us.

Our accommodation was Agung Cottages on Jalan Legian.

Made showed us to our room, which featured two single beds with a pillow and sheet and a wardrobe door that fell off when I opened it. The bathroom had sky-blue tiles floor to ceiling, a toilet with ladle flush, and a shower comprising a piece of hose sticking out of the wall above a cold-water tap.

Paradise!

We had communal breakfast and dinners at the club headquarters on big, long tables set parallel under a leaky roof. The lemon juice was the best in Kuta. We picked out the *semut* (ants) from the jam and scraped it on our tapioca toast.

Nightly dinner was usually a communal BBQ served on plastic plates and garlic bread that you could smell from afar. We all sat together, sharing our daily adventures. Dogs chased cats under the tables, and arms and legs flew everywhere like a Mexican wave as the barking and the screeching meow wafted through the club.

Two nights a week, we ventured to Maxi's Disco. Motorbikes streamed down the narrow gang to an open-air dance floor with a long bar set against one wall. Unisex toilets with very small doors and no lock gave plenty of entertainment as I struggled to keep my newly purchased AUD 3.00 tie-dyed jumpsuit away from the wet floor.

Every Thursday night, the Sunset Club crew would head over to the Bali Hyatt Disco in Sanur. My first experience there was great fun till we had to settle our bar bill. We thought the drinks were the same price everywhere—they weren't—and my travel buddy and I had the biggest argument about how we were going to pay. Then a doctor from Denmark who was staying at the Hyatt intervened and insisted on paying our bill. I wanted to return the next day and pay him back, but he refused my offer as the entertainment factor of our argument was worth it. On the way back to Kuta, our *bemo* (public transportation minivan) ran out of petrol. Never has running out of petrol on the side of a dirt road with a bunch of new friends been so much fun.

One day, we caught the local bemo to Denpasar and promptly got lost and didn't find our way back till late that night. We lazed on Kuta Beach, baked ourselves brown, had AUD 1.00 massages, ate freshly cut pineapple, and drank bottles of Coke with the glass etched from being refilled again and again.

Plastic bottles were rare. A thermos of pre-boiled and cooled water was placed outside our door each morning.

The food was simple: scrambled eggs for breakfast, and the Aussies shared their Vegemite toast. *Nasi goreng* (fried rice) and jaffles were on every menu, along with frogs' legs in various sauces and the occasional veal "Gordon" bleu!

My first visit to Bali was short, but it was amazing.

I met Balinese friends that are still my special friends to this day— some thirty-eight years later!

Bali has given me some incredible holiday memories, but it has also taught me many things.

Bali taught me that you don't have to have material things to be rich in happiness.

It has taught me to appreciate nature, think of others as well as myself, and respect tradition and elders.

I have returned many times, but I would turn back the clock to the early '80s in Bali if I could. There is something about that time that stays with me.

I am so thankful that I experienced that time.

Terima kasih, Bali... selalu! (Thank you, Bali... forever!)

MY ADVICE FOR THE BALI VISITOR ————————————————

Wrap a sarong around your waist and a sash. Place an offering at a temple... close your eyes and give thanks for where you are and what you are experiencing. It's a simple act that will stay with you always.

Parallel Paradise

DORIS CAITAK

Doris Caitak was born in Montreal, Canada. She believes that every life is a canvas each person creates day by day. She has lived in New York City, Italy, Java, and Bali. She met her Italian husband in Bali. Together they opened a series of successful boutiques on the Emerald Coast of Sardinia, Italy where she and her husband imported exotic decorative furnishings for the villas of movies stars and other VIPs. In the cottage industry of Bali, they also produced clothing, jewelry, shoes, and other various accessories for these same VIPs. She has one daughter and lives in a home in Florida designed by her late husband.

Gently she places the flower offering on the statue, accompanied by her hand's subtle, graceful dance-like gesture. She has paid tribute to the gods so that harmony illusively floats through the air.

Stretching out of bed, I fold open the mosquito net, then wrap my sarong around me. I stare momentarily at the thatched roof, whose woven waves have a rhythm of their own. Languid, lazy, feeling the heat of the day, I move. Luca is still sleeping, his long perfect form entangled in fine cotton sheets.

I shower under a brilliant sky, in a bathroom with no roof, with walls made of dark-burgundy coral.

Relaxed and unhurried, I allow the day to envelop me as I walk through the kitchen and smile at Jero. She smiles back, knowing, accepting, sharing, and happy. There is no deception in her eyes. She is who she is, and I am who I am. We both understand, welcome, and cherish the synchronous relationship that we have.

Jero has been there for an hour or so, preparing, cleaning, making sure that harmony reigns.

She asks what I would like for breakfast: French toast, an omelet, or a smoothie? The choice is vast, considering that there was little or no electricity five years ago, and the Balinese were just learning what our tribe liked to eat.

When we arrived, we were happy to taste the exotic daily treats offered by food stands, street vendors, homes, and simple inns. We knew we were in the legendary Spice Islands. We partook with gusto the delicious foods and all manner of flavors, spices, and smells. We have no problem eating with our hands off of banana leaves, squatting near the food stand. Nor do we have any problem eating the freshly caught fish with the fishermen that brought in this morning's haul, sitting on a bench made of a wooden plank, drinking hot, sweet, thickened tea.

Jero brings me my smoothie: homemade yogurt blended with fresh mango and banana. I am sitting at the dining table on the outdoor porch, overlooking a fertile yard—the best way to contemplate the creation of a new day. I hear Luca come down. I see the broad smile Jero has for him. "Mr. Luca, *selamat pagi*! (Good morning!)" He is her favorite. They cook together and often trade jokes. He also asks for a smoothie, and a fresh one is served up, with a smile.

Luca and I are not married. He comes every two to three months from Italy.

We are starting to create a life together. Jero, a mother of three—who married in Balinese style, with a ceremony that celebrates love while affirming the blessings of the gods—looks upon us not as sinners but as two people in love. She sees the love.

Ketut walks in from the office that is just in the building around the bend. He too is smiling and relaxed. There is no shame interrupting our breakfast, as we sit naked underneath our sarongs, with questions about work. His spiritual fabric accepts who we are, how we are, and what we are, in relation to who he is, what he is, and how he is. "*Selamat pagi! Selamat makan* (bon appétit)." He smiles. I know his wife, and in the near future, I will know his children.

Luca and I—and in the future our child, Michela—will be invited to significant religious ceremonies by both Ketut and Jero, for we are members of an extended universal family. We all weave our lives together, and the integrity of the cloth depends on all of us.

We are the seekers, the artists, the craftsmen, the traders. We are members of a tribe that has come from all over this floating globe thirsty for the spiritual beauty that is Bali. They allow us to share their island, knowing that we will not bring disharmony to it. We dance under the moon and stars, we salute the sunset with our pagan joints, we commune with pristine sands, walking miles in a god's costume.

We share in the knowledge that in this space and time we have melded our universes, acknowledged the beauty of the other, reveled in the wonderment of our differences, and seen the splendor of our similarities.

MY ADVICE FOR THE BALI VISITOR

TAKE THE TIME! The Balinese are special. They are happy, playful, and proud. Get to know at least one Balinese person, and you will know more about the island than any tour book can tell you.

Bamboo
and Flute

LUCINDA COX

Lucinda Cox is Anglo-Australian. It's been Lucinda's destiny (or possibly aim) to live somewhat on the fringes, where she likes to observe, discover, and study the connectedness of all life through enquiry, art, music, literature, and geography. She has allowed her various "hobbies" to dominate her time—dismaying some and enchanting others.

As had been my pattern for many years, I once again found myself broke, this time on Bali Island, where I was to spend the next two weeks. I was unable to have my ticket changed to come home early, so with the little money I had, I prepaid a room with breakfast in a bottom-rung concrete hotel at the back of Kuta.

One night, after nine days of heat and boredom, I suddenly remembered meditation. It was late in the fully tiled cubical room where I stayed. I prepared myself, lying down with my body relaxed and straight on my back on the floor, with my arms bent at right angles at the elbow, hands in the air.

This innovation allows me to meditate without danger of falling asleep. If I nod off, my arms fall and wake me up before they hit the floor.

It took me quite a few minutes to "tune in" and "call in the Light," as I was quite out of practice, but soon after I was able to be still. My thoughts as usual drifted here and there, but my intention to return to the awareness of breath was grounded, and I became deeply relaxed in a timeless state of meditation.

After quite some time—who can say how long? — I became aware, on the outer edge of my consciousness, of some very beautiful, faint though distinct music reaching me from far away. I had a definite sense of the direction from which it came. That very day, earlier on, I had walked randomly in the area behind the hotel, and I was sure the music was coming from that direction.

I lowered my arms and rose slowly, as if in a trance, not losing my meditative state. I quietly and deliberately dressed and gently left my room. Even though it was late, the hotel attendant was awake. He confirmed my impression of the direction of the music but warned me there was no light, and I would not find my way back. I was confident, however, that I would both find the source of the music and make my way back with no trouble.

My sarong, wrapped around me in Balinese style, ensured that I moved quietly and slowly with small steps, and so, as I proceeded, my ears became finely tuned. As I had anticipated, the competing sounds of the night sometimes completely overshadowed the delicate sounds of the music, and at times only trust kept me heading on the right track. The path was, in fact, the very path I'd trodden earlier that day, but this time I went deeper into the Balinese territory that in the daytime I had avoided.

Slowly, I came closer and closer, the beautiful music compelling me to approach. The track wound through coconut palms, between huts and shelters, through lanes and alleys. I passed a few Balinese people chattering, candlelight reflecting off their smiling white teeth. As I was nearing the source of the music, suddenly I rounded a bend in the track. Through the branches and playing lights here and there, I saw the musicians. They were still quite far off and very obscured by foreground objects and foliage. I could only see two people who happened to be standing in a doorway, which was within my range of vision. I stood, rooted to the spot, trying to discern the instruments, but I could not. Only the rhythmic movement of their hands silhouetted in the doorway light showed me that they were actually the people playing the music.

Every now and then, there was the sound of a deep gong, and all sound would cease—silence ensuing. Then laughter and Balinese voices splashed brightly into the night air, and again the music would start. This pattern repeated several times.

From where I stood, I could see an old man sleeping in the shadows on a porch. A very cautious cat came slinking out of the darkness, not wanting to be seen, and in the candlelight of a nearby hut, a Balinese washed his hands, sloshing water from a bucket. Eventually, my curiosity and desire to see the musicians and their instruments pushed me out into the electric light radiating from a building ahead. Slowly, step by step, I moved closer, exchanging nods with some old men drinking coffee, who were sitting on the porch of a small shop, while asking them with my body, in silence, "Is it OK? Can I come here?" Their response seemed to be affirmative, so I continued walking slowly past them, where now, in full view, were the musicians.

They sat within a low wall that enclosed an ancient garden, with a raised, open-fronted building about three or four feet above the ground. They were all male. The beautifully intricate ascending and descending music was all around, filling the night with fruity melodies and feather-soft harmonies. I watched and listened in rapture. The clear night vibrated with the sound of insects and buzzed with a calm joy.

Suddenly, someone grabbed my elbow from behind. It was an old Balinese woman. She was pulling me, gesturing, and seemed to be saying that I couldn't watch and led me back to her shop, where she sat me down. I couldn't understand what she said because at that time I only knew a few simple greetings and numbers in Balinese. It seemed from her enthusiasm about my looks that maybe she liked white skin. Then, out of her skirt pocket, she produced a flat, crushed foil parcel whose contents were soon revealed as talcum powder. This she rubbed vigorously on her face and chest. She seemed to approve wholeheartedly of my sarong, denim jacket, and cigarette lighter, but my hair, long and loose, was a problem, which she soon solved by putting it into a ponytail with one of the "*bagus*" elastics she had around her wrist.

Having dressed me appropriately and demonstrated our kinship, she tired and left, and soon after the music stopped too. After saying good night to the coffee drinkers, I headed back to my hotel. I had no trouble finding my way back through the coconut palms and narrow alleyways. It was a beautiful, clear night. All who passed me were friendly and expressed some surprise at seeing a tourist out at night in this area. When I got back to my room, I could hear the boys in the next room slapping themselves, trying to squash mosquitoes. I went in and gave them a mosquito coil and went back to my room. The fact that my Balinese boyfriend hadn't shown up was not really surprising. I slept long and soundly and awoke to the sound of rain.

MY ADVICE FOR THE BALI VISITOR

Try street food, especially nasi goreng *(fried rice). It has never been matched in any restaurant anywhere since. Sometimes I dream of it and would go back to Bali for that alone!*

A Celebrity Guest –
What a Surprise!

PETER DITTMAR

Peter Dittmar is an artist who taught art for fifteen years in Munich, Germany, after which he lived and worked as a freelance artist in Bali, Indonesia. He has had more than one hundred solo exhibitions in thirteen countries and has taken part in international art fairs. His art has been sought by many private and public collections, including the renowned ARMA Museum in Ubud, Bali.

After an invitation from the Goethe Institute, the cultural body of the German government, to teach at the Academy of Arts in Jakarta, my first wife, Jheel, and I traveled with our four-year-old daughter, Vivian, to Bali, destination Ubud. In Ubud I gave a workshop at one of Neka Museum's spaces for my students, who had never been to Bali before. I had started to live in Bali as a freelance artist in 1982 the year before, coming from Munich where I had been teaching art for fifteen years.

We rented Sean Foley's house on the Sayan ridge for six months. The house was, at that time, one of the most interesting ones in design, using traditional materials like woven bamboo and coconut columns. The layout was contemporary, and the views of the Ayung River were breathtaking. It gave us the feeling of living in paradise. On the Sayan ridge were not many private houses at that time. By 2020, the Sayan and Kedewatan ridges had become very well-known and popular, including many five-star resorts like the Amandari, the Four Seasons, and Mandapa (Ritz Carlton). There wasn't a big group of expats of my age group living in Ubud at that time either: Alexander Goetz with his wife, Rebecca, sister Carmen, and their kids; John Hardy and his first wife, Penny Burton; Linda Garland with husband, Amir; Rabik, an Indonesian from Madura; and Made Wijaya.

One Sunday afternoon, we had invited Linda and Amir for coffee and a homemade fruit pie. There was no bakery in Ubud at that time. When the friends arrived, there were four other people besides Linda and Amir—all very interesting people. One of them was a Japanese man who'd come with his girlfriend. The other two were a woman from Geneva and a guy named David. I noticed that he was very interested in painting and led him to the studio and also to our bedroom on the upper floor, where we talked about my work and the art of painting for a long time. After more than two hours we said goodbye and were happy about the visit, which was truly inspiring. We were proud of our house.

The next morning I went to Ubud and met Linda again, who had brought the guests to us. She asked me if I knew who it was visiting us yesterday with whom I had the long conversation about art. I said I had no idea. Then, to my almost shocking amazement, Linda said it was David Bowie with his friends and his assistant Coko Schwab.

David obviously refreshingly enjoyed that I hadn't known who he was and was happy to have such a carefree conversation about art. He then invited us for dinner at the Tandjung Sari Hotel, where he was staying, and a few days later, we went together to a trance performance at the court of the prince of Kerambitan.

We had never experienced anything like this, and if I had not been there myself, I would never have believed what we saw. This was a full moon ceremony with a *Rangda* (a demon witch), and some Balinese went into a trance. The incredible thing was that a participant of the ceremony attacked a bare-chested participant at a distance of about twenty-five meters, holding a large dagger. The attacker ran full speed to the man and tried to stab his bare breast with the dagger, but the weapon ricocheted. We were all sitting no more than ten meters away from the performance, so we could see everything close up. There was no trick. We were incredibly impressed, actually shocked, and at the same time enchanted by everything we saw.

I am so thankful that I have been able to spend thirty-seven years in Bali and get the inspiration for creating all my artwork to present at more than a hundred solo exhibitions in thirteen countries and art fairs. I am most thankful to Agung Rai, my first collector in Bali, who bought major pieces for his ARMA Museum, and my friend Tony Raka, who runs a high-quality gallery in Mas south of Ubud.

Altogether, Bali, with its people and ceremonies, and our wonderful staff—Wayan Lastri, Wayan Weni, and Pak Chandra—have made our lives very rich and special.

MY ADVICE FOR THE BALI VISITOR

Escape the south and stay at the idyllic "Cilik's Beach Garden" in Air Saneh/ Singaraja, including great food and service!

Nyoman,
Our Angel

MARIE LASOURCE

Marie Lasource was born in Marseille, France. She has traveled the world as a photographer and lived in Bali for thirty-seven years. She has two daughters that travel around the world also, and both are divers. Today she lives a peaceful life on the island of Gili Meno in Java, which reminds her of Bali in the old days, and feels connected with the cosmos.

In November 1983, my eight-month-old daughter, Julia, fell seriously ill. When I got home, I found her burning with fever, over forty degrees Celsius, and vomiting continuously. Her skin was red, and she was very dehydrated. I was only twenty-two at the time, and Bali had only one hospital, Sanglah, located in Denpasar.

We went to see three different local doctors (thanks to Thora's car). These doctors gave me three different diagnoses, so I decided to take the advice of my Chinese business associate, who told me to leave immediately to Singapore for a more professional diagnosis. He suggested taking Julia to Gleneagles Chinese Hospital.

At the time there were very few expat babies, yet Julia was well known to the small community that we formed. I felt very supported by my friends, and they helped to organize my departure as quickly as possible, as Julia was rapidly dehydrating.

I arrived just before midnight at Singapore Airport with my unconscious baby in my arms. I had to take a taxi to go to this hospital. It was my first time in Singapore, so I didn't know anything about this city.

On arrival at the hospital, it seemed to me very empty. There was a reception area but no nurse—no one except the night porter, who I asked about seeing a doctor. He told me that at this hour of the night there was no doctor and that I should come back tomorrow. So, I found myself completely lost, in this large corridor with my unconscious baby, crying all the tears I had in me.

During this time in Bali, a miracle was happening.

My pembantu (housemaid), Nyoman Artini, who became my karmic sister, searched through my belongings and found my travel insurance contract. She was twenty-one years old and didn't speak English and, of course, not French either. At that time in Bali, the only phone we had access to was at a small booth at the airport handled by a local operator. Calls had to be placed through to an operator in Jakarta, and sometimes it would take hours to reach the party one was calling. Despite all these complications, Nyoman managed to call my insurance company in France and explain to them (and I still to this day wonder how she tackled that) that my daughter was very ill and that we had flown to the Gleneagles Chinese Hospital in Singapore.

In the meantime, I was crying in this big hospital corridor, when the hospital telephone rang. The porter answered, and a few moments later, he came to me asking my name and saying that the phone call was for me, to my astonishment.

On the phone, a French man asked me if all was well. Of course, I told him the whole story and that Julia was in a critical condition. He told me not to move and that an ambulance would arrive in five minutes to pick us up. He then hung up.

To this day, I don't yet know what Nyoman did, and I wonder how this doctor from my insurance company knew we were there.

The ambulance arrived very quickly, and ten minutes later, we were at the American hospital and were immediately taken care of. The doctors told me that Julia had an amoebic infection. They said she was more than sixty percent dehydrated and that if we had spent the night waiting, she would have probably have died overnight.

Julia was in a coma for seven days. A week later, she had become a bouncing, sparkling, healthy baby again. She had been saved.

When we came back to Bali, the community came to check on us every day. The owners of Made's Warung restaurant sent Julia large bottles of fresh carrot juice mixed with rice water to drink. She was daily becoming stronger and stronger.

I will never forget that it was because of Nyoman that my daughter is alive today. I will never forget all the support I had from my friends who showed up for us then. Every time I look at my daughter, who now is thirty-seven years old, all the emotions of that time are still present inside of me.

Thirty-seven years later, I thank you all from the bottom of my heart once again.

Nyoman became Julia's second mom, and now we are one family. Nyoman's children are my children, and my children are her children. The magic of Bali is always present between us. I am eternally grateful for her help.

MY ADVICE FOR THE BALI VISITOR ──────────────────

Go to Pura Luhur Batukaru Temple, located in the village of Wongaya Gede, Penebel Sub-District, Tabanan Regency.

Learning More
Than Carving Wood

ALISSA STERN

Alissa Stern was born in New York and is the founder of BASAbali, a collaboration of artists, writers, environmentalists, and language advocates who aim to keep the cultural, linguistic, and physical environment of Bali strong. Alissa and her husband live outside of Washington, DC, and just became empty-nesters after having raised three wonderful boys.

Every morning, I'd go to his house and take a seat at a wooden table in his outdoor pavilion. A young boy would bring me coffee, at the same time sweet and bitter, with a little plastic conical cover to keep out the mosquitoes. Ida Bagus Putu Raka ("Pak Putu") would come out a few minutes later, in a short-sleeve button-down shirt with a pack of clove cigarettes and mechanical pencil in his breast pocket, sit down across from me, smile, and unroll his set of chisels. Silently, we would begin.

It was 1983, and I was in Batuan, Bali, for one month of a six-country yearlong study-abroad program. Since 1958, the International Honors Program has been giving American college students an opportunity to experience social, political, and environmental issues from the perspective of societies around the world. In my year, the theme was the transition from colonialism to tourism. In Indonesia, we were placed in the temple compound in Batuan, Bali, with one light bulb shared between the sixteen of us.

Each morning I would go to Pak Putu's house. I would learn to carve three-dimensional panels, with the idea that by learning from an expert carver, I would get some glimmer of understanding of how panel carvings were evolving from the Dutch occupation to modern tourism. It was a project for a Ph.D. thesis, but we had only a few weeks, so, if nothing else, I'd get to learn how to carve.

The first thing I learned was not carving, but how to respond to the three questions I was always asked by locals on my way to the woodcarver: "Where are you going?" "Where are you from?" and "Are you married yet?" I soon realized that the importance of the questions was not the answers but the interaction itself, like responding "fine" to an American cashier at a fast-food restaurant who asks, "How are you?" while ringing up the bill, not really expecting to hear about anyone's well-being but enjoying the chitchat.

The second thing I learned was that there was no way I would be able to learn Balinese, the local language—or even the easier national Indonesian language—in only a few weeks. I was going to have to learn as much as possible from Pak Putu without using words.

Each time we sat down together, it was roughly the same: Pak Putu sorted through his set of twenty or so chisels without breaking the impressively long fingernail on his pinkie finger. He'd choose a chisel and, with a mallet in the other hand, demonstrate how that particular chisel carved wood in a particular way. He'd hand me the chisel; I'd inevitably break one of the delicate leaves or even more delicate intertwining branches. Pak Putu would patiently take out his pencil and redirected the branches to camouflage my clumsiness and would demonstrate again. After two weeks, I was able to carve a single three-dimensional well-shaped leaf.

Practice was over. With only a few weeks, there was no time to spare. Out came a large block of suar wood, which I later learned comes from the Albizia saman tree, a plantation tree brought to Indonesia by nineteenth-century colonialists. With a few quick strokes, Pak Putu drew Saraswati, the Balinese goddess of knowledge. I had a feeling the Saraswati I was going to be able to carve would look nothing like the

Saraswati Bapak drew, but he saved me from mangling her by relegating me to carving the leaves in the background. *I could carve leaves*, I thought. *At least, I could carve a leaf.*

It took going to tourist shops to really understand that tourism was unwilling to support, or perhaps was ignorant of, the quality Pak Putu was able to create, settling instead for much simpler two-dimensional pieces than his more intricate carvings.

But what I really learned from Bapak went beyond market forces and tourism, and well beyond patience and perseverance—although there was plenty of that to be gleaned from his pavilion in Batuan. Pak Putu literally showed me how to redirect when facing obstacles, broken branches, and mangled leaves.

And maybe that's one of the many things that Saraswati, the goddess of knowledge, has to teach us all of us, whether we are in Batuan in the '80s or elsewhere in world coping with the 2020 Covid-19 pandemic: the fortitude, power, and resilience of the ability to redirect.

MY ADVICE FOR THE BALI VISITOR ──────────────

Check out old and new Bali photos and more in the 'Places' section of dictionary.basabali.org. Lost Bali Facebook group has sponsored this section and has earned its own shelf.

Bali High

ALEXANDER LEON

Alexander Leon was born in Cuba. Alexander's family moved to Sydney, Australia, via San Salvador, Guatemala, and Melbourne. He has lived in Bali; Austria; the Amazon jungle with shamans; and Sri Lanka, where he ran a post-tsunami charity. He trekked to Everest base camp. He currently resides in New South Wales, Australia, with his wife and second child. Music is his passion.

I do not know about you, but there are only a few times in my life where a feeling, an experience, or a space in time stands out to me so strongly that when I close my eyes, I can feel myself back there.

I had a few of these magical moments on my travels. One was at the end of 1983 in Bali, and the band Yes had just released their eleventh studio album *90125*.

It was my second time in Bali. The first time we had departed from Kingsford Smith airport was in December 1980 from Sydney on a world tour. We had tickets for seventeen destinations, and our first stop was Bali. My friend Laurie and I traveled all the way through Asia up to Nepal, where we went trekking. We got about five hundred meters from base camp on Mt. Everest, when altitude sickness first got me and then Laurie, and so that trip ended in Nepal. We never got to use most of the tickets, but that again is another story.

Anyway—back to Bali and our second trip.

I had become friendly with Agus at Mahogany in Legian. Agus was one of the bunch of five or six Bali boys whom we used to call the "Bali Cowboys." They were all good-looking and had long hair, and were always popular with the women. I would frequently go there to have a yarn and a laugh with him, while sampling all the new releases of music that could always be found. Of course, the shop always had one or two pretty women in there.

One day I fell in love with a particular song called "Owner of a Lonely Heart."

To my mind, this song was revolutionary, changing the direction of rock 'n' roll.

Interestingly, over the years, numerous people, from Michael Jackson to Frank Zappa have sampled it. Needless to say, I bought the cassette.

One sunny morning Laurie and I hopped on our motorcycles and headed up into the mountains toward Ubud, which in those days was a one-dusty-road village. Armed with our Walkman's hooked onto our belts and our favorite cassette tapes to play along the way, the feeling of freedom was overwhelming.

Back in the early '80s, there was still no overload of tourists in Bali, and we shared the road up there with no one.

I distinctly remember it like it was yesterday. Riding up through winding roads past beautiful green rice fields dotted here and there with stands of palm trees, no helmet on with the wind blowing through my hair with my headphones, listening to "Owner of a Lonely Heart" turned up to almost full volume. I would repeat and repeat and repeat it. All the time I was listening, I was in awe of the stabbing guitar sounds, all of these new keyboard sounds, and the way in which they were used.

The feeling of twisting and winding up the mountain, the breeze through my hair, and my favorite song of the moment playing loudly in my ears is a memory, a feeling that has never left me and that will live with me till my final breath.

MY ADVICE FOR THE BALI VISITOR ───────────────────

Leave the major cities and suburbs. The true and authentic beauty of Bali lies further afield—the paths least trodden.

The Blessing

ANTHONY PABLO GENTILE

Anthony Pablo Gentile was born in New York City. Pablo attended the New York School of Visual Arts, where he studied fine arts, graphic design, and 3D design, and studied literature at New York University.

He first came to Bali in 1973 on a trip around the world over land and sea (no planes!) between high school and attending university. When he returned and was asked where the most beautiful place was, he answered without hesitation, "Bali." Those sixteen months on the road were the beginning of more than thirty years of travel to all corners of the earth.

His paintings and sculptures have been widely exhibited and appear in collections worldwide. He currently divides his time between studios in New York City, Stockholm, and Bali.

Nobody had seen Steve for ages. Seemed strange—he was a regular on our circuit, which meant he could have been anywhere: India, Nepal, Thailand, Ibiza, or the States. During this time, few if any one of us had permanent residences, much less telephones. The Internet hadn't yet been invented. Our pipeline was word of mouth and various Poste drops around the world, yet still, everyone somehow kept in touch.

It seemed strange Steve should miss a season in Bali, where he—as did most of us at that time—produced a small but very high-quality number of handmade garments for European and American customers.

They were highly valued by those in the know and a staple at flea markets from Goa to Ibiza, Amsterdam, and New York. Usually, the foundations were made from antique batik sarongs dating from the 1940s, which were readily available in the marketplaces of Jogjakarta or from the massage ladies who combed the beaches in Bali.

Oddly, right about the time we were wondering where Steve was—as often is the case with people you don't see for a while—he showed up. He appeared at my door in Golden Village with suitcases in his hands around five-thirty p.m. with a new girlfriend, just as we were sitting down for a sunset drink and rollin' one.

"Where have you been?" I asked. "We were just talking about you yesterday."

Steve explained that he was getting a strong sense of déjà vu, so much so he wanted to find out about his past lives, and if he had a past life connection to Bali and decided to see a *mangku* (Balinese high priest) about it. He sought out one of the highest, most ancient and renowned, most powerful of shamans, Pak Jagra of Singaraja, on the northern coast of Bali, about ninety miles from our shack in Seminyak. He was interviewed and instructed by the shaman that should he really want to get in touch with his past lives, he needed to change his ways and go through a strict cleansing ritual that would last a year. The instructions were for him to drop out of all worldly pursuits for a year, no business or travel, and follow a strict regimen of yoga, fasting, and meditation, then come back to see him exactly one year to the day, and the priest could help him.

He had rented a small place in the desert on the outskirts of Taos, New Mexico, and lived accordingly for the last twelve months. These were the first few hours his girlfriend had ever been in Asia, and I thought this trip would be a lot for her to deal with. She seemed to be doing fine.

Steve was one of the more rational of our group, and this kind of stuff surprised me coming from him. A Harvard grad, he did have a few eccentricities. For one thing—although in his mid-thirties and well-traveled, he had somehow never managed to learn how to drive!

He was a little stressed as he related how he messed up his reservations and lost a day in the air, traveling directly from New Mexico to LA. To catch a plane to Singapore and transit through Jakarta to Bali and go directly to my house, he needed to jump in a car and try to make it over the mountains to Singaraja, North Bali, in order to get there on time. They had been traveling for more than twenty-six hours, and they must have been exhausted.

He had to get there before midnight in order to follow the priest's instructions to the letter, and he needed a lift there. I thought this would be interesting, and we agreed to do it, which meant leaving directly.

"Wait till you meet this guy—he turned himself into my dead grandmother!" Steve said as he jumped into the front passenger seat. I rolled my eyes and tried not to smirk—skeptical, to say the least. And off we went, in my open-aired convertible yellow Jeep. We took little more than a toothbrush, a blanket, and a bag of fruit.

Ingele's snow-white Nordic radiance appeared to me as an angel in my rearview mirror. The golden sunset lit her from behind, and she appeared to be surrounded by a glowing halo illuminating the tiny white peach fuzz on her cheeks and golden hair blowing in the breeze. (Now my wife, an angel she remains to me today...)

We sailed over cratered roads devoid of traffic into the late sunset. The mountain shadows softly blended from verdant greens into gradients of ultramarine and ambers. Always breathtaking, from any angle—Bali in the '80s.

We drove past various temples and realized it was a moonless night, and the Balinese were observing the ritual of *Tilem* (black moon). The priest must have calculated this as an auspicious day for their meeting. The road was devoid of traffic, but we were delayed by processions of Balinese going either to or from the countless temples we passed along the way, carrying offerings piled upon their heads, decked out in their ceremonial finest.

Steve popped a cassette into the player, and on auto reverse we listened to unintelligible repetitions of Hindu mantras and bells and gongs for the hours the ride would take us. He sat in the front seat, squeezed into lotus position and tried to meditate as we chugged and lurched along. A look in the rearview mirror revealed our companions. His girlfriend (I just met her once and can't remember her name) was jetlagged and tired. She was falling asleep on Ingele's shoulder, which was close to impossible as we careened over potholes the size of small craters on the moon and lurched and leaned into sharp corners, by now through the cold, dark mountains. I stopped the car and dug out a blanket for them as Ingele rolled her serious eyes with the look of one who had unwillingly gotten herself into an adventure she wasn't ready for when she happened to stop by for a sunset drink.

We caught our breath by the road in the fog and the darkness. There were no streetlights in Bali at that time. Suddenly a family of monkeys appeared. The largest one leaped into our car and grabbed the bag of fruit we had brought along for the trip. The girls screamed. Steve, deeply into his meditation, hadn't stirred. His girlfriend shrieked, and I bumped into the stick and threw the Jeep into gear, into the darkness. We lurched the car and skidded to a halt, coming only a few centimeters from the cliff's edge that would have sent us over the mountain into the blackness and depths below. The frightened monkeys screamed as they jumped away.

We took this to be an omen. "Let's stay focused and slow down," I told myself. Nobody had a watch with them, but we figured we still had a few more hours until our midnight deadline. Onward we drove. Eventually, we cleared the mountains in a series of twisting hairpin turns on the single lane with broken asphalt that served as the main road, leading through the mountains that connected the northern and southern coasts. When we finally reached a lower altitude, the fog, and clouds behind us, we were greeted with a vision of the ocean sparkling below us. It was illuminated by no light other than the thousands of stars out on this moonless night. There, above us in plain view, the constellation Scorpio stood perfectly visible. I stopped again to take this in and for a rest.

Steve finally came to. I couldn't tell if he was sleeping off his jet lag or deeply into his meditation. At least he finally hit the eject button and turned off the mantras. "Where are we?" he said. Below and before us, from our perch in the foothills, was the town of Singaraja. Its few electric lights revealed a couple of Chinese shops, a Chinese temple, a mosque, a Balinese temple, and a gas station—our next destination. We gassed up and found an open shop that sold ice cream bars, then we shot through the town and headed to the village of Lovina. Steve decided that we should rent a couple of rooms by the sea and leave the women there, an idea they gladly went along with.

The next stop was to find the translator. The shaman spoke only Balinese, and our limited knowledge of Bahasa Indonesia would have been useless. We drove through the dark streets until we came to a little house with a faded and cracked powder-blue doorway, barely large enough for my six-foot-tall friend to get through. We had to squat in front of the door and start knocking. It was around eleven-thirty p.m. In Lovina, 1986, the streets were deserted and dark, and from the car, I just realized how odd this call must appear. When the door finally opened, a little man greeted us in perfect English. He seemed to recognize Steve and took our arrival matter-of-factly, not surprised to see us and thought nothing strange about our request. "I've got to see Pak Jagra," he whispered.

There was still one more stop to make before we could get to the shaman's door. We needed offerings. Steve explained that Pak Jagra didn't accept cash for his services, and the translator, his assistant, led us to a tiny warung dimly lit by a flickering oil lamp. The odd thing was they only sold a few basic products but had just what we needed. We stocked up on flowers, incense, bottles of sweet Balinese *brem* wine, chewing gum, and tiger balm. I was suddenly itching all over and found a bottle of talcum powder there. I thought it was strange to find just what I was craving and put it down to coincidence.

The assistant eyed me warily as I proceeded to put the powder all over my skin, which was breaking out in little red bumps everywhere. By the time I reached the door of Pak Jagra's house, I was inflamed with a rash that just sprang up and an accompanying migraine. Maybe it was all the driving or that last *arak madu*, I thought.

Steve broke out a couple of sarongs for us to respectfully put on before entering the pure grounds of his temple complex. We wrapped them over our jeans. "Leave me here. I'll wait in the car. I'm ready to pass out," I protested. The itching became unbearable, and my headache was getting worse by the minute. The assistant shot Steve a sharp and knowing look as they pushed me closer and up the stairs through the narrow temple gates.

The inevitable Bali dogs snarling and howling in the darkness announced our arrival. The compound consisted of a few small family spirit temples and a bunker-like cinderblock building consisting of two rooms and one window. Outside, a few kids were watching a tiny black-and-white TV; battle scenes blared that, with my headache, seemed to be at full volume.

When we entered, there in this stark room sat Pak Jagra, perfectly composed, in front of a small table on which lay a large open book and an oil lamp. The clock on the wall behind him said 11:55! He pointed to the last line on the open page, and there, in bold English writing, was written Steve's name.

"I've been expecting you," he said, with no idea of the distance Steve had come to make this appointment. We piled the offerings on the table. I looked around the room. Nothing special, I thought: empty walls but for a round clock, the kind you might come across in a post office or the office of some government official. A dim and flickering oil lamp illuminated the room. There was only one window with some thin curtains in front of it. The room was airless and stuffy once the door was closed, and the TV was outside in one of the pavilions but sounded as if it was right in there with us. Mosquito coils and sweet incense choked me. Outside the door, chickens squawked and dogs barked in the darkness among the sounds of crickets and frogs. My head was bursting, and I started sweating profusely. Before us stood the most powerful of Balinese white magicians.

He is credited with supernatural powers beyond comprehension, but to my mind didn't really look like much. A small man, dressed immaculately in white, slight of build, bald. He had the unlined face of a newborn baby. His tight skin stretched around his bony open face like a living skull. He stared at us purely and clearly from deep-set eyes with the kind of depth that looked right into your soul, as only one with a foot in both worlds can do. His spotted hands were scaly and wrinkled, and his fingers looked like the legs of a chicken and revealed an undefined age that could have been centuries.

I was still sort of skeptical but found it strange that when he spoke, I understood practically everything he said, better than the useless translator could, and all of the background noise floated off in a vast distance. It was a kind of direct, no chance of misinterpretation, perfect communication. Or was I just imagining this, exhausted from the long ride, or shaken from almost driving off the cliff? I wondered. Exhausted, I drifted off into a half-sleep. My mind went back to New York.

Just ten days ago in New York City, a cold night in a Kennedy Airport parking lot, Cindy and I parted with a kiss. She handed me a list of production notes and things I had to do for our clothing business. She sadly remained behind to mind the office. The last-minute instructions were but a way of not mentioning what was really on our minds.

The last few months, some strange changes had occurred in her. A fashion model who became my business partner and fiancée, she truly represented the left-brain part of the business. Chinese, a sharp business sense, quick with numbers and calculations, her contribution to our business was the perfect complement to my intuitive, creative compulsions.

She was tall and graceful on the runway—a successful fashion model. She was spending more time representing our fashion line than modeling, to build a career and a future together. An empire was born and ruled from the expanses of the freezing five-thousand-square-foot loft that served as our studio, office, shipping room, and home.

But those weren't the changes that worried me. In the passing months she had developed shaky hands, a quick temper, puffy cheeks and hands, and a host of symptoms that interested our family doctor. He recommended a specialist, a friend of his that was researching lymphangiomas, which sounded very scary to us.

Basically, it's a growth on the spleen that usually affects kids but rarely people into their twenties, and rarely seen in someone as healthy as her. "It's not serious," he said to me, lying, as I offered to delay my departure to Bali. Tomorrow she would be starting a series of tests that would get to the bottom of her condition. A tight production schedule had me booked on that flight.

"And for God's sake, drive carefully," she'd warned, referring to the still unhealed broken wrist I brought back from Bali as a souvenir of my last trip, from a motorcycle accident on Jl. Legian.

This floated into my head in my delirium as I sat entranced in the presence of the shaman. He and Steve and the translator spoke for a while, and then they disappeared into the next room. I poked my head in to get a glimpse and was pushed violently out by his assistant. I got a quick look at the second room. The room was dominated by a large altar packed with offerings, ceremonial bells and objects, vessels of holy water from the sacred spring of Tirta Ganga, and clouds of incense. I put up no resistance and fell back into my chair in the next room, by now almost delirious with exhaustion, a migraine, and itchy welts that covered every inch of my sweat-soaked body.

I was nodding off and didn't realize they had eventually reemerged. I was awoken by a gentle nudge by Steve. The translator sat on the floor before me as Steve plopped down in the chair to my right. He looked visibly shaken from this meeting that he had prepared a year for. The priest looked at me and said, "Who is he?" as if aware of me for the first time. I understood immediately. "I'm just the driver," I answered meekly.

He looked at me for a second and held my hand. The headache melted away immediately, and for the first time in hours, the itching stopped. He indicated we needed to meditate together, all of us, as if something big had just transpired in the next room, and we were all part of it.

As I went into the lotus position and attempted to turn my palms upward, he noticed my inability to turn my right wrist due to the motorcycle accident. He stopped us and looked at me deeply. "Tell me about your life!" he demanded. I said everything was going fine, my business was doing well, and I had a beautiful woman I was going to marry. In a flash, he looked at me again and said, "She is very ill." I hadn't told anyone about Cindy in New York and that she had just gotten out of the hospital. It blew my mind.

Now focusing intensely into my unblinking eyes, he asked, "Does she look like this?" and right before our eyes, his face became hers. I was struggling to swallow as Steve nudged me with a look that said, "See, I told you so!" The old man got up, stood straight, and asked, "Does she walk like this?" and this mad little old man gracefully and elegantly proceeded to do what I called the "Cindy Shuffle"—her signature strut I had seen on the fashion runways and catwalks of New York, Paris, and Milan.

I found myself fighting back tears and shortness of breath. With that, he grabbed my wrist, held it outstretched, and proceeded to furiously rub his palms together. When he built up the desired amount of friction, he held them over my broken wrist, and the heat they radiated allowed it to effortlessly relax and rollover. I had seen the X-rays—my wrist needed to be rebuilt with bone grafted from my hip, and the procedure was scheduled after my return to New York. The possibility of moving my wrist defied the acupuncture and physical therapy treatments I was undergoing in the hope of avoiding this operation.

"There's black magic in your wrist," he pronounced, casually and matter-of-factly, like someone who sees this stuff every day. He went on to explain that dark forces had tried to keep me away from him by striking me with a headache and itching. This gave me the chills. He explained that my skepticism had kept me closed to these threats, but the energy can bounce off a closed nonbeliever onto the person closest to them who is open. Which sort of made sense to me at that moment, under those circumstances.

He announced that he could help and send healing energy to her, from here in Lovina. In a little dark hut, in the middle of nowhere, in the middle of the night?

He motioned for the three of us to sit in a lotus position again. By now, my wrist had gone completely numb, no feeling in it at all, and the annoying outside sounds had drifted off like they were miles away.

The shaman instructed us to breathe in and out—controlled breathing, in unison. As we breathed in and out, with each inhalation, the little old man seemed to grow larger in posture and in stature, until he was towering over us in the flickering lamplight.

As he grew, his face became twisted, lines appeared, and veins on his arms, neck, and forehead popped out. His eyes rolled back in his head until they were only whites, and his shaky hands reached into another world, arms moving wildly as he deftly rearranged things in some other dimension that, for an instant, we all were fully aware of. He seemed to reach through this vortex, and his hands grabbed and struggled with forces we can only remain skeptical of for our own sanity. His shadow was perfectly projected by the little oil lamp on the wall behind him. It seemed to be growing larger too.

We continued breathing in unison. He seemed to grow larger and larger every time we inhaled. He finally reached a crescendo and let out a loud retching cough conjured up from his innermost depths. I was certain he would have a heart attack. At that moment and for the first time that night, a breeze blew into the room, moved the curtains into the room, swept around us, and moved the curtains on the way out. The lamp flickered as it blew by, and the old man collapsed onto the floor, taking the table, book, offerings, and oil lamp with him.

"Get out!" I screamed, "Fire!" as the kerosene spread on the cement floor. Steve quickly removed his sarong and smothered the flame. The kids came running into the room and picked up the priest and carried him out, came back, then cleaned up the mess and the smoldering sarong. I looked at the clock: 1:45 a.m.

When we finally stopped shaking, the priest explained what had gone on and what forces he had to contend with. I hardly heard him now, as I was completely focused on the situation with Cindy in New York. Finally recovered, we drove back to our rooms, woke up the girls, the owner, and probably all of the other guests, paid our bill, and checked out. I had to get to a telephone; I had to reach New York and see what happened.

At that time, the only available public phone capable of making long-distance calls could be found at the airport, which was located far on the other side of the island. We sped through the jungles and over the mountains, over deserted dark roads in silence, arriving at the airport around four in the morning. The time difference between Bali and New York is twelve hours, making it around four in the afternoon in New York.

We woke up the man at the desk in the telephone office and told him it was an emergency. Then we waited the thirty or so minutes it took to get the connection through the series of operators relaying the call through Jakarta, Singapore, and Hong Kong. Because of this impossible system, international calls were rarely made, and being out of touch except via telex was pretty much a given.

Finally, I heard a faint ring as the mosquitoes circled my head. The ringing in my ear then became louder. After just a few rings, Cindy answered, and her voice, as clear as a bell, said, "Hello!"

I shouted to be heard, and she asked, "Why are you shouting? I can hear you perfectly."

She related the events of the past few days, when she went in for the tests. They had rushed her to the hospital, where a serious growth was removed from her spleen. She had been in the hospital a few days and returned that morning, feeling bad and barely able to get up. Around 1:30 p.m. she got up to answer the phone. It was her mother. During the conversation she blacked out and collapsed into the chair, and had been there at the desk for the last few hours. Funny, she said in a perfectly clear and even cheerful voice, "Somehow, right now, I feel great! Better than I have in weeks."

More testing baffled the doctors in New York, who never witnessed a speedier and more complete recovery from her condition.

X-rays and further testing also made it unnecessary for me to undergo a painful wrist surgery. Though I've not regained full mobility of my right wrist, it's only a slight problem, and no surgery was ever prescribed again. The doctors say it must have been the acupuncture or physical therapy.

Who knows?

MY ADVICE FOR THE BALI VISITOR ──────────────────────

Magic and mysticism are still very alive in Bali and should not be taken lightly. As a tourist, stay away from it and don't trouble priests with Eat, Pray, Love *trivia—there are plenty of "advisors" around who will be happy to help you with that.*

You Missed
the Best of It

DIANA DARLING

Diana Darling is a freelance writer and editor. She is the author of The
Painted Alphabet, *a novel based on a Balinese tale, a former editor-in-chief
of* Latitudes *magazine, and has published numerous essays on Balinese society. She was born in the United States and moved to Europe in 1973, where
she lived in Italy and Paris, carrying out independent work as a sculptor. She
has lived in Bali since 1980 and is married to A. A. Alit Ardi of Ubud, where
they live with their children and grandchildren.*

If you came to Bali as a young thing in, say, 1976 (or in 1980, as I
did), you would have seen things that you can't capture in a selfie. You
would have seen the movement of the invisible. But these days the old
holy has become shy.

It used to flash out everywhere—at springs and by dusty roadsides,
on stone steps, in magical drawings on cloth. It surged up through trees,
bounced on fireflies, and glowed at the bottom of a dirty glass of arak. It
danced in public. The Balinese were playful with the holy in those days,
with their rough trance and bawdy ritual theatre. Their religion was an
unselfconscious, multi-dimensional gorgeousness, which to the Balinese
was just ordinary life.

Now modern Balinese are becoming pious, and their religion is becoming a venue of identity politics. For the tourists, it's wallpaper. The

official face of Balinese culture is no longer a farmer but a grotesquely made-up dancer, often dancing for travel agents or guests of the government. The spontaneous magic and natural glamour of art performed for the gods now appears as just another entertainment item, before or after dinner. The 'sacred' is now a branding theme, applied to tour packages, spa treatments, cocktails.

Cultural tourism—conceived by prominent Balinese in the 1970s— was a strategy for somehow sharing their culture with tourists without ruining it. In those days, Balinese culture was a rural way of life with a peculiarly spectacular way of engaging with the spirit world. Then, slowly, what a tourist could see of the culture became obscured by the visual noise of new buildings and traffic jams; and the tourism product shifted from 'culture' to self-indulgence.

But life is like that: it keeps changing, and it tends to get worse as you grow old. Tourists have been complaining about the ruin of Bali since the 1930s. These days there is a generation of expatriates who remember the 1970s and '80s as a time when Bali was still infused with the old holy.

Things looked different then. Before the advent of cement blocks in Bali, people built their houses from what was on hand: stone and bamboo from the river gorge, mud bricks made in the back yard, and tough wild *alang-alang* grass for the roof. For Balinese, the 'bathroom' was the pigpen and the river. For foreigners, the bathroom was under the eaves, with a bin of water filled every day by a girl carrying a bucket on her head from the nearest stream.

This girl, your *pembantu*, did everything for you, because you yourself couldn't carry water (or firewood or market produce) on your head. You didn't know how to wash your clothes in the river. You rather felt like you couldn't cook rice. Your pembantu would come to work at dawn and sweep the packed-earth yard around your house of the blossoms that had fallen in the night, and then spend the day cooking, laundering, doing your errands. But the main reason she was there was to make the daily offerings. She was probably the daughter or niece of your landlord, who was concerned about all the demons that would be attracted to the house of a foreigner. So she was there to keep harmony on the land. (Her doing everything else for you foreshadowed the pampering style of resort hospitality.)

In your little bamboo house, lighting was kerosene lamps that your pembantu cleaned and filled at the end of every afternoon, after sweeping up again before the swift fall of night. You listened to music on a little cassette player that ran on batteries. You also needed batteries for your torch, which you carried in a woven Dayak bag—along with a sarong and temple sash—whenever you left the house. You wrote on a little portable typewriter, or by hand.

Your bed was built of bamboo and it wobbled. The mattress was thin and lumpy, and it had to be aired regularly by your pembantu. Your Chinese bed-linen from Singapore was baked fresh in the sun. If something really had to be ironed, your pembantu did it, of course, with an iron heated with burning charcoal. This sometimes scorched the cotton-rayon clothes that everyone wore and many expats designed.

The weather was always with you. Nowhere was truly indoors. In the hot dry months of September and October, the world was coated in fine dust. In the rainy season your feet were always wet, and your leather shoes (which you never wore except to go to Immigration) turned green with mould. Often in the rainy season you would be soaked to the skin in a sudden downpour. Then you would dry yourself at the fireplace in your kitchen, with a glass of muddy coffee, and wood smoke swirling in your hair.

In those days before telephones and fax, much less the internet, important business communications were conducted by telex at somebody's office. But if you wanted to talk to anyone in Bali, you went to their house. To get there, you might walk along the beach or through Ubud and the occasional rice field. If it was far, you'd go by motorbike. If you had to go into Denpasar, you might take a *bemo*—a tiny truck with benches in the covered thing on the back—which plied vaguely defined routes and picked up anyone who waved it down. If your day in Denpasar was to be a busy one—say, the bank and then some shopping on Jalan Gajah Mada, then picking up airline tickets at the Bali Beach

Hotel, followed by lunch at the Tandjung Sari—you might hire the bemo for the day for your private use and feel like a lord.

Time was slow in those early days, when nothing was truly comfortable or convenient and entertainment was scarce. People looked for the extraordinary in the subtle things around them. In your bamboo hut, you lived with the earth, amidst its smells and sounds. There was the sound of water running through ditches in the rice fields outside your house; the sucking sound of a buffalo pulling a plough through the mud, and the rattle of its wooden bell. There was massive birdsong in the morning, and the soft whooping of owls in the night, and the sound of wind rattling the leaves of coconut trees. The croaking of frogs was so large a feature of the night that the frog orchestra was a popular theme in the carving of wooden souvenirs and stone statuary, with each frog carrying a musical instrument. And you lived with the sky, ever alert to the weather and the time of day and the age of the moon. Would you get home before dark? Would there be enough moonlight to light your way?

In your sooty kitchen, you learned that the gods had resting places there—in the firewood rack above the stove, by the big terracotta water jug, in the rice basket—and your pembantu gave them little offerings every day after the cooking was done. She also put offerings at all the important points around the house where the invisible tended to cluster: by the gate, on the seat of your motorbike, on the ground in the middle of the well-swept yard, and on the little purpose-built shelf above your bed. Your landlord would have insisted that your house have its own temple, perhaps just a single shrine, before building began on the house itself. On certain days the offerings would be more elaborate and you might be encouraged to put off going to Denpasar for another, more auspicious day.

It was a time of oblivion about the rest of the world, partly imposed by Suharto's military dictatorship which permitted only news that flattered it. International newspapers and magazines were censored and always out of date. Bank transfers and letters from your family took weeks to arrive. Sometimes you felt like you lived on another planet.

Yet it was a warm, voluptuous, and spacious planet. There was plenty of room for everything, and great freedom to move around in it. You could go anywhere you wanted, could drive up or down a street as you pleased and park at the door of wherever you were going, stop right outside the gates of a temple festival, where there was room for everyone to mill about in the ritual clutter. In the 1980s you could fly from Bali to Jakarta on a nearly empty DC-10, drinking whisky and smoking kreteks.

In those days, only the main roads were paved, and if you stuck to them you'd never get lost anywhere on the island. You always had a view of Gunung Agung. On the coast, you could walk from your bedroom down a dirt track straight onto the beach.

And, if you liked, you could stroll along the beach completely naked, for this was also a time of astonishing personal liberty. The Balinese may have thought you were mad, or barbaric, but they didn't appear to mind; or perhaps they were just too courteous to say anything. If you made a mess of yourself on magic mushrooms, they cleaned you up and called in a healer.

Very early on, there was a special relationship between the Balinese and the foreigners. It was not equitable, but it was collaborative and extremely fertile. This had much to do with the fact that, especially in the 1970s, Bali was very poor. Its economy was agrarian and its technology was neolithic. A decade earlier it had been devastated by mass killings and famine. And the national government, which permeated everything, promised that riches would be brought to Bali by international tourism—so foreigners were to be welcomed.

The early expats were not what the government had in mind, however. Indonesia was preparing (with great slowness) for a style of high-end tourism where visitors would stay in an enclave of five-star hotels, spend their dollars on souvenirs, and quickly be on their way. But in the 1970s, Bali was also a fabled destination on the hippie trail that extended from the Mediterranean through Afghanistan and India to Southeast Asia. It was about drugs and surfing and mysticism, and Bali was the jewel at the end of the rainbow.

These unanticipated visitors could hardly believe the glory of Kuta beach and its rolling surf and sunsets that soaked the world in red at the end of every day. And they were fascinated by the Balinese — by their beauty and dexterity, by their outlandish intimacy with the gods, by their fearless and tender care of the dead. Above all, they were delighted by their exuberant welcome. Whatever a wasted hippie might wish for, the impoverished Balinese competed to provide. A place to stay? Come stay at my house! A cold beer? We have the coldest! Or maybe you'd like me to climb a palm tree for a coconut? No problem!

Before long, foreigners and Balinese entered into a long love affair of many guises. Some of course were simply love affairs, and some resulted in marriages. Many of these produced little businesses, such as food stalls that catered to the tastes of surfers, hippies, and the growing tide of Australian students on holiday. Some grew into destination restaurants. The famous Made's Warung took off in 1969 when the Dutchman Peter Steenbergen fell in love with the nubile Madé Masih, and they began serving food that foreigners craved, like bacon cheeseburgers and lemon sorbet soaked in vodka. Others saw the potential for producing handicrafts or jewelery or simple clothes. Or furniture. Or artwork in shells or glass. Or whatever. Some became rich in logistics businesses, exporting whatever people thought up to sell. Foreigners provided ideas and marketing, while the Balinese provided labor and land. Investment cash came from wherever you could find it, and many Indonesians from outside Bali flocked to get in on the action.

Expats in Kuta set the pace for going modern. They were the first to devise hot-water showers (say, from a coiled black hose on the roof of the bathroom), the first to design chic houses of timber and polished cement, the first to get air-conditioning, the first to venture into gastronomy. They partied hard at discotheques until breakfast time. Their Balinese partners opened petrol stations and supermarkets.

The scene in Sanur, on the other hand, was about gentility. Whereas Kuta's expats were young and ardent, Sanur's expats were sedate and exclusive; many lived in a park of private villas in Batujimbar. The focus of chic in Sanur was the Tandjung Sari hotel, which began as a few little huts on the beach, and whose brand evolved as barefoot epicureanism for rock stars and royalty, in contrast to the hulking Hotel Bali Beach up the coast, whose main market was international sales conventions. Hotels and expat houses in Sanur were large, fan-cooled bungalows and open-air pavilions surrounded by coral walls and masses of bougainvillea. Sanur's most notorious expatriate was the Australian painter Donald Friend, who lived there in the 1960s and whose household was run, or perhaps overrun, by young boys. This idyll was perfected in the 1980s by the Australian landscape designer Made Wijaya. But aside from serving in houses or hotels, the native population of Sanur remained aloof from the foreigners, and devised their own, sometimes clueless, local restaurants and souvenir shops according to what they imagined the tourists wanted. They mostly kept to their own quiet way of life, their coral temples, and their discreet black magic.

Meanwhile in Ubud—which conceptually included the villages of Peliatan, Mas, Celuk, Batubulan, and Batuan—the tourism scene was all about 'culture'. Already in colonial times, Ubud had been known to tourists as 'the village of painters' while Peliatan was 'the village of dancers', Mas 'the village of woodcarvers', Batubulan 'the village of stone carvers' and Celuk 'the village of silversmiths'. Batuan was good at all these things. But the village of Ubud had the nous of marketing culture to tourists, thanks to the enthusiasm of Puri Ubud, its ruling family, for engaging with foreigners since the 1920s. Its most glamorous guest in those days was Walter Spies, the German painter, musician and amateur ethnographer who became the model for later generations of Ubud expats of how to 'be' in Bali — that is, you must be erudite in all things Balinese: the inscrutable multi-level language and peculiar calendars, the impossibly complicated music that made your heart ring like a bell. Visiting anthropologists found Ubud a good base from which to conduct their studies: the local people were used to foreigners and happy to elucidate what they understood from Puri Ubud to be Balinese culture.

In the 1970s, Ubud's tourists were accommodated mostly in homestays, little huts in people's backyards, which allowed visitors to participate in the life of the host family. The Balinese took pleasure in helping

their guests put on traditional temple dress in order to fit in more respectfully with local religious ceremonies, and both sides did their best
to understand each other's strange cultures. Lasting friendships often
arose, and of course businesses, too. Perhaps the most exemplary of these
is Threads of Life—an endeavor started by Jean Howe and her husband
William Ingram, with the help of I Wayan Sudarta—which is devoted
to indigenous textile traditions of Indonesia. The friendship perhaps
began when Jean saw the ghost of Sudarta's late father sitting in the
family courtyard.

No matter where they were, Bali's expats of the 1970s, '80s, and even
'90s seemed to ride a tsunami of success. This was a time when if you
had an idea, you could carry it out. Start something, design something,
build something, stage something. Creativity was burgeoning, and everywhere there were bright young Balinese to help you turn it into a
business project. The Balinese were caught up in the excitement. They
contributed their talent and their connections, their genius for team-
work. Jewelers and woodcarvers and dancers and builders brought the
knowledge they'd inherited about the old way of doing things and an
eagerness to do things in a fresh new way—and make money!

For this was also a time when money was surging into the island.
Everything multiplied—the population, the tourist arrivals, the hotels
and art shops, the banks, the villas, the malls and spas and gourmet
shops and car dealerships—and urban Bali is now almost choking on
money. The only thing that has not multiplied is the land, but there are
plans for that.

In this newly rich and crowded world, the Balinese see money as
the metric of success, even a virtue: if it makes money, it must be good.
Yet the people of Bali have not lost their bearings, nor their memory of
poverty. Money—a new form of life's abundance—is gratefully recycled
back to the gods in religious ceremonies, always on a scale beyond their
means. Ritual extravagance is a sign of devotion. And big ceremonies
make a point about Hindu pride.

Yet to some outsiders, excess and the holy do not go together.
Foreigners have always had their own notions about what Bali should

be; in general, they think Bali should be the way it was when they first got there. Some foreigners today feel that the Balinese should be spending their new wealth on education, health care, waste management, low-impact public transport, and animal welfare shelters.

But the Balinese have always known how to manage the universe. The difference between now and then is that in the olden days, the entire universe seemed to fit into the little world that was Bali, and to us the fit looked perfect.

MY ADVICE FOR THE BALI VISITOR ───────────────────────

If you want to discover the "lost Bali," slow down. You will see more, and people will appreciate your courtesy. Meanwhile, for a part of Bali not yet spoiled by tourism, check out the old neighborhoods in Denpasar.

ACKNOWLEDGMENTS

During the process of compiling this book, there were some friends who enthusiastically supported me along the way to whom I express my gratitude. Soma Temple and Ananda Hart had a similar idea for a book years ago and mailed me a recording of the two conversing in Bali about their Bali memories. Listening to this recording brought the spirit of Bali into my home in Big Bear, CA. Pablo occasionally called me offering creative ideas. Carolyn Tyler and Diana Darling helped to round up some writers living in Bali. Roger Hughbanks helped me to proofread a few stories. My children helped me greatly: Anouk, gave me wise insights; Katya backed me with her excitement with the project and social media advice; Yos helped me with my cover concept; Morena referred me to my incredible art director, Natasha Berting. I would like to especially thank Bruce Carpenter, who contributed in many ways to the book with his kind and professional advice.

I am eternally grateful to my loving Higher Power who gives me more than I could ever deserve.

NOTE FROM THE EDITOR

The Lost Bali Stories – Volume I and *Volume II* contain only a fraction of stories that lie within the hearts of those that loved Bali back in the day.

I am welcoming submissions for *Volume III*. If you have a story to submit, please email me: lesliefranklinlcf@gmail.com.